To my husband for his patience
and to my family,
both immediate and extended,
with thanks

Contents

List of Illustrations   ix

Acknowledgments   xi

Introduction   xv

Abbreviations   xix

1

The Early Days   1

2

The Captain, the Wedding, and Elmwood   18

3

The Early 1920s: First Big Sales   34

4

The Rim of the Prairie   47

5

"There Is Nothing to Do but Go On"   61

6

A Lantern in Her Hand   76

7
A White Bird Flying   94

8
Miss Bishop and the Early 1930s   113

9
The Mid-1930s and *Spring Came On Forever*   128

10
The Late 1930s and More Best-sellers   151

11
The 1940s, A Movie at Last, *The Lieutenant's Lady,*
and the 1950s   174

Notes   201
Aldrich Bibliography   225
Index   231

Illustrations

Following page 104

The Streeter family, c. 1886

Bess around age 10

Graduation picture from Iowa State Normal School, 1907

Charles S. "Cap" Aldrich

The Aldrich family, c. 1920

Bess Aldrich and children, c. 1920

Cap Aldrich

Bess, c. 1926

"The Elms"

Bess Streeter Aldrich, 1920s

Mary Eleanor Aldrich, 1926

James Whitson Aldrich, 1929

Charles S. Aldrich, 1930

Robert S. Aldrich, 1937

Bess Streeter Aldrich, 1942

The Aldrich house in Lincoln, Nebraska

$\mathcal{A}$cknowledgments

Those who have helped me have been of major importance in the work and the pleasure of writing this book. Two who were instrumental in the very beginning for suggesting that I write a biography of Bess Streeter Aldrich were Susan Rosowski and Bruce Baker. Sue has provided invaluable comments, assistance, and warm friendship, as she has through many years; she has my very special thanks.

The board of directors of the Bess Streeter Aldrich Foundation in Elmwood, Nebraska, also suggested that I write a biography of Aldrich, the nationally acclaimed author and hometown personality they had known so well. These board members were Chet and Valda Bornemeier, Elaine Bornemeier, Rob Clements, Muriel Fischer, Eleanor Fleishman, Ross McCormick, Mary Miller, Jean Reinke, Don Skalak, Mary Skalak, Earl Stander, and Shirley Wenzel, all of whom also supplied quantities of information. I am grateful for their consideration and assistance.

I began my research by talking with Aldrich's daughter and son-in-law, Mary Aldrich Beechner and Milton, who not only gave me great insight into the warmth, humor, and philosophies of Mrs. Aldrich, but also became my friends. Mary and Milton Beechner also gave me access to three boxes of Aldrich materials, noted as Beechner Boxes in the notes and now housed at the Nebraska State Historical Society. Robert Aldrich and Charles Aldrich, two other Aldrich children, answered many questions on the phone, in person, and through letters, as did Dorothy Beechner Mapes. Without the input of the Aldrich family, this work could not have been accomplished.

I am indebted to the Nebraska Humanities Council for their grant and for their continuing interest in Aldrich, and to Molly Fisher in particular, who answered so many of my questions.

I thank Anne Billesbach, Cindy Drake, Ane McBride, and Martha Miller of the Nebraska State Historical Society, and the many others there who answered questions or delivered to me box after box of material. Rosie Peterson of the Cedar Falls Historical Society was a great help, as were Vopal Youngberg and Julie Bailey, both of whom have done much research on Aldrich, and Jean J. Card, who supplied me with information on the family. Those in the library field who answered many questions were Laura Dixon, of the University of Nebraska, Omaha, Library, Ellen Van Waert, of the Nebraska Library Commission, and Margaret Blackstone, Barbara Lehr, and Alice Station, of the Omaha Public Library.

So many people in Elmwood made it a point to give quick informational additions to my knowledge and understanding of Mrs. Aldrich or their town, and I did not always get their names, which I regret. I feel that I could list each resident of Elmwood; everyone has been so helpful and supportive. Since this is not possible, to all of them—more thanks than these words can convey. There are a few individuals I would like to thank for interviews or specific information: Marie Clements, Dwight and Marge Clements, Frances Buell, Gladys Buell, Opal Clements, Donald and Mary Gonzales, Ted Hall, Marge Julian, Doris Greene Lamb, Mary Linhardt, Charles Miller, Carolyn and Walter Oehlerking Jr., Donna Greene Reuter, and Theresa Seiker. Should I have missed including some names, I am sorry; please know that I appreciate all assistance.

I am deeply grateful to my family, who have been so important in this work. Being with them in person or by phone or mail, sharing the warmth and concerns of family life, have enabled me better to understand the life I was writing about. Their thoughtfulness and encouragement have made so much possible; thus, a very large thank-you goes first of all and especially to Al Petersen, my patient husband, and to Sheri, Rich, Jessica, and Lillian Tillson, Jerry, Joan, Wesley, and Travis Petersen, Mark and Ann Petersen, and Pat and Jim Petring. Finally, my gratitude goes to Charlene Fletcher, who has always had faith in my writing.

Introduction

The more I got to know Bess Streeter Aldrich, the more I grew to enjoy and respect her. Outwardly she wore a Victorian courtesy and reserve, but this front covered a keen sense of humor and a shrewd Scot's business sense, seen by friends and business associates. There were those who spoke of her work as that of a Romantic; others argued that she was a Realist. It seemed to me that such a determination could be made only by a combined study of her writing and her life.

Aldrich was a generous woman and was willing to share of herself with other writers. People wrote to her in large numbers to ask advice on writing, and she answered them all, undoubtedly sending many to correspondence schools for writing lessons, for she had taken such training herself after she had become an established writer. The owner of the school had soon told her that he could help her very little as she did "not seem . . . to need very much help."[1] Ever the teacher, she made suggestions to aspiring authors to help them avoid some of the problems she had had to work through, and she devoted talks to university students and writing organizations on the how-tos of writing; she also contributed articles to *Writer* magazine that are still primers for budding authors.

Aldrich stressed that writing should be undertaken "first of all about the thing you know very best, the thing that lies closest to your heart, and to write it with no thought of pleasing anyone but yourself, with no thought of acceptance or rejection." She knew of this personally, adding: "When I began to write about the things I knew best, noisy youngsters, ordinary folks who have to plan to stretch their incomes, old grandmothers who have lived through hard days, my market began to concentrate, and I began to sell more readily."[2]

Aldrich was pragmatic about writing. She could see "no reason why art and checks should be considered oil and water . . . we should write like inspired artists and sell like shrewd Yankees." Enlarging on this, she said: "The main thing is to write first for the sake of writing, what Kipling calls the joy of working, living up to one's own ideals, saying the thing he wants to say with no thought of what the trend may be or what he believes some editor wants—then find a market for the finished product when it has passed the test."[3]

Bess Streeter Aldrich stayed home to write her stories, and when they were ready, she sent them forth herself. She got into print without agents and without traveling to New York and knocking on doors. If her submissions came back she sometimes reworked them; however, if they satisfied her, she retyped the first and last pages to make them look fresh for the next editor and sent them off again until they found a publisher. She made her plans, chose her targets, and refused to be denied. She believed that, in many ways, one could shape one's own destiny.

It is tempting for a biographer to see her subject's life in the written legacy; and that is true in this case. There is in Aldrich's work a reflection of the author's own kindness and of her subtle humor, a "running laughter," to use words Aldrich applied to James M. Barrie. One can have little doubt that, in *A Lantern in Her Hand,* Aldrich wrote the scene of Will Deal's sudden death much as she lived through the sudden death of her husband, Charles Aldrich. Charles died of a cerebral hemmorhage, and although the cause of Will Deal's death is not specified, that very lack suggests this is how the husband dies so instantly and devastatingly. Aldrich's description of the banker's importance to the rural community unquestionably stems from her awareness of

Charles's value to his community. Similarly, when Aldrich writes dialogue between a teacher and a student, it is likely that such dialogue took place between Miss Streeter and one of her pupils. This is not to suggest that Charles or Bess Streeter Aldrich or their family are reproduced in the Aldrich works but that it is possible to catch glimpses from time to time of how Aldrich viewed her world and how the family reacted to events. The mythology of her Grandfather Streeter runs through Aldrich's prairie novels; the rhythms of the King James bible, with the words changed but with the meanings retained, echo through her longer fiction; the contemporary "psychology" of childrearing appears in family stories side by side with her ideas on that subject; an awareness of human imperfections is often presented, mediated with an over-all belief in the goodness of others.

It is perhaps this last point that most shapes Bess Streeter Aldrich and her work. She believed that people strove to do the right thing, that people were basically moral and well intentioned; these were the people she knew. She also believed that there were those who chose a world very different from hers: one that was not, to use her word, clean. She accepted this as fact, but it did not deter her from writing about the world that she knew and in which she lived. Her own life was filled with hard work, family joys and tragedies, friendships, and deep satisfactions.

Because she did not write of the sordid, she has sometimes been called a Romantic; yet she wrote of what was fact to her, which places her in the Realist field. I believe that her writing has connections to both schools, and that her life, viewed as if it were fiction, melds both elements. In this biography, I have tried to show the quiet drama of an ordinary woman whose writing made her extraordinarily popular. I have come to see her and her life as exemplars of the Romantic Realist.

Bess Streeter Aldrich's home in Elmwood, Nebraska, has, for several years, been listed in the National Historic Register. In 1993, the house was given by the latest owners, Dwight and Marge Clements, to the Bess Streeter Aldrich Foundation. From across the United States people have visited to see where this writer lived.

They have traveled to Elmwood also to attend the Bess Streeter Aldrich Remembrance Day, held in the village yearly the first Sunday in October, a day sponsored by the Aldrich Foundation, which, in conjunction with the Elmwood Library Board, has constructed a joint Library and Aldrich Memorial Building.

The Aldrich literary legacy continues, also, in new editions, reprints, of her books and short stories. Her first novel appeared in 1924; her last work, a compilation of Christmas stories called *A Journey into Christmas*, came out in 1949. Both of these books and all those that came between are still available.[4] New generations are finding pleasure in her writing and finding also the factual history of an earlier America. This continued readership far exceeds Aldrich's hope that the second and third generations after the pioneers would read and understand the struggles and strengths in the lives of their parents and grandparents.

Abbreviations

ALIHH *A Lantern in Her Hand*

BB Beechner Boxes

BSA Bess Streeter Aldrich

CFHS Cedar Falls Historical Society, Cedar Falls IA

CSA Charles S. Aldrich

DCHS Douglas County Historical Society, Omaha NE

DIR Draft of "I Remember"

GSB Grace Simpson Bailey

HIMS "How I Mixed Stories with Do-nuts"

JB Julie Bailey Files

JLBW John L. B. Williams

LHJ *Ladies' Home Journal*

MAB Mary Aldrich Beechner

NSHS Nebraska State Historical Society, Lincoln NE

RBJ Rutger Bleeker Jewett

RSA Robert S. Aldrich

UNIA University of Northern Iowa Archives, Cedar Falls IA

Bess Streeter Aldrich

1

he

Early Days

When the telephone rang that Sunday morning, 3 May 1925, the clock showed 11:45. The caller told Bess Aldrich that Cap had been taken ill during church service and that a car was coming for her. She pulled off her apron as she hurried to the door and down the steps to the walk. The car arrived, and she slid in. Before they had gone the three blocks to the church, the few murmured words had told her. Cap was gone. Bess was a widow with four children.

Aldrich later closed a chapter dealing with a similar sudden death in one of her books by writing that real life is a "relentless master. If its hardest blow be dealt at three o'clock, then four o'clock must be met, and five and six,—the first dark, agonizing night and the first pale, torturing dawn."[1] And, as with the character in that book, Bess Aldrich must get on with the business of living and making a living.

Aldrich provided with her pen the necessities and the extras for five lives, telling the stories of her family's experiences. The stories portrayed immigrants pioneering into the Plains and reflected those lives so accurately that her readers felt she was writing of their own families.

Where did it begin for Aldrich? How did she become the writer to express the extremes of pioneering joy and anguish and all that lies between? The stories that Bess Streeter Aldrich would interpret began in Iowa, where her parents had pioneered and where she was born. Bess's father, James Streeter, was a part of a family that had been moving to new areas almost all his life. In 1852, when James was twenty-five, this westering spirit brought her grandfather, Zimri Streeter, to Iowa. He was a man old to be pioneering still, for he was in his fifties. With him came Lucinda Dean Streeter, his busy, wiry, worrying little wife, also in her fifties, and their children. Iowa was what they had been seeking: they moved no more.

A great influence on Bess Streeter Aldrich was that grandfather she never met but whom she knew well. Aldrich's later writing suggests that her Streeter grandfather, "gnarled and weatherbeaten as the native hard timber," became family myth, personal legend, and perhaps even archetypal pioneer.[2] He died a few months before her birth, but the stories about him were a part of her childhood. As pioneer and politician, hero and humorist, he was the prototype for Jeremiah Martin in *Song of Years*. Aldrich acknowledged that from his side of the family "has come to me a trait of seeing the funny side of things" (HIMS 32). Her grandmother, Lucinda Dean Streeter, "energetic, humorless and intolerant of fun-making," was the model for Sarah Martin. They were, Aldrich said, "with no disrespect for . . . the dead, a vaudeville team" (HIMS 32). Although they provided elements of humor for her writing, she had great respect for and pride in them because theirs were pioneering spirits.

Aldrich once described the Streeter family as being of "good old Revolutionary stock," adding, "in fact, there seems to be a conviction in the family that our ancestors *swam* here and were drying their clothes around a bonfire when the *Mayflower* docked" (HIMS 32). The family lore provided stories that were full of patriotism and politics, peopled by such individuals as a colonist of pre-Revolution days who married into the famous Adams family, another whose cousin was Ethan Allen, another active in the Green Mountain Boys' efforts against the British, another who put the lantern in the Old North Tower, and still others whose everyday toil cloaked adventurous spirits that finally broke free and sent them moving west with the opening of new lands.[3]

Aldrich was well acquainted with these family stories. She commented that she had heard them so often from the long-lived aunts and uncles who had made the trip that they seemed almost to be a part of her own memories.[4] She knew the Streeter wagon train averaged only about five and one-half miles per day on the last hundred miles of the trek because the spring rains and marshy ground slowed and sometimes halted travel. Family legend describes the little caravan moving through an almost unimaginable emptiness, where the only remarkable sights on the prairie were scattered trees along the occasional watercourse or the next rise of land at the horizon. In those last hundred miles, the travelers seemed to be in a world without other human beings. Only one structure, a log tavern at Independence, Iowa, suggested other immigrants. These are the kinds of stories that many people in Aldrich's generation had heard, and her descriptions in such books as *The Rim of the Prairie*, *A Lantern in Her Hand*, and *Song of Years* provided a bridge for succeeding generations.

Near the Cedar River, Iowa, a few miles "between the two clusters of cabins . . . which became the cities of Cedar Falls and Waterloo," Zimri bought government land for $1.25 per acre. There he and his family built their first primitive Iowa cabin, and it was the largest in the area (HIMS 32). Because Zimri Streeter "had the leadership which some men naturally possess," the other pioneers rushed to his cabin at the (false) reports that the Indians were coming to fight the immigrants.[5] This was another of the family stories that would later find its way into Aldrich's writing (*ALIHH* 22–27).

As noted above, the story of Zimri Streeter is the story fictionalized as Jeremiah Martin's in Aldrich's 1939 *Song of Years*. Zimri was a firm supporter of the new Republican Party, loved to talk politics to any available listener, and willingly interrupted his work to go to town to urge, argue, and debate his views. In writing about her grandfather and grandmother, Aldrich described astringent Mrs. Streeter as giving short shrift to Zimri's politicking; she was known to call to him as he left for town not to "even speak to a Democrat today or you'll never get home."[6] Voters of the area, however, respected his views and enjoyed his dry wit; they elected him to the first Iowa legislature when the capital was moved to Des Moines in 1857.

Aldrich wrote that

> every life has its big moment, and Grandfather's came during Lincoln's campaign for a second presidential term. Governor Kirkwood appointed him to go down into Georgia, contact General Logan's Fifteenth Army Corps, and bring back the [Cedar Falls/Waterloo IA] soldiers' votes. . . . He left with his flowered knapsack and arrived in Atlanta just as it fell. All communications to the north were cut, and he was bottled up with the army and had to march with Sherman to the sea. Sixty-four years old then, he had to endure all the hardships of the march, subsisting at times on corn from the fields. But his only complaint when he returned was that he lost his hat.[7]

Although this is undoubtedly the way the story came into family history, there is a slight discrepancy. Grandfather Streeter probably arrived in Atlanta during preparations for Sherman's march to Savannah, which was begun on 15 November and which would have been a week after the election. Zimri's collection of ballots, whether he was aware of it or not, in all likelihood was not counted until after Lincoln was declared winner on 10 November.

However, Zimri had campaigned hard for Lincoln in Iowa and was proud of his role in having helped reelect him. When Aldrich describes Zimri's reaction to the president's assassination, her writing takes on the tone of one repeating a legend: "He idolized Lincoln and on the day the news of the assassination came, in his grieving he went out alone into the timber and cut the initials A L in a tree, where they remained a half century, the rough bark growing in and filling the scars long before those other scars made by the fighting were healed" (*Journey* 241). This story is another part of the family myth of "Old Blackhawk," Zimri's nickname in the state legislature, given to him because he was from Black Hawk County and also as tribute to the respect he had earned. Perhaps due to his intimate relationship with the land, his philosophy was that, although altered, nothing is destroyed, telling Bess Streeter's mother that "I'll [always] be in something around here, even if it's the prairie grass or the wind in the timber" (*Journey* 241). His granddaughter provided a tangible *something* when she placed him in her *Song of Years*.

A few years before she paid tribute to her father's side of the family, Aldrich had created a similar tribute to her mother's family in *A Lantern in Her Hand*. The Anderson family history was also full of adventure and helped shape the romantic side of her imagination. These family histories-cum-legend blend the reality and romance that Aldrich confronts in her stories.

Aldrich's recounting of a typical childhood visit to her Grandmother Anderson indicates how she romanticized her grandmother. Aldrich writes of her visit as an "interview" for which she was ushered into her grandmother's presence in "the sunny east room. *And there she was* . . . in a big chair with a hickory staff at her side, and her full skirts forming a gray calico pool around her. She was in her eighties, short and dumpy, shaped like the pictures of Queen Victoria." Aldrich added that "she seemed the personification of Wisdom" (*Journey* 249–50) [At this time, 1888, Queen Victoria was seventy].

Aldrich surrounds with a fairy-tale aura her Scottish grandmother's early life and courtship: Margaret Stevens [the future Mrs. Anderson] "lived with her parents in their humble cottage on the Scottish moors. In 1820 when she was sixteen, a young man rode up one day and asked for water for his horses. He was from the gentry and had become separated from the rest of the hunting party." They talked. Before he left, he promised he would return, which he did often, even though "the neighbors

[were] wagging their heads and saying no good would come of it." The young man was Basil Anderson, and he fell in love with and married "pretty Margaret," taking her "to live with his mother in the large ancestral home." Basil's mother was "not too pleased with the little peasant daughter-in-law," but did her best to make the girl into a "lady," "dressing her differently and teaching her the duties of her new station in life." When Margaret grew homesick, she would change from her finery and throw a shawl over her head, have a horse saddled, and "ride across the moors to see her people" (*Journey* 250–51). Aldrich had in her possession a piece of that shawl, which remains a family memento.

The older woman, Basil's mother, remained mistress of the house for fifteen more years; upon her death (probably in early 1835), Margaret assumed that role. Shortly after his mother's death, Basil took a trip to see America. Word came that the ship had been lost at sea. Before he had left, Basil had co-signed notes for a friend, guaranteeing payment on a debt; when the creditors heard the ship was gone, they "closed in on the estate to confiscate it. *Roup* (i.e., auction) signs were posted that the house and its contents were to be sold. Because the horses could not be removed from the stable under the *roup* sign," Margaret, pregnant with her sixth child, took two of the other children and walked the fifteen miles across the moors "to get her parents to come and bid on some of her personal belongings" (*Journey* 251–52). She or her family succeeded in buying back her set of Chelseaware china and some blue beads, but little more.

After the auction, information came that the vessel had not gone down, but legally the information came too late; the transactions forcing Margaret and the children from the estate could not be rescinded. Basil was safe in Liverpool and sent for the family to meet him. With her children and her china, Margaret made her way south to Liverpool, and from there the family left on the "wild and perilous" six-week voyage to North America and up the Saint Lawrence River to Quebec, where in 1835 Margaret bore a girl whom they named Mary Wilson Anderson. Mary would become Bess Streeter's mother (*Journey* 252).

The Andersons remained in Canada four years before moving in 1839 to Illinois, where Margaret's "peasant blood asserted itself." With her oldest son, seventeen-year-old "dependable Uncle Jim, she became the real manager of the family, while [Basil] fitted for no work, remained the white-shirted gentleman to the end" (*Journey* 253). A few months after his death in 1839, Margaret gave birth to their last child, a son. About this time they received word from the authorities in Scotland that, with certain proofs, they would now be allowed to reclaim a portion of Basil's land, but the family had neither the money nor the desire to return to Scotland. By 1854, Margaret, having heard of the fertile soils and generous rainfalls of the new area called Iowa some two hundred miles to the west, believed it was again time to move. She was forty-nine years old, and daughter Mary was eighteen.

This story, "with its endless details," fascinated Aldrich. In a work published in 1949 she recalled: "My grandmother became many things. . . . She was Wisdom. She was Romance. She was Adventure. And through her, too, came a dawning realization of change. . . . Grandmother had been slim and sparkling, pretty and sixteen. Here she sat, fat and toothless, blind and eighty-four. It was almost impossible to reconcile the two pictures. So came my first conception of life moving continuously on and with the moving, great changes taking place" (*Journey* 253).

Aldrich remembered also the funeral for this grandmother, detailing "the dusty grass and the 'hoppers getting up under my dress and leaving their tobacco stains on its whiteness." She recalled also her reaction to the minister's words, " 'Her life was filled with labors, *but was uneventful*.' Uneventful? To go from a peasant home to an aristocratic one, only to lose it later and go back to the soil for a living? To take the perilous six weeks voyage across the sea and pioneer in the new midwest? To make the trek later to a still newer state through the prairie grass and creek beds and unchartered woods?" (DIR 21). The tribute to this "uneventful" life appears in *A Lantern in Her Hand*.

Lantern is also a tribute to Aldrich's mother, for Mary Wilson Anderson drove one of the family's teams on the long trip from Lockport, Illinois, to Iowa. In a 1952 *Christian Herald* article, Aldrich wrote that her mother

> would recall the scenes of that trip: the ferrying across the Mississippi, the horses and oxen plunging up and down the bridgeless creekbeds, the tipping over of one of the wagons with the eight precious sacks of flour slipping into the water and the feather pillows floating downstream like so many geese, while the younger children chased after them with hilarious laughter. She would tell the happenings merrily as though there had been no hardship at all. The camping on the edge of the woods, the sounds of the night winds, the odors of the prairie grass—all these she pictured so clearly that I could almost see and hear and smell them myself.[8]

There was little creature comfort when the Anderson family reached Iowa, for they lived in a cleaned-out sheepshed while they built their cabin in the timber. Because the shed had no door, they hung quilts over the opening. Eighteen-year-old Mary, who had little formal education, taught in one of the first log-cabin schools in the area, "boarding around" and earning $20 for each three months.[9] She met James Streeter much as recounted in *Song of Years,* and they married 1 January 1855. Their wedding was in a log cabin from which much of the furniture had been removed to make room for the guests. This setting was depicted in *A Lantern in Her Hand.*

After the wedding, the couple began farming across the road from the Streeter place, on land that James had purchased from the government. They had farmed for twenty-some years when James and Mary decided to move into nearby Cedar Falls, Iowa, where James took a job with a milling company. Of their seven children, all but their married son, Norman, moved with them to the house on Franklin Street.

They had lived in town only a year or so when Mary found she was to have another child. Bessie Genevra Streeter was born 17 February 1881, the last of the eight children and the only one not born on the farm. Her parents were fifty-five and forty-six at the time of her birth. Through the years, the name Bessie dropped from general use, to be replaced by Bess to all but a few relatives and close friends.

Bess later described her childhood and recalled much of her families' histories in an article entitled "I Remember," published in the November 1926 issue of *McCall's*. The work later appeared as a chapter in her 1949 book of Christmas stories, *Journey into Christmas,* and is the closest she came to writing an autobiography of her childhood. Many vignettes of these years appear throughout her fiction. In an article she wrote at the request of the Waterloo, Iowa, *Daily Courier* for its centenary, Aldrich noted that "a child unconsciously absorbs much of the adult conversation around him, and so, without realizing it, the stories of the early settling of Blackhawk County became a part of my youthful knowledge. For years they did not interest me very much, and by the time I had reached my teens, they frankly bored me. But life changes as we grow older, and in my adult years I began to see the drama in them."[10]

In "I Remember," Aldrich wrote that "because my parents were of such mature age and had grown and growing children I had a great many bosses." There were four older brothers and three older sisters, and she learned how to turn their numbers to her advantage: "With impunity, one can always tell some inquisitive adult member of the family that certain other adult members have given their permission to do thus and so. It usually stops all further annoying questions and is a method which was frequently employed by me" (*Journey* 230).

She described the big, rambling, family home on Franklin Street as a good place in which to grow. It began, she said, as a "white-painted, green-shuttered type of eastern wing-and-ell house, but . . . additional bedrooms had been built onto it and atop it," until ultimately it became a house painted a practical gray, of no certain architectural style; however, it "was plain and comfortable," and had seven bedrooms. Inside were "tall glowing coal stoves and many glass lamps, china wash bowls and pitchers, center tables and high bureaus, and an organ until that most wonderful of childhood birthdays when draymen backed up and unloaded a piano, leaving me stunned with surprise" (DIR 3). In *Lantern,* Aldrich recalled the childhood joy and excitement of receiving a piano. When "the wonderful shining affair" was unloaded, the daughter who would play it "would not have exchanged places with the first lady of the land" (188–89). In Aldrich's childhood, organ-playing required steady pumping of two pedals to keep a supply of air going across the reeds to make the sound, creating "a windy accompaniment" (*Lantern* 188).

The furniture in the Cedar Falls house "was substantial and unmatched, a chair being a thing to sit upon and not a Louis-something *objet d'art*" (LHJ 11). She added that "on the floor of our home were sale flowered carpets which had to be taken up every spring and fall, beaten almost thread-bare, and put down again over a layer of newspaper and a load of fresh [oat] straw" (IR 11). These details also would later appear in her 1925 novel, *The Rim of the Prairie.*[11]

The comfortable old furniture was welcoming to a little girl, and Aldrich would recall that from "the cushioned depths of big worn chairs I have sunk into the apple orchard of the March sisters in *Little Women* [Louisa M. Alcott] and into Caddam Wood with Babbie and the little minister [James M. Barrie]" (DIR 3). Because she spent a great deal of time with them, "the characters in those books were as close and friendly and well known to me as the neighbors" (IR 86). Years later, Aldrich wrote to a poet friend: "I love anything whimsical and I note that undercurrent in so many of your things. That's what I always saw in James Matthew Barrie,—a sort of a laugh under the surface even when he was most tender."[12]

Bess did not always curl up in a large chair to do her reading. Theirs was a large house with many bedrooms, and she would often slip a book under her apron and volunteer to go upstairs to make beds. That gave her ample opportunity to read undisturbed for long periods before anyone thought to wonder where she was.

Aldrich wrote that she grew up "among older people, reading, dreaming, fancifying, singularly free from care or responsibility," but she also helped with the household chores (DIR 11). And she spent time with her mother out-of-doors, where the front and side yards were Mrs. Streeter's special domain, and she "could revel in flowers to her heart's content" (DIR 4). With her mother to teach her, Bess learned the names of many flowers and how to tend them. On the nearby edges of native prairie, on farmland, and on timber-grown creek banks grew great varieties of wild flowers that Bess came to recognize. Later her books of pioneer days would name and describe flowers, cultivated and wild, often evoking also the scents of the flowers. Aldrich believed that scent—even description of scent—was one of the most powerful tools of memory, deepening the reader's absorption into the story.

Besides reading, Bess also cultivated her imagination in play. The backyard had a barn, carriagehouse, chickencoop and yard, woodshed, small plum-thicket, grape arbor, gooseberry and current bushes, sidewalks, and, best of all for young Bess, a playhouse her father made for her. The playhouse had a window that worked and "a discarded sewing machine, upon which one could pedal furiously, pretending long journeys over land and sea and air" (DIR 5–6). Young Bess created stories of kings and queens, knights and ladies, and the playhouse was a favorite place to make up such stories and to read them to a friend.[13]

Also in the backyard was her father's large vegetable garden, which supplied produce for the family and frequent guests. Parents and sixteen sets of Streeter and Anderson brothers and sisters remained in the vicinity, and the home on Franklin Street became a welcoming place for visitors. These visitors provided "a great deal of talk and laughter and fun" (*McCall's* 11). In Aldrich's words: "There were a great many relatives constantly coming and going to and from our home: big brothers and their wives, big sisters and their husbands, uncles, aunts, cousins, second cousins, cousins by marriage, and those always welcome, if vaguely known people designated by our parents as 'early settlers we used to know.' Constantly another plate was to be put on the table, an extra can of fruit brought from the cellar, more potatoes pared" (DIR 5). The conversations that took place when the relatives and early settlers gathered at the Streeter house provided a wealth of story material that Aldrich drew upon in her fiction.

Helping with the housekeeping, the food preparation for many people, and the canning from the large garden was a supply of young Danish women from Cedar Falls. Aldrich admired these "fine people whose thrifty boys were to become merchants and bankers, and whose young girls were not then averse to working in kitchens" (DIR 5). One of the young Danish household helpers was a dentist, "smartly professional," who wanted to learn proper English before practicing her profession. Aldrich wrote that the family was amused at her choice of homes, because "the conversation [at our house] was a bit careless, if sprightly" (DIR 6). She would later make similar comments about family conversations in *Mother Mason* and *The Cutters*.[14]

Bessie Streeter was a blonde-haired, active child. When she was a little girl, native prairie remained in scattered areas at the edge of town, and she and friends played in it but went in "only a few yards and scuttled back to the safety of fences" (*Journey* 243). Her reaction to the deep grasses and the unknowable fears that lay in the wilderness of prairie, as well as the sense of safety that comes through fencing it out, is recalled in *Lantern*. Cedar Falls had existed for about fifty years when Bess was born, and the original prairie grasses that remained were due to foresighted landowners who had left them untouched. In *Rim of the Prairie*, Aldrich stresses the importance of retaining portions of such living history so that future generations know something of what the original immigrants saw and felt (285).

The secure world of her childhood included church and Sunday school. With the other youngsters, Bess heard the stories and sang the songs the teachers taught them, including "Jesus Loves Even Me." The child Bessie for a long time assumed that the words were "Jesus Loves Eve and Me," confident that she and the biblical mother of races were particularly noteworthy (*Journey*, 258–59). Her family were devout Presbyterians. Phrases or paraphrases that reflect the King James Bible are scattered throughout Aldrich's work; however, Aldrich suggests in *Rim* that there is often too much of man's interpretation in religion and that "kindness . . . [should be] all there [is] to it" (122).

Bess's world was also one of local town events, such as the yearly excitement of the commencement program at the teachers' college. This was a three-day activity in which the townspeople took lunch baskets and picnicked on the campus, and student orations mingled with student-acted Shakespeare plays. This was a dress-up affair, which meant "the other dress was brought and donned," and the "width of your hair ribbon established your social status."[15] Bess's world also consisted of going to school, winter bobsledding, school debates, the joys and embarrassments suffered under one guise or another by all children, and, finally, the beginning of friendships that would last a lifetime.

Bess Streeter was an outgoing individual, active in many extracurricular high-school events, including athletics, cooking, and Shakespeare. Years later, writing in answer to a request from Cedar Falls High School, her alma mater, she described the introduction of basketball as a game for Cedar Falls High School girls. She noted that among her memories,

> none seems funnier to me now than the time basketball was introduced. The game was very new, and there were nine on a team. We had practiced in the old gymnasium, and then someone decided the game should be played outdoors. When word trickled forth that we were actually to play outdoors in *bloomers* where the whole world could look on, there were many and sundry discussions and shaking of heads concerning the moral and ethical aspects of this great venture. . . . Each pair of bloomers contained six yards of wide flannel, that when raised at the side would form a fan-shaped mass of drygoods as high as the shoulders with no visible sign of parting.[16]

The girls drew a large crowd; the fact that they could play at all in such clothing speaks well for their physical abilities. In her writing,

Aldrich often noted the resistance of the older generation to the clothing styles and mores of the younger, "modern," generation.

At Cedar Falls High, English classes read Shakespeare plays aloud. Almost all of Aldrich's books, as well as many of her short stories, contain references to Shakespeare's work. Bess's introduction to Shakespeare had come when she was a young child, attending with her family and many of the townspeople the lengthy graduation activities at the college. Now, as a high-school student, she belonged to the Shakespeare Club.

In a draft of an article about her high-school days, Aldrich describes her senior class as having thirty-three of the two hundred students in the school and the entire school having only six teachers. She recalls one teacher in particular and one event. The teacher was Grace Norton. Small, Eastern, and old when she moved to Cedar Falls, and unchanged years later, Miss Norton was formidable. Aldrich writes of an occasion when the senior Shakespeare class was reading *Hamlet* in the study hall for want of a better place. Other students in the hall were whispering and rustling papers, and Miss Norton wanted no distraction for her class. Bess, as Hamlet, had just read, "Never to speak of this that you have heard, / Swear by my sword." Clyde Parks, the Ghost beneath, responded, "Swear." Abruptly Miss Norton turned to the restless juniors and sophomores, took off her glasses, and gave one of her famous, acrid lectures about not making disturbances when others were working. She stopped; the silence was awesome. She turned back to the players and told them to continue. Bess Streeter heroically declaimed Hamlet's next line: "Well said, old mole!" The roomful of students erupted with laughter, and even the redoubtable Miss Norton joined in.[17]

School was also the beginning of writing for Aldrich. In her 1922 short story, "Josephine Encounters a Siren," Aldrich tells of twelve-year-old Josephine who loves to make up stories. After writing them out, Josephine reads them to her friend, much as Aldrich read her childhood stories to Grace Simpson [Bailey]. One of Josephine's stories is "The Knight of the Great White

Castle"; another is "The Quest for the Golden Lily." When her stories are completed, Josephine reads them to Effie, who, "loving the stories almost as much as their author, was a most satisfying friend." In the story, Josephine loves "juggling with words. 'When words are put together right, they're just like singing.' . . . And she was right."[18]

Josephine's experience in writing stories and receiving notice from adults seem to be outgrowths of fourteen-year-old Bess's excitement when she sent a children's story to the *Chicago Record* and won a camera. Aldrich recalled that "it was then when I first tasted blood; for the intoxication of seeing my name in print was overwhelming" (HIMS 33).

In high school, Bess wrote for the yearbook, the *Tattler*, and composed a poem, "Choosing the Motto." That same year, a former high-school classmate sent Bess, age seventeen, a clipping telling about a *Baltimore News* sponsored short-story contest that would give five prizes. Bess wrote and entered "A Late Love." She later admitted she wrote a love story even though she had thus far never loved a man. The story was, she said, "heavy as a moving van. It oozed pathos. It dripped melancholy. And it won the fifth prize—five dollars. I have always had a sneaking suspicion that there were only five manuscripts submitted." The excitement of the win sent her out immediately to cash the check and buy a parasol with "chiffon ruffles from stem to stern [with which I] had nothing whatever suitable to go . . . but if there is a heaven for dead parasols, that one has surely gone there" (HIMS 33). The parasol was bright red, and her sisters teased her that she had certainly got her money's worth. Some forty years later, in writing about the sisters in *Song of Years*, Aldrich used the idea of a parasol as not only protection from the sun but also an item of finery and source of personal gratification.

On 9 June 1898, Bess graduated from high school and in the fall enrolled at Iowa State Normal School, later to be known as Iowa State Teachers College and still later as the University of Northern Iowa. Iowa State Normal had solid academic as well as education courses and was considered an excellent school for training teachers. Bess continued to live at home while in college, daily walking the four-mile round-trip to and from classes.

Despite the distance from her home, she took part in many college activities. All students belonged to an English group or took part in debates, orations, and other "English activities," for, in order to graduate, students were required to participate in three major English programs, to which faculty and other students were invited. Bess chose the Alpha Society, serving successively as corresponding secretary, society reporter, and president. For the Greek program at one of Alpha's annual "open sessions," she wrote and delivered "an oration"—"Xanthippi"—that the student newspaper described as "especially worthy of commendation."[19] Bess again participated in basketball and acted in plays. She completed a primary education course and a two-year high-school Latin course, graduating in 1901 with a Bachelor of Didactics degree (B.Di.).

Bess Streeter's first teaching job was in the primary grades at Boone, Iowa, where she stayed for one year. The following year, she took a position at Woodbury Elementary in Marshalltown, Iowa, where teaching third grade earned her $450. During the 1903–04 and 1904–05 school years she taught first grades at the same school but with a $45 per year raise in salary. The following schoolyear, 1905–06, she moved to Salt Lake City, Utah, and taught first grade at Lafayette School. A note in her college files states "S[eerle, president] recommends Miss Streeter for primary work at Salt Lake City—One of I.S.N.S.'s strongest primary graduates."[20] The following year, she returned to Iowa State Normal School and worked on an advanced degree. During this learning and teaching year, she also wrote stories for the *Young Citizen*, a publication geared to children's reading levels and needs. Several of these stories were published: "The Holy Night" is a Christmas story; "The Highland Shepherds's Chief Mourner" tells about a dog who loses his master; "Discovering America" describes some of Columbus's activities; "Abraham Lincoln's Boyhood" relates events of Lincoln's childhood; and "One May Night" points out the value of sharing with people whom one can help. The last theme was an integral part of Aldrich's personality.

Aldrich often used her imaginative talents in conjunction with events in her own life. For example, the house in which she lived while teaching school in Marshalltown became one of the models for the Bee-House, a boardinghouse in *The Rim of the Prairie.* However, one boardinghouse event did not find its way into her books. Bess and a friend, who also taught school in Marshalltown, lived and boarded in a stately, remodeled old home called the Robbin's Nest. There were two dining rooms at the Robbin's Nest, and the mores of the Victorian era, which had a great influence in rural areas at that time, recommended that one dining room be used for "the ladies" and the other for "the gentlemen." However, occasionally the numbers were not evenly divided, and so it happened that at one dinner the men's dining room was filled; thus, two "dashing and handsome" young men were sent to eat in the women's dining room. Miss Streeter, watching their approach, turned to her friend and murmured, "Lola, there's one for each of us," just as the men arrived. They were introduced as Captain Charles Sweetzer Aldrich and Mr. Frank Harridan. Bess's comment was prophetic, for Bess would marry Aldrich, and Lola would marry Harridan.[21]

2

he

Captain,

the Wedding,

and

Elmwood

Charles Aldrich was born in Tipton, Iowa, on 7 September 1872, to William W. and Mary B. Aldrich, who, like the Streeters and Andersons, were pioneers in this new Iowa area. Charles's father was a farmer, stockman, and, for ten years, owner of a local hotel, the Aldrich House. Charles's grandfather and grandmother homesteaded a mile west of Tipton when Charles's father, William, was fourteen. Ten years later, William determined he, too, wanted to go west, and, traveling to California, spent three years there, from 1850 to 1853. He returned to the Midwest and married Mary Whitson in 1855. Mary bore thirteen children over the next twenty-four years. Charles was the ninth.

Charles grew into an athletic young man and was one of the leaders of the University of Iowa football team prior to his 1895 graduation. He received his law degree (LL.B.) from Iowa in 1896 and became a practicing attorney in Marshalltown, forming the partnership of Boardman, Aldrich, and Laurence. During the day he worked at his law practice; in the evenings he helped organize and train a group of Marshalltown area men, who became, in June 1898, Company H, 49th Iowa Infantry Volunteers. In that month they were called to duty in the Spanish-American War. A few months later, Aldrich and the rest of Company H were in Havana, Cuba. One of the youngest captains in that war, he was known as a good officer. He was concerned with the welfare of his troops, visiting the sick, making rounds at night to talk to his men, securing blankets for those who had none, and generally providing whatever assistance he could. While in Cuba, Aldrich was stricken with typhoid fever so severely that some doubted he would recover. He did, however, and he and his company were sent back to Savannah, Georgia, and were mustered out in May 1899. Aldrich returned to Marshalltown and resumed his law practice.

Charles Aldrich's pioneer spirit was not satisfied with his adventuring in Cuba. In 1900 the lure of the Alaskan goldfields, coupled with the realization that attorneys would be needed there, sent Cap Aldrich, as he was now called because of his army commission, to Nome, south of the Seward Peninsula, where he opened a law office. Aldrich, always innovative, organized a literary society that met every week during the long dark of the Alaskan winter. The meetings became so popular that often there was not enough room for all who attended. In July 1903, Aldrich accepted an appointment as U.S. Commissioner and moved to Candle, Alaska, a town above the Arctic Circle; however, in the summer of 1904, he received word that his father had died and that he was urgently needed in Iowa. Aldrich went home, settled the legal issues of the estate, and returned to his law practice in Marshalltown. It was then that he met Bess Streeter.

Bess and Charles found they had many mutual interests, including their pleasure in literature. Their courtship was full of laughter, good talk, and fun. They attended church together; they read Shakespeare to each other.[1] The pair followed the stringent proprieties of the respectable Victorian code, which, in the early 1900s, set strict guidelines for the moral behavior of a school-teacher and her suitor. Cap proposed marriage, wanting Bess to go to Alaska where he had again been offered a one-year post as commissioner. But Bess refused the Alaska offer, for her sister Clara, who was twenty-six years older than Bess, and Clara's husband, John Cobb, had already asked her to accompany them to Salt Lake City, Utah, where John would represent Burrough Brothers, a Baltimore pharmaceutical company.

Clara and John were special to Bess, who was young enough to have been the daughter they did not have. They had supplied her college tuition, and Bess, in turn, regarded her sister as a combination of mother, sister, and friend. She promised to write to Captain Aldrich. She also planned to "annex the Aldrich name when the year should be up."[2]

Bess took a teaching position at Lafayette Elementary School in Salt Lake City and later described having her class gather foodstuffs to send to the people of San Francisco after the devastating 1906 earthquake There was much that was different in Utah from Iowa, including, as she noted in a story draft, chil-dren for whom discipline problems seldom arose. Unlike other experiences that Aldrich was to draw upon for her fiction, her Salt Lake year receives only slight attention. In *A White Bird Flying,* an unmarried young woman who wants to become a writer con-siders the possibility of living as companion and surrogate daugh-ter to an elderly aunt and uncle: she would remain with them and care for them for the rest of their lives; in return, they would make her sole heir to their substantial fortune.[3] This is an exaggerated version of Bess and the Cobbs in Utah.

On returning to Cedar Falls, Bess also returned to classes

at Iowa State Teachers College. To earn the advanced Primary Training Certificate, she took the necessary courses and worked as a "critic teacher" and assistant in the Training Department, receiving $600 for the term. Some of the year's lessons were later reflected in her short story "Pie."[4]

In the spring of 1907, she received her certificate but did not accept a teaching position; she had made more exciting plans. Bess and Cap planned a September wedding. They had been engaged since August 1905.[5] When Bess's eighty-year-old father died on 6 March 1907, she, Cap, and the rest of the family discussed postponing the wedding to allow for a longer mourning period. They decided, however, to continue with current plans, knowing her father would have wanted that.

While she taught, Bess also continued to write. "The Madonna of the Purple Dots" is the story of Miss Felicia Brown and a five-year-old student, whose personal class Christmas project is a small picture of a Madonna. The boy provides the figure with a red and orange halo interspersed with purple dots. Recognizing the great effort that went into his work, Miss Brown tells him to give it to the one he loves best. Love (and Aldrich's imagination) bring the characters together. While taking the Madonna to his teacher on Christmas Eve, the boy is injured in an accident. The young doctor who attends him has also been on his way to Felicia with his Christmas offerings, love and marriage, and she accepts the gifts of both.

"The Madonna of the Purple Dots," the first of many Christmas stories Aldrich was to write, signaled the responsive chord she struck with a wide readership—beginning with the editor of the *National Home Journal.* After the *National Home Journal* accepted her story for $5, Aldrich received a letter saying that the editor had decided the story was worth more than that and a check for $10 was enclosed.[6]

At 8 P.M. on Tuesday, 24 September 1907, Bess Streeter and Charles Sweetzer Aldrich were married at the Streeter home in Cedar Falls. Following the contemporary customs, John and Clara Cobb and Charles and Bess greeted the sixty-five guests as they came into the house. Bess, whose wedding dress was of lace-trimmed white chiffon, carried red roses. Among those who gathered, she was was especially glad to see Mrs. Frank Harridan, the good friend from the Robbin's Nest to whom Bess had murmured, "Lola, there's one for each of us." Lola was another of the friends with whom Aldrich would remain close through correspondence.

When the bride and bridegroom took their places before the minister in the parlor, a niece began playing Schumann's "Traumerei," the piece that would serve as the musical theme of Aldrich's life. After the wedding supper and a reminder to their guests that they would be "at home" in Tipton after 15 October, the Aldriches left on the late-train to Chicago.[7]

The young couple were ideally matched by both heritage and interests. The generations of pioneers and the stories of their experiences on both sides of her parents' families had filtered down to become the myths and legends that were a part of Bess. Her mother, Bess, a sister, and at least two of her brothers would write poetry and stories.[8] Charles, too, whom she was later to describe as the "most admirable and attractive man I had ever known," also descended from adventurers, had been one himself, and enjoyed reading and literature. Charles encouraged Bess's writing.[9] As a couple, their future was bright. The elements that would shape her literary future were in place.

After their wedding trip, Bess and Charles returned to Tipton, where Charles had been born. Charles began working in the bank and practicing law, and Bess settled into marriage, concentrating upon setting up a home and becoming active in the church and community. They also discussed the future. The Aldriches and the Cobbs shared both a mutual affection and a desire to live in a small town. Thus Charles and John made several trips to investigate business ventures, finally deciding to purchase the American Exchange Bank of Elmwood, Nebraska, founded twenty years earlier (1889). Bess did not go with them: pregnant women did not travel much in 1909, and she was expecting the first Aldrich child.

Of the four planning this move, Bess probably looked forward to it least. Nebraska conjured up childhood memories of the agricultural depression of the 1880s and the church basement filled with bundles of old clothes and sacks of dried apples for the Nebraska destitute.[10] But the move was one of those happy accidents preparing her to write. Reluctant to leave her home even while willing to accompany her husband west, Bess gained insight into the emotions of the pioneer women who had preceded her. Cap moved to Elmwood after the 10 February 1909, birth of their daughter, whom they named Mary Eleanor for Grandmothers Mary Anderson Streeter and Mary Whitson Aldrich. Bess, finding it harder than she had expected to have Cap gone, soon followed, arriving in Elmwood on 16 April, with her infant, her widowed mother, and her sister.

Bess Streeter Aldrich's introduction to Nebraska was as grim as her memories of a land where people needed missionary gifts. A gritty wind blew into their faces and onto her closely-wrapped infant, carrying rough particles of dirt and straw and everything else that a heavy dust storm could pick up. The trip from Tipton had been long, and Bess was not prepared for this added weather assault. Cap, John, and Si Maris, whose two-seat surrey and team had been hired to take them to their new home, were at the station to meet them, but the surrey couldn't hold everyone. Because of the dust storm, Bess would not let her infant ride in its carriage, so the baby, the grandmother, Bess, and Clara rode with Si, while Cap, pushing the empty baby carriage through town, walked with John. In the dim light of the late afternoon dust and gloom, Si was not sure which cottage at the end of the main street Cap had rented. As Bess Aldrich recalled the event, "it didn't take me long to pick [the cottage] out, for through the blasts of dust I could see my best upholstered rocking-chair, a wedding present, sitting on a little porch with an arm hanging limply down at its side, evidently broken in shipping."[11]

Alighting from the surrey, they hurried through the wind-blown dirt and dust to the front door and were greeted by Si's sister, who had come in and prepared dinner for them. Aldrich wrote later: "On my own stove and with my own dishes, she had prepared a delicious meal for the strangers, that they might feel welcome." Aldrich recalled that she had "experienced it a thousand times since—that warm-hearted hospitality, loyal friendship and deep sympathy of the small town. And it is these characteristics and others of the better features of the small town and its people that I have tried to stress in my short stories and books."[12] The families settled quickly into their new community, Cap and John Cobb at the bank, Bess with her baby, Clara with her activities, and Mrs. Streeter, who had her own room at each daughter's home, dividing her time between them.

The transition from Iowa to Nebraska was easier than Bess had expected, for the winds died down, spring came, both Clara and her mother were in Elmwood, the townspeople were kind, and Bess was meeting women with whom she was becoming good friends. Elmwood became home. Bess and the family joined the Methodist Church and took part in town activities. By 1911, she was ready to resume writing. She decided to enter a contest sponsored by *Ladies' Home Journal*, writing "The Little House Next Door" during the next few afternoons while Mary Eleanor slept. The story concerns a young woman, Betty, visiting her aunt and uncle in their small town. Through the years this annual visit has become a ritual for Betty, as has the teasing and growing up with childhood friend Bob, who is now an attorney. Betty, or Midge as friends call her, is a college graduate. Bob asks Midge to marry him, but the choice is difficult as it would mean exchanging the city's excitement for rural quiet. When a famous and wealthy woman comes, incognito, to look at the empty little house next door to Betty's relatives, Betty accompanies her through it and learns that the woman and her husband had begun their married lives there. The woman feels that if they had remained, she would not have become a "cross, discontented woman." The woman's visit helps Midge make her decision.[13]

When Aldrich finished writing the story in longhand, she went to the bank to type it, for she did not have a typewriter of her own. As she did not know how to type, it was slow work. Compounding these difficulties was the fact that when one of the clerks needed to type something, Aldrich had to take her manuscript out of the machine and wait until the bank work was finished. She later recalled that Cap, "in sheer self-defense, bought me a second-hand [typewriter]. Later, of course, I purchased a twelve-cylinder, sixty horse-power affair" (HIMS 33). Nearly twenty-three hundred writers entered this "Girls' College Prize Competition," but for unexplained reasons, the contest was called off. Aldrich, who had written the story under the pseudonym of Margaret Dean Stevens, received a letter from literary editor Franklin B. Wiley saying that "The Little House" story "appealed so strongly to us that we wish to use it in the Journal." The *Journal* sent her a check for $175. Aldrich, who continued to view the story as a contest entry, noted that she could "well remember the day I received notice of the prize award. My mother was with us when my husband brought home the letter. . . . I was wild with delight, but Mother said to look again—'It must say $1.75.' I looked but there wasn't a sign of a decimal point in the figure."[14] She also felt

> that proved it—I could write! I had arrived! It was all very very lovely. How easy! Just a few afternoons of writing. . . . So I sat down and wrote another story, much better than the first. Already I had the second check mentally invested —it would probably be for two hundred dollars this time.
>
> It was like a slap in the face when that story came back. I began trotting out all the excuses that disgruntled writers use. I felt sure that the editor himself had not read it. But it seems that he *had* read it. The letter said so. And right then and there I received my lesson: that you have to work to be a successful writer, just as you have to work to be a successful groceryman, or a successful anything else. . . . [Writing is] sheer labor. (HIMS 33)

She acknowledged, however, that "from then on I had something in print most all the time."[15]

In January 1912 she had another baby, this time a boy

whom they named James, after her father. Another life in her household did not slow Aldrich's writing, for that same year she entered two more story contests in the *Ladies' Home Journal*. "The Greatest Experience of My Life and How I Met It" won her fifth place and $100 out of the almost five thousand contestants, and "How I Knew When the Right Man Came" brought $150. Both were published anonymously as were the other winners because of what the editors called the "sensitive" nature of the material. "The Greatest Experience of My Life" describes the marriage of a town girl to an educated young farmer and the growing understanding that how one lives, not where, is important. "How I Knew" explains how a young woman made her marital choice. On other manuscripts for the next few years she was using the pseudonym Margaret Dean Stevens, a combination of her grandmothers' names. She chose to hide behind a pen name because "I felt a timidity in having my stuff read—the typical amateur's print-fright, which is the writer's stage fright."[16]

Not all of her writing garnered hundred-dollar-plus checks. In 1913, her total earnings came to $79. Aldrich sold three more short stories for $20, $45, and $5 respectively, received $2 for a recipe in the *Armour Cook Book,* $5 for a picture game in the *Omaha World-Herald,* and $1 each for "Criticisms" and "Feminist Experience," which appeared in the *Delineator.* An inveterate contestant, in 1914 she received checks from several such sources, including a "Yellow Page Contest" and the *Omaha World Herald's* "Booklovers Contest."[17] During this year she was pregnant with her third child, Charles, born in September. She was now thirty-two years old.

In 1914 Bess Aldrich and some friends realized the value of the growing National Federation of Women's Clubs. She helped start the Elmwood Women's Club and was its first president (the group would affiliate with the national organization in 1919). She also was among the founders of the first library in Elmwood.[18] She continued to write, and stories describing the activities of small-town club women came from personal experience, as did the stories she wrote about the church work, kensingtons (women's sewing circles, see *The Cutters*, page 29), and the personalities of the people involved.

Aldrich was more than clubwoman and writer: she was also a good neighbor and friend, thoughtful of others' children as well as her own. Typical was her concern for five-year-old Donna Greene, daughter of across-the-street-neighbors the Harry Greenes. Donna had her tonsils out—in the doctor's office as they did in those days—and had to stay at home and be quiet for seven days, a long time for an active child. The house-stay was eased by Bess Aldrich, who brought a large box with seven gifts, each individually wrapped, to be opened one a day for the prescribed seven days. In later years, Aldrich would advance this young woman enough cash, which was repaid, to assist her in meeting a deadline at the beginning of her college career when the state university could not accept her parents' check because of the bank holiday of the 1930s.[19]

Aldrich's stories continued to sell slowly over the next few years. She placed "Grandpa Statler" with *Harper's Weekly* in 1914. This is one of the early brief sketches of her grandfather, Zimri Streeter, although she used a Nebraska setting rather than Iowa. In 1916, Aldrich received $100 for each of two stories, but she also sold one for only $1 and another for $30. Aldrich was learning the market and serving her apprenticeship. In 1917, she had five sales, the largest of which was $75 from *McCall's* for "The Box Behind the Door" and the smallest was $3.84 from *Housewives League* for the "Crete Plan of Domestic Science."

"The Box Behind the Door," the story of a young woman who has something of a dual identity and heritage, is an early casting of the plot that Aldrich used in her first novel, *Rim of the Prairie* (1925). "The Box" had been to innumerable editorial offices prior to *McCall's*. She persisted in revising it, later noting that "nothing was too hard for me to attempt if first results were not satisfactory." It was the first work to appear under her own name, for by now she had the confidence to write to *McCall's* and other magazines that she would like to stop using Margaret Dean Stevens and would write under her own name, Bess Streeter Aldrich. *McCall's* responded with the helpful comment that she needed to tell editors to whom she sent future material that her stories "have been appearing in such and such magazines for the last five years." However, the editor of another periodical, upon receiving word of her name change, queried plaintively, "But are you satisfied with 'Bess' Streeter Aldrich? If agreeable to you we should like to use the full name Elizabeth which is so beautiful. But of course if you have adopted the name 'Bess' for your stories, you will want the name to be uniformly used."[20] She did, indeed, prefer Bess.

Another of her activities in 1917 was being society reporter (as she had been in college). Writing for the *Elmwood Leader-Echo*, she described the wedding of Marie Lorenz and Guy Clements, who bought the house across the street from the Aldrich home. Marie would become one of Bess Aldrich's best friends; and Guy, hired by Cap Aldrich, would become president of the American Exchange Bank of Elmwood. Still later, when Aldrich prepared to move to Lincoln, she sold to the Clements her Elmwood home, which is now on the National Historic Register. The house has since been donated by the Clements's son, Dwight, to the Bess Streeter Aldrich Foundation.[21]

Most of the time, however, Aldrich directed her writing to the magazine audience, a market in which she was determined to find acceptance. In 1917, Aldrich wrote to Dr. J. Berg Esenwein of the Home Correspondence Course in Springfield, Massachusetts, asking about his writing course and telling him of her successes. He responded that, inasmuch as she had already sold some work, he recommended his book, *Writing the Short Story,* to her and said she should enroll in the advanced course if she chose to study with him. Esenwein assured Aldrich that "If you decide to undertake the work, I shall handle all of your criticisms personally." She enrolled, worked seriously on the lessons, and incorporated his comments and suggestions. Within the year, he wrote that he was pleased with her progress and that he liked the way she developed her stories through atmosphere rather than frantic action. At this time she was outlining and writing drafts of stories that later appeared in major magazines. One story he particularly applauded, in 1918, was "Freedom from Her Mountain Height," an "adventure" for a typical American mother. This story would later become the first of the "Mother Mason" series in *American Magazine*. Others published in large circulation magazines were "Across the Smiling Meadow," recounting the story of a little girl and her mother (*Ladies' Home Journal*); "The Two Who Were Incompatible," about a determinedly professional woman who decides to marry (*McCall's*); and "A Long Distance Call from Jim," the ordeal of small-town women trying to make a reception "elegant" for a returning son (*American Magazine*). Eventually, Esenwein told Aldrich that she was a born writer and that he really could not help her anymore. He asked her to let him know when she had stories published so that he could note them in his magazine, the *Writer*.[22] In later years, she allowed her name and picture in an ad for Esenwein's course.

Another challenge of 1917, and for the next few years, was writing to motion picture companies, enclosing synopses of stories that had been accepted by magazines. One that went often was "The Cat Is on the Mat," and while many companies liked it, they generally felt that it did not contain enough conflict. These were the days of silent pictures, and one company wrote that "Cat" would need too many printed explanation lines with the pictures. At one point, the story was being worked into synopsis for a major filmstar, Constance Talmadge, and John Siddall, fiction editor of *American Magazine*, sent congratulations, telling Aldrich he hoped she would acquire the scenario writing style so she could use her skills in that direction.[23] She had hoped to sell "Cat" and other stories as two-reel films. Producers would write that they had a star ready to take the lead role, only to write later that the plan had fallen through. She was often asked to submit further materials and was contacted by agents, asking her to tell them when one of her stories appeared in a magazine, and they would take it from there. The disappointments hurt, but they did not stop her writing.

The year 1918 was a landmark year for Aldrich. The first

important year had been 1911, when *McCall's* purchased "The Little House Next Door"; 1918 was the next year of major importance in her writing. In February, Aldrich received a prize for the best story in the 1917 issues of *Black Cat Magazine*: "The Rosemary of Remembrance" tells of the recall of youth for a group of college graduates at a campus reunion. Aldrich considered prizes to be an affirmation that she was doing well, and each success in a contest provided stimulus to her writing. In March 1918 *People's Home Journal* accepted a story; in May, *American Magazine* accepted another; and *McCall's* capped the year for her with a December purchase. The May acceptance, originally titled "Freedom from Her Mountaintop," had earlier been rejected by the *Delineator*; Aldrich revised the manuscript, and *American Magazine* retitled it, publishing it in December as "Mother's Dash for Liberty." This is the story of Mother Mason, wife of a small-town bank president, her banker-husband, and their family. Mother Mason's family, church, and social obligations suddenly seem to her to be impossible, and in everyday situations she can no longer see humor, a trait that has been a mainstay of her life. She makes a dental appointment in neighboring Capitol City and stays for three days, after which she returns home refreshed and with her sense of humor restored. Aldrich won reader acceptance and pleasure because Mother Mason, the doer, the mover, the action leader, was recognized by readers coast-to-coast as the mother in their own families.

In May 1918, John M. Siddall, editor of *American Magazine*, wrote to Aldrich that the portrayal of the mother in "Mother's Dash for Liberty" was one of the best such portrayals he had ever read (as "Freedom," this was the story that Esenwein, too, had particularly liked). "Mother's Dash" had exciting repercussions. John Siddall wrote to Aldrich that he had received a letter from a young soldier, a Private McNeill, stationed with the American Expeditionary Force in Europe, saying that the story had reminded so many of the men in his outfit of their own homes and mothers that they had worn out his copy of the *American Magazine*. The soldier asked if they could have more such stories.

Siddall wrote to Aldrich, enclosing the letter and adding, "The boy is right. You've a real family there and personally I hope you'll keep them alive for a long time." Siddall also pointed out reasons for the popularity of the Masons when he told her that he and his wife "are small town folks—the big cities are full of us. Your stories take us back, renew our youth and our early associations. You don't merely create characters, you create people with whom we are familiar."[24] At this time, Aldrich already had "Mother's Excitement Over Father's Old Sweetheart" (1919) accepted as *American Magazine*'s second Mason family story: she, too, had recognized their possibilities. Siddall asked for still more of the stories about the mother who had made the dash for liberty; thus in January, February, April, May, July, September, and October 1919 Aldrich sold more of the Mother Mason stories. Each story appeared on a double-page spread with illustrations. "The Theatrical Sensation of Springtown," a story of sixteen-year-old Eleanor Mason's first brush with love, was illustrated by Norman Rockwell. Accepted in May, it appeared in *American Magazine*'s December 1919 issue. Aldrich is believed to have been the first or among the first to have placed a family series in the magazines.

This was a time when Aldrich was finding what worked for her, and what didn't. She wanted to write a Junior Mason story and tried several versions. She reworked one story twice before changing the names and sending it to the *Ladies' Home Journal*, which published it under the title of "Ginger Cookies." The story centers on Georgie Billings, whose favorite treat was ginger cookies, but who found even that most desired pleasure could be overdone. Aldrich finally was satisfied with Junior in "Last Night, When You Kissed Blanche Thompson," and Siddall, who wanted "each Mason story to 'be a gem', " was pleased.[25] In 1919, Aldrich sold ten stories—a substantial achievement for one who had never been to New York or seen a magazine editor's office.

Most of the ten sales were tales of the Mason family, and that Aldrich had created them delighted Cap: he was proud of her work. Bess and Cap read aloud almost nightly with the children. One evening Cap read them one of the Mason stories; concluding it, he smiled at Bess and said that her writing was becoming so well known that perhaps she might become the family breadwinner. Bess, however, wanted to write only when and as often as she chose. Further, both the bank and Cap's work as an attorney were prospering. More important to Aldrich was that she was doing what she wanted. She later would say that, while writing was work, it was also the result of a "desire so keen that there are no obstacles which you will not surmount to carry out that desire."[26] Life and work were very good just as they were.

The Mason series closed in March with "Father Mason Retires." Siddall was pressing for another series and urged it often in his letters: "What else have you in mind for us after this series is over? You had better get busy and start another family. I want you in the magazine all the time. I am glad to hear Mr. Davis [editor of *Ladies' Home Journal*] wants you to do a series of six boy stories. Even if you don't think you could do the series there is nothing like trying, and personally I think you will get through with flying colors." This last was in reference to a comment in her letter telling him another magazine had asked for the boy series. Later in October she wrote to him, expressing her gratitude for his help. He replied, "I cannot tell you how much I appreciate what you say in your letter about me having done more for you than any other editor." Her acknowledgment of his help was undoubtedly true, although she had also learned from the comments she received from many editors, including those who had rejected her work. An example of this occurred in 1916 with "The Box Behind the Door"—rejected because, the editor (name unknown) wrote, "It takes one quite a little time to get into it. That . . . is a mistake, as it causes the reader to lose interest. . . . [It is] a pretty good story. . . . Let us see something else whenever you can." Below this, Aldrich writes, "I like his criticism. I cut the first [part of the story], plunged right in and sold it to [*Ladies' Home Journal*]."[27]

Aldrich's 1919 successes were not limited to the Mason stories: she also sold three other tales to national magazines—one to *McCall's* and two to the *Ladies' Home Journal.* No story in that year brought less than $100 and the top was $200—good prices.

Total sales were $1,575, triple her previous high. Aldrich understood the marketplace and did not hesitate to tell an editor that the price offered was not enough, that she felt a story should bring more than the offered amount of $100, $150, or $175. Generally she received her price. In order to put these sums in perspective, one needs to realize that in 1919 a loaf of bread cost ten cents. Publishers were doing some subtle bidding, for in August 1919, Mary B. Charlton, managing editor of *People's Home Journal,* asked for more stories from Aldrich, adding, "as to boosting of prices—we are in that boosting game ourselves." Aldrich was sending to major magazines where substantial funding was available, and they were willing to pay. She was reaching the point that magazines to whom she had previously sent stories and hoped for acceptance were writing to her, requesting her material, asking why she had sent them nothing recently. Other acknowledgments of her growing recognition came. Late in 1919 she was invited to the University of Nebraska, Lincoln, to give advice to aspiring authors about writing and selling their work, and she enjoyed the task tremendously.[28]

As she learned in 1911 after the attempted sale following "Little House Next Door," "you have to work" at writing. Publications proved she was slowly achieving the success for which she strove. However, while some stories were selling, many still came back with the familiar rejection slips—enough, she said, "to fill an old-fashioned bedtick. . . . [however,] I wrote story after story, beginning a new one soon after each had been sent out" (HIMS 33). Finding the time to write cannot have been easy, for she was fulfilling the social responsibilities of a banker's wife, mothering three active children with a fourth on the way, participating in church activities and the Women's Club, and doing much of her own housework and preparing meals at a time when there were few shortcuts. All the while, she continued writing and rewriting her stories and corresponding with editors; indeed, she corresponded so often with some that one noted that she seemed almost like one of the staff. That was all right with Bess Streeter Aldrich. She was doing the things she wanted to do.

3

The

Early 1920s:

First

Big Sales

In January 1920 Aldrich received a long letter from John Siddall, editor of the *American Magazine*, predicting that Aldrich would some day start on a serial-length story. When she did, he told her, he wanted to have the first chance at purchasing it. He continued by discussing the possibility of bringing out the Mason stories in book form and suggested three editors and firms among top-ranked publishers who might be interested; these were Ferris Greenslet, of Houghton Mifflin, George H. Brett, of Macmillan, and George H. Doran, of Doran Publishing. Siddall suggested Aldrich could do much because "yours is a case of stored up energy."[1]

Prior to Siddall's suggestion, Aldrich had not considered publishing the Mother Mason stories as a book, for she saw her field as the short story. Further, she was hesitant because she knew that books of short stories did not fare well with the buying public. However, such a venture was a challenge she could not resist, and the Mason manuscript began its travels. The first publisher (Houghton) rejected the series because the stories seemed too "individual," which told Aldrich she needed to include introductory and transitional material. Because "Mother's Dash for Liberty" had had such an impact on magazine readers, she knew it should appear as the first chapter. In the original magazine form, each story had been given an "introductory description of one member of the family," but this would not work with the combined stories. To make the needed changes, Aldrich "pulled all those descriptions to the front of the book and wove [them] into something resembling novel formation."[2] This became chapter 2, Introducing the Family, and gave a brief sketch of each of the Masons. Succeeding chapters focused on the activities of individual family members as they lived their independent yet interlocked lives.

The second publisher to whom she sent the manuscript (Macmillan) also rejected it, but in this case declared that it was because of a current severe paper shortage. The third publisher (Doran) kept the manuscript many months longer than the others, and her hopes were high; then this company, too, returned it. At this point, Siddall wrote Aldrich asking her to send it to him; a woman in the office, he said, although not an agent, felt so badly that the stories they all liked so much could not find a publisher that she had decided to find one. Apparently this was not to be, either, and after several tries on their part, Aldrich requested Siddall's office to return the manuscript to her. With typical perseverance, she decided to send the Masons out until they found a home. From an alphabetical listing, she wrote publishing company names and addresses. D. Appleton was first on that list, and it was to them that she next sent the manuscript. They accepted it quickly, and to the excitement and delight of the whole family. Bess Streeter Aldrich was the author of a soon-to-be-published book. She had first offered the Masons to a publisher in 1920, and, finally, it reached bookstores in 1924. None of her other books would take so long; nor would she ever have to write another such list.

By the early 1920s, through nationwide newspaper syndication, many of the Mason stories had already been published, creating an interest that would boost book sales. Aldrich's work was also receiving attention overseas. Near the end of 1920, A. P. Watt and Son, a London literary agency, wrote and requested that they be her agent in England and America. Their credentials spoke well for their firm, for they represented, among others, such writers as Rudyard Kipling and Arthur Conan Doyle. She apparently approved, writing in 1921 that she was "presently re-selling my stuff in England."[3] She was also giving permission to U.S. film agents to sell her short stories to silent-movie companies, but she did not actively employ agents in the United States until later years, when she wanted to sell her longer fiction in Hollywood.

While the Masons were searching for a publisher, Aldrich continued writing. Siddall had asked her for a personal story, and in May 1920 she sent him "How I Mixed Stories with Do-nuts," for which the *American Magazine* paid $300, a substantial sum. In this article, Aldrich explained a great deal about herself, both as a person and as a writer. She wrote that her forebears were of Revolutionary stock, described living in a "tiny Nebraska town," of having received "enough rejection slips to fill an old-fashioned bedtick," and of finally selling "a story on its twenty-third trip." She also described working in a spare bedroom that, according to her plan, was to be her private writing room. However, her husband began keeping his newspapers and law magazines in there, her daughter housed a doll family under the desk, and her sons tucked kite-strings and tin soldiers in the desk's pigeonholes. "Thereupon," she wrote, "I decided that *my* writing, at least, could never be separated from the family life."[4]

Siddall had asked that Aldrich write her personal story so that readers could get to know her better, and she did more: she wrote her article to show readers that they could shape their own lives and could do what was important to them, as she had done.

Aldrich wrote that she had "found time in the past few years to write and sell nearly sixty stories, while raising my babies and doing a great deal of my own housework" (HIMS 33). Under the title "How I Mixed Stories With Do-nuts" appeared a quotation from the article, reflecting her philosophy: "People are always telling what they long to do more than anything else in the world. If they really did, they would go ahead and do it, because you can always find time for the thing you most want to do" (HIMS 32). In the first five months of 1920, Bess Streeter Aldrich wrote and sold two short stories and an article. In June, Bess Aldrich gave birth to her fourth (and last) child, a son whom they named Robert.

There were a number of reasons for readers to welcome and enjoy Aldrich's writing, among which was the temporary escape from the nation's relentless mechanization and urbanization. The end of World War I marked major changes. Young men returned to the United States and home. They had been in trenches, had seen death, and had seen new ways of life, new ideas, new peoples, new countries. Young women had found jobs outside the home in greater numbers than ever before yet were confused by their new roles as wage earners and by their new freedoms—for example, to have an alcoholic drink with little censure. They had few role models in this changing world other than the vamps on movie screens. Further, the tenets of religious faith and the old morals were under attack. A good deal of brashness and braggadocio masked the diffidence and timidity many younger people felt when they moved to more urban regions. The parents and grandparents who remained on the farms and in small towns were troubled by what seemed to be the denial of their lives by the younger generation. But Aldrich took her readers back to their growing-up years and to the safety and solidity of youth on farms or in country towns; she affirmed the older generation and offered models of grandparents, spouses, offspring, and siblings.

"Mother's Dash for Liberty" offered such a model. The story is told with humor, yet underlying it is the truth that great amounts of effort are expected of local volunteers. This is particularly true in a small town but true also in city neighborhoods, with their overlapping volunteer groups, as letters from many readers attested. "Mother's Dash" also presents the sympathetic treatment that Aldrich always accords the local banker—a character who will appear in other short stories and will be an important player in many of her longer works. The bank cashier was to be the main character in a series of half a dozen stories she would write over the next decade for *McClintock's Magazine,* the publication of a company manufacturing bank equipment.

Molly Mason, protagonist of "Mother's Dash for Liberty," is a woman who has reached a comfortable middle age. She has a successful husband, an active, attractive, nearly grown family, and she prefers to set [make] her own bread ("Mother's Dash" 12). Perhaps most important, she has a sympathetic humor that allows her to see the fun and lightness of most situations. The story opens, however, on a Mother Mason from whom joy has temporarily fled, who sees herself only as fat, near-sighted, and generally flawed. She is presented as a creature of artifice—glasses, porcelain teeth, and a switch of somebody else's silky gray hair that makes her coiffure only seem full and rich. She is, on the night the story opens, tired and irritable, unable to recognize that her skin is clear and fine, that her blue eyes are attractive, that humor and character have molded her features. Mother Mason is disenchanted with life and feels a slave to family and world. Having set up the conflict, Aldrich provides the resolution. Mother Mason determines to make a brief escape to nearby Capitol City by telling her family a small lie: that she needs dental work done. Kneeling for her bedtime prayer, she ramblingly explains her feelings to God, who she knows understands and who she accepts is looking upon her as he would any other little fat girl with a thin pigtail and a vague complaint.

Aldrich's language reflects the times, for World War I was in progress when Aldrich wrote this story; and at the time of publication, the war had been concluded only a month. Therefore, her announcement of the trip to the Capitol City for the denture repair "was like a hand grenade in their midst," and their response was like a "shrapnel return." Aldrich also reflects well-known music when one of the girls paraphrases a long, popular, rather doleful song called "My Reverie." In honor of her mother's dentures, a daughter quickly fashions a poem about the visit to the dentist; the poem concludes "My Crockery, My Crockery!" Mother Mason reacts to their humor with "tragic dignity" (10).

When she reaches the city, Mother Mason goes to the best hotel, registers for a three-day stay, and walks to a nearby department store and purchases a nightgown, robe, and slippers before sending her husband a wire explaining that the dental work will take until Friday, when she will return home. Her obligations in the week ahead include leading the Tuesday afternoon missionary meeting, hostessing her regular Tuesday evening card-playing guests, reading her paper on "Pottery—Ancient and Modern" at the Women's Club Wednesday afternoon, attending the church supper Wednesday evening, the library board meeting Thursday afternoon, and, on Thursday night, Junior's Sunday school class party. Most of these events also called for Mother (Mrs. Henry Y.) Mason to prepare and serve food, an activity she usually enjoys but that now makes her feel burdened and put upon. Abandoning all of this is quite daring for Mother, who rarely leaves her family or travels alone.

In Capitol City she attends movies at which she eats candy as she laughs and weeps over the actions on the screen, wanders into and out of stores in which she makes purchases for herself only, orders dinners without looking first at the price, attends a concert, goes to an art exhibit, and each time thinks with glee of the various activities at home that she is missing. She also fields a call from Henry, who wants to join her until she is through with the dental work. She assures him all is well and tells him she wouldn't consider letting him come.

As she returns to Springtown late on Friday afternoon, Mother mentally clutches the secret and satisfying knowledge that she can on rare but necessary occasions do this again. She is met at the train station by the entire family. They happily give her the good news that all of the events have been postponed until the following week so that she would not be left out. The last piece of news is that they have company coming for dinner that night, and Father would let no one but Mother fry the chicken because she does it so well. A "tidal wave of chuckles was forming somewhere inside Mother's stout interior," as her lost sense of humor returns. Kneeling later that night at her bedtime prayers, her rambling complaints of a few nights earlier are gone: "Dear Lord: I always felt that You must have a humorous side and now I am sure of it. The joke's on me . . ." (61).

The story, which, as noted above, won her wide attention and acceptance, is an outgrowth of Aldrich's own experience of a day's freedom in the city. In a 1925 newspaper interview Aldrich commented: "A person who hasn't four children and a house to take care of can't imagine what it means to be away all day long to do just as you please. Well, I did just as I pleased and had a good time, and when I went back home in the evening ready to start another day, I evolved a story in my mind that could be worked out."[5]

Although Mother Mason continued to bake her own breads, store-purchased bread was widely available. Other conveniences, too, that have long been considered commonplace were beginning to be available. Families were acquiring indoor plumbing and electricity, which, for example, allowed housewives to do their laundering more easily and not have to carry the washwater in and out. Thus, women were indoors more often; hence, they were also more isolated. Electricity made ironing easier, too. Many women no longer had to heat heavy "sad irons" on a roaring stove. More women now had some degree of leisure-time, giving them a chance to read, to live vicariously in the written word.

Magazine circulation grew as work became less labor-intensive and advertisers allocated increasing funds to the medium. Originally, advertising had been relatively simple and straightforward, but in the late 1880s it had become a partner with U.S. business. Forty years later (1920), it had become a giant industry, reaching an annual sales total of $1 billion. During the the 1920s, advertising continued its growth and became one of the country's major businesses, becoming 2 to 4 percent of national income, a level it held through the 1950s.[6]

The magazines in which Aldrich's work appeared increasingly aimed their advertising at female readers. For example, the issue in which "How I Mixed Stories with Do-nuts" appears advertises "Dustless Dust Cloths" made by the Three-in-One Oil Company. Another advertisement suggests that one can choose between "Old-Time Drudgery or New-Day Efficiency . . . for the price of four or five brooms" and the choice clearly is efficiency through the purchase of Bissells' Sweepers. Other ads tell women to "Cultivate Your Beauty," or purchase a "Rolling Bath Tub with Heater . . . that closes up in a space 3 ft. square." The same issue of the magazine also carries self-help ads: "Become a Nurse By training at home"; readers are also presented with the possibility "Of all things . . . another Raise!" by studying the "Tulloss School of New Way finger training" for secretaries. These publications were not restricted to women; they carried both articles and advertising directed to men. Further, wives could be expected to call their spouses' attention to suggestions such as "Get Into Advertising, Learn Quickly by Mail in Spare Hours"; "Learn Wireless at Home by Mail"; and testimonials in which "my $5,000 a year income, my home, my family's happiness, I owe it all to my spare time training with International Correspondence Schools."[7] Aldrich, in all likelihood, read of Dr. Esenwein's writing course in his monthly publication on writing, the *Writer*.

Because magazines depended on stories for readership and on readership for advertising revenue, good writers were essential, and Aldrich was a good writer. Thus, in November 1919, Siddall was jubilantly telling Aldrich that the *American Magazine* cover of January 1920 would claim circulation of one and one-quarter million. He added that they were already over that number.[8]

At one time Aldrich noted that she was successful because she studied the market and understood what would sell. One reader said that Bess Streeter Aldrich "has given the best story of a midwestern home and the kind of people we know." Aldrich was a close observer of humankind, and her characters were the kinds of people she knew; she understood that their lives were duplicated throughout the nation. For example, the Mason family story titled "Mother Mason Gives Some Good Advice" is renamed in the *Mother Mason* book with Aldrich humor, "Bob and Mabel Meet Tragedy." The title is a tongue-in-cheek description of the seriousness with which a young married couple view an unexpected second pregnancy—one they had intended to postpone for a while.[9] They feel temporarily disillusioned with one another and with marriage as each reacts to the news of this event, Bob with glum silence, Mabel with exhaustion and tears. Mother Mason, on her way to a missionary society meeting, drops in to show her new parasol to daughter-in-law Mabel and visit briefly before going on to the church. She finds the house, the child Betty, and the young mother all in the rare state of untidiness because Mabel has little energy in her early stage of pregnancy to get her usual work done.

While the story dwells principally on Bob and Mabel, it touches on characteristics of the entire family, noting, for example, that Bob and Father Mason are *all* Mason in that they "keep still about things the longest of any one I ever knew," in contrast to Mother, Marcia, and Junior, who talk about everything, and Katherine and Eleanor, who share traits of both (*Mother Mason* 189). The story contains advice from Mother Mason's Scottish-born mother, "Every Jennie has a-muckle to do wi' her own Jockie" (every wife has problems with her own husband), a quotation Aldrich undoubtedly heard from her own Scottish mother, and as most female readers heard similarly from their mothers or grandmothers in varying accents. Further, in the story, Mother Mason points out that each person is "inclined to think we have a monopoly on each new sensation . . . but [most couples] are no different from Isaac and Rebekah" (190). Having assessed the problem and the family, Mother Mason proceeds to take action to help the young couple over this stretch of difficulty: she whisks Mabel and the baby off to the big Mason home for a five-day visit; Bob, too, lives there, when not at work, for the five days. Mother

Mason also sends her own resident domestic and friend, Tillie, to clean the young couple's house. The strategy of rest and renewal works, and Bob, Mabel, and Betty return to a sparkling home, grateful to have again their privacy and quiet after the noise and clamor of the Mason family house. Bob and Mabel also realize they are both now pleased and excited about the prospect of the coming infant.

The Tillie who is sent to clean the house is probably a first in short-story literature: there had not previously been live-in domestics who were friends as well as employees. Tillie is drawn more fully in "Tillie Cuts Loose," which appeared in the April 1920 *American Magazine* and is included in the *Mother Mason* book. She serves as the determinedly unwed and humorless foil for Molly Mason's deeply satisfying marriage and almost unquenchable humor. The rare occasions Tillie demonstrates even a slight approach to humor come only when she is surrounded by her adopted Mason family.

By the early 1920s, Bess was so involved in literary work and correspondence that she hired a housekeeper. As indeed she might: she answered every fan letter she received, and in 1921 that amounted to more than twelve hundred letters.[10] In a letter to long-time Cedar Falls friend Grace Simpson Bailey shortly before Christmas in 1921, Aldrich explained what her life was then like:

> Am *in* the writing business so thoroughly now that I don't even do all my mending. I have my housework arranged just fine now. Keep my Gussie *Rosenkoetter* [*sic*] all the time for cleaning, dishes, ironing etc. Then my next door neighbor does part of the baking. She's a dandy cook and all I have to do is to call her up and say I want a crock of beans and a pie and two dozen rolls and they come over looking so lovely. Then Gussie's sister takes a basket of mending home with her, another woman does the sewing and I have all my own clothes and Mary's from the ready-made.
>
> Now I know you are wondering what there is left for me to do. Well, to tell the truth I do have it lots easier

now than when I was just trying to get in the magazines and do my work too. Right after breakfast I get my dinner ordered and do something in the cooking line toward it myself, get the children all off to school and Gussie's work laid out and then Bobbie and I go in the writing room and I work for several hours at my desk while he plays with his things. After dinner when he has his nap I put in a couple more good hours of work at the desk and then shut it up and take Bobbie out in his cart or go to club or a kensington or something. I make so much more money at the writing than I pay out to hire this work done that of course it would be foolish for me to plan it any other way. And with those people all working for me it keeps everything up nicer and cleaner and going along more smoothly than if I tried to do more.

Referring to her writing, she noted, "Have just finished a contract of eight short stories [the Masons],—have been under contract to turn out one a month. After New Years I begin on my first serial, and believe me I don't know whether I can do it or not, as it is such a new thing for me. It may turn out to be a postum cereal, I can't tell."[11]

Other serials had been proposed as well. One was the boardinghouse series for the *American Magazine* and another was the series of six stories requested by H. V. Davis, of *Ladies' Home Journal,* the managing editor who had purchased "Ginger Cookies." Davis had asked for half a dozen stories about this boy on a one-per-month basis. However, in 1922 she sold only three stories to the *American Magazine.* "The Masons" went to the Boston Post Metropolitan Syndication, and she wrote only a few other new pieces. Her London agents remained active, however, and the year included three sales to British publications. Her hopes for a motion picture production were raised in September when she received a telegram requesting her price for picture rights to "Last Night, When You Kissed Blanche Thompson," which had appeared in the August 1920 *American Magazine.* As author, she was guaranteed "screen and exploitation credit" and she responded in high hopes. But in January 1923, Palmer Photoplay telegraphed again, apologizing for the delay and regretting that the sale would not go through.[12]

In 1923, the "First Nebraska Authors' Week" included Bess Streeter Aldrich as a short-story writer. That year, Aldrich sold four stories, all to the *American Magazine,* receiving $450, a considerable increase, for each one. There was little need to sell more, for her British republication rights were steady (she was receiving $35 to $50 at a time for these). Further, she was writing "because I like to" and not for the financial reward, believing she should be paid a fair price, yet considering the income to be, in her words, " 'pin money.' "[13]

The year had begun with Aldrich's January sale to the *American Magazine* of "The Victory of Connie Lee," setting the tone and theme for her first novel, *The Rim of the Prairie.* The story's locale is Ourtown (Aldrich's use of *Ourtown* predates Thornton Wilder's 1938 play of that name by fifteen years). The story outlines some of the major characters she will later use in *Rim* and also uses the Realist concept of Fate; other times she will call fate "the gods" or "the stars." Many of Aldrich's works include this concept that individuals have relatively little personal control, that they are subject to the decrees of destiny. In this story, the protagonist is driving aimlessly about the country and must decide, after he crosses the railroad tracks, on which road he will continue his rambling drive. His future hangs "on that finely balanced decision." That he does not know this is the Aldrich reality: "we never do." Then Fate "laid a bony hand on the steering wheel," and his life makes a major turn (20ff).

Another story, "The Woman Who Was Forgotten" was sold to the *American Magazine* in October but not published until three years later (1926). (In 1926, immediately after publication, the *National Education Association Journal* wrote for, and was granted, permission to reprint the story; also in 1926, she received $500 for the photoplay rights to the story, but nothing came of it at that time.) The story is about Miss Miller, who had been a teacher and school principal for over thirty years. As the story opens, she has been retired for a year. Miss Miller had expected to spend her last years back East with the niece she financed through college, but, having spent her first year of retirement with the niece and her family, she realizes that such an arrangement is not to be. She is confronted by the spectre of having too little money if she lives very many years, resulting in, as she thinks with a rising sense of panic, "*Dependent* Old Age." Her return to her hometown and to her house, which wisely she had not sold before going East, has gone unnoticed by all but one or two neighbors. Opening the newspaper one evening, she discovers that, in a week's time, the old high school at which she taught is to be torn down. Both she and the school building, she realizes, are too old to be useful.

This was Aldrich's first experiment with the schoolteacher who would become the title character in the novel *Miss Bishop* (1933) and the movie *Cheers for Miss Bishop* (1941). Aldrich had firsthand experience in teaching, and she had been happy with it. But her acquaintance with many teachers who had dedicated decades to children and who faced impoverished old age would always haunt her. In this story, she made her first attack on the neglect of adequate retirement for educators.

The following year, 1924, saw sales of only three new stories or articles: "Easy Money," "I Remember," and "The Ring of the Piper's Tune" ("The Ring of the Piper's Tune" was sold to the *American Magazine* but never published). But the Aldrich energy had not diminished. That she wrote any short stories at all is astounding, for she was working on her first real novel.

4

The

Rim of

the Prairie

By January 1924, Aldrich had "Easy Money" in the mail to *McCall's*, who paid her $500 for it. She then began the serious planning of her first extended narrative, which she had probably been considering since late 1923. The new work, *The Rim of the Prairie*, would be the first she would write as a novel, unlike *Mother Mason*, the collection of short stories. She settled on the book's theme and content by February and then began the fifteen months of writing. She had not previously tried any work so extensive and was not sure she could finish: "All the time I held in my mind the reservation that if the tale became too complicated I would use it for short stories, and at one time, I almost broke it up into eight or nine of them."[1] The occupants of *Rim*'s boardinghouse may well have been personalities she worked out when she considered following the Mother Mason series with the boardinghouse series that she discussed with Siddall for the *American Magazine*.

Six months after *Rim*'s 1925 publication, Aldrich

gave a talk about the book at Iowa State Teachers College, her alma mater. She had wanted the story to be "a little bit old fashioned," by which she meant it would be a "clean" story. Hence, she told them, "I wove my story around the love of an unmarried young man for an unmarried young woman. Real pre-nuptial love. I got away from the love of an old man with a wife and family for a young girl, away from the love of a man for his neighbor's wife and wrote a simple wholesome tale." She added that she did not believe in the "Pollyanna type . . . mushy and sentimental" but did believe in the "cleaner stories that were true to life . . . no story can stand by itself, so I interwove a secondary theme of the old pioneer people who settled Nebraska in the early days."[2]

On another occasion, when discussing the novel's secondary theme, Aunt Biny and Uncle Jud, Aldrich said that "there had to be something beside a love element in the book, [because] even Romeo and Juliet would pall if there were no scene which contained Friar Lawrence and Tybalt and the nurse and so on." Biny and Jud served still another purpose, for Aldrich "felt that there was one characteristic of this wonderfully courageous person [the pioneer] which had not been caught between the covers of a book, or having been caught, had not been stressed enough—the intense love which he holds for his home place, for the furrows which he turned from virgin soil and for the trees which he planted a half century or more ago."[3]

By the time Aldrich gave her talk at Iowa State Teachers College in Cedar Falls, *Rim* was already a best-seller. It was hailed by the highly regarded *Boston Transcript* newspaper as "among the greatest books ever written." The *Chicago Post* described it as "the other side of Main Street," adding that "Mrs. Aldrich has the happy trick of writing an interesting story." Other reviews, too, were positive. Under the headline, HERE IS A GREAT BOOK, a Decatur, Illinois, reviewer said: "Unheralded and unsung, this story makes its appearance and should, if novels depend on their merits for greatness and not on authors' names, rank with the best works of the year." From the South (Nashville TN) came word that "This book is one of the new and better conceptions of the West, a type

which has been slowly coming forward, a strong appetizing antidote [to] . . . stuff which disguises as representative Western life,
type and customs." Three years later, *Rim* was still the best-selling
book for Christmas in Nebraska bookstores, and high schools
and universities were reported to be using it in English classes.[4]

Two of Aldrich's earlier stories were reflected in *Rim*. One,
"Mother o' Earth," subtitled "An Old Fashioned Love Story," she
had sold to the *Delineator* in February 1916; the other, "The
Victory of Connie Lee," was sent to the *American Magazine* in
1923. "Mother o' Earth," one of the two Aldrich/Stevens stories
mentioned in the *Best Short Stories of 1916,* is an early example of
Aldrich's knowledge of the stereotyping that was imposed on
rural and urban lives. One of the main characters, Marcia, as a
city dweller, might have been expected to be the one with a broad
understanding of others and to have wide intellectual interests; in
fact, in the story, she is far more narrow than Alec, the young,
college-educated farmer she meets. Alec understands not only the
musical and literary arts as does she, but also understands nature's arts of the outdoors. Aldrich often stressed (for example, in
the short stories "My Life Test" and "Their House of Dreams" and
in the later novels, *A White Bird Flying* and *Spring Came On
Forever*) that a person living in the country can as readily learn
and enjoy the arts as can one who lives in the city, and that the
greatest personal growth comes from the individual's active interest and participation in his or her world, regardless of place.

"Mother o' Earth" begins with Marcia spending the summer in the country with her Grandmother Cox, ostensibly to
recover her health. Marcia has not been ill but has been in a slight
auto accident, and both her physician and her wealthy uncle feel
she should summer in the country to "rest and rusticate" (11–
12). When she precipitously slides down a haystack, the event
introduces her to Alec Brown, who works his parents' nearby
farm. Alec's sophistication is unmistakable. He takes quiet pleasure in discussing poetry and in listening to classical music, distinctly different from the ideas that Marcia (and, Aldrich implies,
the nonrural public) holds about men of the country. At one

point, Alec tells Marcia that "you belong to that class . . . who thinks a farmer's a brainless nonentity" (11).

During the summer, the citified Marcia spends her days performing rural household chores; the evenings she spends with Alec. Alec teaches her to look beyond the labor of farming and see the beauty of sky and stream and field. At their first meeting, at the base of the haystack, Alec accuses her of being a city person, which she does not deny. Near the end of the story she confesses that she had lived on a farm until she was fifteen, raised chickens, and knew a lot about farm work. By now, of course, the couple are deeply attracted to one another; however, it is time for Marcia to return to the city. She must choose, between the city and wealth or the farm and love. She chooses love.

The confrontation between love and wealth, country and city, for a young rural-cum-urban woman was one that continued to interest Aldrich. She returned to this theme in the *American Magazine* publication of "The Victory of Connie Lee" (October 1923). This, too, is a story of a young woman who returns to her rural childhood home. Her plan is to spend a year with the grandparents who reared her before she marries the young scion of an Eastern establishment family. It is a Cinderella-like tale, in the best tradition of rags-to-riches-to-love. "Victory," however, is a larger reworking. Aldrich goes deeper and explores the results of the two people's lives after marriage, the passage of time, and the arrival of children. Aldrich probably began the story in late 1922 and usually spent three weeks writing a piece of short fiction. The *American Magazine* purchased it in January 1923.

Most Aldrich magazine stories begin quickly: a person or an action is thrust immediately into focus for the reader. However, in "The Victory of Connie Lee," Aldrich, who described herself as one who told stories, experiments with the techniques of the oral storyteller. She opens with a long, almost reflective, paragraph, followed by the information that the story actually began sixteen years ago in Ourtown. Thus, the reader is drawn into the story, knowing it will unfold as a reminiscence. Following the tradition of the storyteller, she personifies Fate, calling her "that old woman who pushes her human checkers about [with] a bony hand" (21).

The story opens with almost the same words as those at the beginning of *A Lantern in Her Hand*: "Ourtown sits complacently beside a great highway where once there were buffalo tracks. . . ." After the opening paragraph, Aldrich describes Norman Harper, bachelor superintendent of the Ourtown schools, and concludes her introduction by defining briefly the story's perimeters: "[T]his is the story of Norman Harper and his love for Connie Lee" (21). The story then proceeds, particularly in its descriptive sections, by allowing the repetitions and cadence of the oral traditions to work through the reader: "His way lay past orchards, / where little pincushions of apples / clung to sapfilled branches, / past alfalfa fields / ready for the first cutting, / past corn fields / in which green shoots / were already ankle depth." (line breaks mine) (21). In contrast to the background information, the conversations are crisp. Aldrich describes the accidental meeting between Norman and crotchety Old Man Lee and his gentle wife, Mrs. Lee. The latter's hands, despite their years of work, are still "as slender and pointed as a Gainsborough['s]" (21). The couple have pioneered the land on which they still live and work. In the farmyard, the buildings are scattered about; the house, with its surrounding petunias and zinnias, sits as a fenced and protected oasis behind white pickets.

Norman has gone out to visit the old couple several times and discovers a vantage on a bluff overlooking the far country. Dusk drops across the land, and suddenly a young woman approaches, running up the path but not seeing Harper in the shadow of the trees. At the edge of the bluff, she stretches her arms outward and calls, "Connie, Connie Lee, come here!" This strange behavior causes Norman to wonder briefly if she is deranged; but when he steps from the shadows to let her know he is there, her poise reassures him. She laughs and explains to him that she had been calling to bring back the spirit of herself as a child. The conversation progresses. Connie tells him she will try to get a job teaching school and that she needs the money because she does not want to burden her grandparents, the Lees, with whom she will live this coming year. Harper, as school superintendent, is at first wary, but later persuades the board to hire her to teach at Whittier Elementary.

The parallels between this story and *The Rim of the Prairie* are noteworthy, for *Rim* opens with the return of a young woman, Nancy Moore, from her life in Chicago to the rural farm-home in which she spent her childhood. She had left the farm in anger and denial on her eighteenth birthday. Nancy is to be married the following year to a friend's father, a kind and wealthy older man. However, before her marriage, Nancy wants to return for a short time to the farm pioneered by Aunt Biny and Uncle Jud Moore, the elderly couple who reared her after her mother's death and whom she believes are her aunt and uncle. The Moore's farmyard in *Rim*, situated on the outskirts of the small town of Maple City, is described much as the "heterogeneous collection of buildings" found in the Connie Lee story, including the house surrounded by its white picket fence (23). Uncle Jud and old Mr. Lee are similar types who hide their warmheartedness behind irascible pretense, while Aunt Biny and Mrs. Lee are of "finer texture . . . gentle of speech" ("Victory" 21). Nancy Moore and Connie Lee have both been reared by older people; have both returned from a city to spend time in their rural, childhood homes before marriages to wealthy urban men; and both take temporary teaching positions at small-town schools named "Whittier." Both also change their minds about the wealthy city men to whom they are engaged and, instead, marry educated men who have moved into the small towns to which the women have briefly, as they believe, returned. Both short stories, "The Victory of Connie Lee" and "Mother o' Earth," share themes with *Rim*; "Mother o' Earth" shares with *Rim* the further connection that the female protagonist denies her rural heritage immediately after meeting her future spouse following a speedy slide down a haystack. *Rim*, being a longer work, allows more leisurely development of these shared elements.

The man whom Nancy Moore meets is Warner Field, a

character Aldrich named purposefully. For Aldrich, with her deep feelings about the country, *Field* expresses many of her own reactions to the Plains, as indicated in her articles and stories. She also believed Midwest people to be both heroic and strong, sensitive and artistic. Warner Field is all of these.

Warner, the reader is told, was reared in Omaha, graduated from an Eastern university, and went from there to Chicago, where he worked successfully as a freelance writer. After his father's sudden death, Warner feels morally bound to assume his father's huge debt; in order to repay the creditors, he must have a steady job. He chances to meet an old friend of his father's, Maple City bank owner and president O. J. Rineland, who, after some discussion, offers a position to Warner. Here again is Aldrich's belief in Fate, for the offer comes at the conjunction of many negative circumstances for Field and is made to him "at the only time in his life when he would have given serious heed to it" (60). Warner accepts the position, but later he will be forced to make a decision about staying with the bank, and its assured opportunity and security, or returning to his less certain but more fulfilling work as a writer. Aldrich's consideration of Fate may stem from her turn-of-the-century Calvinist-Presbyterian rearing. It is particularly apparent in such short stories as "A Long Distance Call from Jim," "Marcia Mason's Lucky Star," and "He Whom a Dream Hath Possest," in each of which Fate plays a major role.[5]

Her first morning home, Nancy decides to slide down the haystack—something she had done often as a child. Just as she hurtles down, Warner walks around the haystack on the way to his car. Nancy lands, realizes that someone has appeared beside her, and looks up, recognizing Warner as a man she has met more formally in the city at the home of her future husband. Field does not recognize her, nor does she remind him they have met. She has told her aunt and uncle of her marriage plans but wants no one else in Maple City to know. As the weeks pass, she and Field enjoy each other's company, but Alice Rineland, the bank president's spoiled daughter who has planned to marry Warner, works to thwart any complications due to Nancy. Ultimately Nancy gives up her Chicago fiancé to marry Warner and take her chances with him on his making a living as a writer.

Uncle Jud and Aunt Biny present a contrast to the younger generation in both age and point of view. They are an old pioneer couple who migrated into the area many years earlier. During Nancy's year in Maple City, Uncle Jud's health declines, they decide to sell their farm, then reject the plan because Jud cannot leave the land he loves. The process of sale and repurchase provides Aldrich opportunities to describe how the land looked before the first plow broke into it, what their world was like for the early settlers, and to question the benefits of "progress." Aldrich views progress as something of a dichotomy. Uncle Jud rejects automobiles because they go too fast to allow one to see the roadside flowers, a metaphor for the increasing pace of life he sees threatening his world. He also refuses to plow or change ten acres of virgin prairie so area children will always be able to see how their land looked when the first pioneers arrived. In a later book, however, Aldrich approves the achievement of paved highways and the state's new and beautiful capitol. She further reflects pride in the tremendous advances in crop diversity and harvests as the result of "progress."

When Aldrich discussed the book in her Cedar Falls talk a few months after its publication, her comments suggest that she felt the primary story was that of the young couple, and that the pioneering aspect was subordinate. She added that "then a strange thing happened. When the reviews began to come in, they all said much more about the attractiveness of the old pioneer couple than of the young one. In other words, intending as I did to have the young couple the leading characters, I found that the old pioneer couple had run away with the show." She had, however, emphasized the importance of the pioneers in Nebraska who had, in one lifetime, "builded an empire, builded civilization, brought wealth, education and culture" to the area. Aldrich touched again on her deeply held belief that while most of these people could be termed "only small town midwesterners," they were basically little different from the people of the cities.[6]

Aldrich said that as she worked, she stopped often to determine if her portrayed world was as the pioneers would have lived it, if her described colors and the sunlight were as clear as the settlers would have seen them.[7] She also paid careful attention to her minor characters. For example, the pompous, opinionated Major Slack, a lodger at the Maple City Bee-House at which Nancy and Warner also live and board, is the same type as Judge Pendle, who appeared in an earlier piece, "The Weakling," sent to the *American Magazine* in November 1923, the second of the two Connie Lee and Norman Harper tales. She described such characters in depth, mentioning a walking cane or a part of an army uniform to add the touch of reality.

The Rim of the Prairie is probably the most personal of Aldrich's novels, for here she expresses her philosophies and also her deep regard for her husband more overtly than in any other work. In *Rim*'s foreword, Aldrich identifies herself with those of whom she writes and challenges again those who feel superior to her Midwest: "Blind souls, they call us—struggling spirits who can never find deliverance from sordid surroundings. Poor thinkers! Not to know that from tangled roots shimmering growth may spring to the light in beautiful winged release" (ix).

Her deep love and respect for her husband come through clearly in the character of O. J. Rineland. He is among the contemporary individuals who live in this small community on the rim of the prairie. During the period when Aldrich was writing this book, Cap was attorney, cashier, and partner in the American Exchange Bank in Elmwood. Very often Cap is defined when Aldrich describes Mr. Rineland: "No one is capable of measuring the influence on a community of a man like Mr. Rineland. Placed as he is with his hand on the financial pulse of the people, his position is one of physician to the various businesses. He is also a combination of teacher, preacher, lawyer." (155–56). Aldrich's recognition of the banker's importance to the community was verified by townspeople. It was Cap Aldrich who made the speeches at important events like Memorial Day and the Fourth of July, who helped organize the Chautauqua, and who arranged bank loans for those with collateral and personal loans for those without. One longtime resident of Elmwood commented that Mr. Aldrich was "a good neighbor to all of the people in the town. He helped everyone every way he could."[8]

Bess Aldrich and Cap shared many attitudes and beliefs, and, through Rineland, Aldrich voices some of these. For example, both Cap and Bess enjoyed works by Shakespeare and Dickens: Rineland has been reading *Macbeth* when Warner Field comes to visit; Rineland admits to having "a sense of pleasure in thinking that Mr. Pickwick and Becky Sharp and a dozen other old friends are up there [on the library shelf] ready to come at my bidding" (25). Both Cap and Bess believed in "clean" literature just as they believed in the high quality of the people who live in small towns.[9] Aldrich is probably reflecting Cap's belief when she has Mr. Rineland tell Warner,

> You can't please a lot of us with a gruesome episode in life or a salacious experience. I'm tired of a lot of that stuff. . . . They call it real life. . . . Are indecency and slime all that constitutes real life? Here's Maple City . . . nobody is rich as counted now, and yet everybody is rich as compared with the old pioneer days. Nobody is highly successful as the world counts it. There's nothing here out of the ordinary. Yet, there's drama here. There's deep grief here . . . the quiet kind . . . there's service . . . great joy . . . deep love here (75–76).

Other beliefs they shared would also emerge in *Rim* when Aldrich, through Nancy Moore's thoughts, suggested that religion needed simplified rituals: "Whatever one did, one ought to have a love of humanity with it, a watchfulness and care for the people about one. . . . The churches with their ponderous creeds and their eternal question of beliefs . . . did they make the whole thing more weighty and complicated than it really was? After all, wasn't it merely that kindness should leaven the daily life?" (122).

In this first full-length novel, Aldrich also made observations about the importance of work: " '[N]o woman in the world will ever find happiness for herself if she doesn't work.'" Why? "'Because it's part of the scheme of things.' [Biny's] philosophy was simple but it would admit of no modification" (69). On Midwestern architecture she could say: "[H]ere on the prairie . . . we've a wide-porched, hospitable kind of architecture of our own" (86). And on teaching: "'Remember that children are not empty buckets that you have to fill with something. . . . Get every brain to thinking for itself and every hand to doing for itself. . . . They will all be living, as Kipling says, 'Each for the joy of the working'" (91).

Some of the details that Aldrich used came from personal experience. The couple who came to town in their big car with the husband at the wheel and the wife "sitting stiffly on the fine upholstery of the back seat" were her brother-in-law John Cobb and her sister Clara (107).[10] In all likelihood, the child remembering the grown-up lady who wore a "cameo pin as big as a waffle iron" was straight from Aldrich's years of teaching (103). Aldrich, always factually correct, recorded the importance and the humor of the telephone in those party-line times; for, when one turned the crank to get the operator, the telephone rang in each home on the same line, and neighbors would lift their receivers to listen and catch current information. It brought people together in time of need and served as the "daily newspaper in many a country home" (21). Another event given specific description was the tornado, one of the major events in *Rim*. Aldrich describes, from firsthand experience, both the frightening sounds and the graceful but menacing movements of the storm. She pictured the tornado that she had seen and heard, writing to a friend that she had watched as it went just south of Elmwood.[11]

Aldrich not only revealed much of her own philosophy and firsthand experience in *The Rim of the Prairie,* she also revealed a great deal about her writing. As storyteller, early in the work she expressed the frustrations of many writers at the limitations inherent in the art of creating a work: "The telling of a story is necessarily as flat as the paper on which it is penned. It has no third dimension. Like a picture on canvas there is no back side to it. And for that reason it will never show life in its completeness. . . . If one could only walk around back of it and see these other incidents that are happening simultaneously, the story would become more complete and real" (9).

Working within these limitations, she did, however, try to enhance the sense of multiple action, providing vignettes of events occurring simultaneously. On one occasion, the action moves from Nancy's thoughts in the old farmhouse to Aunt Biny's thoughts, then to the boardinghouse in Maple City and a conversation between three characters, then to the city, finally to the streets in Maple City (317–18). Together, these provide a sense of the continuity for which Aldrich strove, a the sense of the flow of life.

A glimpse of Aldrich as writer comes through her use of characters as channels through whom she talks about writing. Through Aunt Biny, for example, she describes how difficult sometimes is the struggle to get the words just right: "I can feel them all in my heart, beautiful things that sing. But when I put them down on paper, it seems they're little wild things . . . they're gone" (23). Aldrich also describes the joy of concluding a work she believes is well done. Warner feels "the pleasure and fear of calling his work finished. In a small way he had the sensation of the Creator, who, looking upon his handiwork, beheld 'that it was good'" (213).

Near the end of *Rim*, after the book Warner is writing has been accepted, he "had that feeling of elation" that Aldrich also knew when work was accepted. Further, from her earliest comments about writing, she maintained that sympathy was essential to an author in order to understand the life of each character about whom he or she wrote. It is, therefore, no coincidence that Warner's editors congratulated him on "a vein running through [the work] . . . a sympathy, a human understanding which made it stand out" (243).

In no future book would she so clearly state her personal thoughts and beliefs. *The Rim of the Prairie* is important in other ways also. For in a deeper strata of her writer's mind lay the history of Zimri Streeter's coming into the new land. The short story genre did not allow for more than a quick glance at the influences that had produced the contemporary lives about which she wrote, but the slower pace of the novel allowed not only mention of historic tangents, it also provided time and space to develop them. Thus, much of Aldrich's grandfather Zimri is in Uncle Jud. Writing under her Stevens pen name, in the June 1915 issue of *Harper's Weekly*, she had portrayed Grandpa Statler as a "tall gaunt man . . . big and massive as the native timber in whose clearing stood his weather beaten house."[12] This is the pattern she used for Jud Moore in *Rim*, just as it would fourteen years later be the pattern for Jeremiah Martin in *Song of Years* (1939). In all likelihood, the words that define Uncle Jud also define Aldrich's image of Zimri: "The big head with its shaggy graying locks, the swinging arms that had held scythes and plow handles, that had planted and husked, seemed suddenly to belong to the partiarch of a people. He appeared . . . as the victor of a vanquished race, as the conqueror of a new world . . . an aged John the Baptist who had prepared the way in the wilderness for a new civilization" (68).

Aldrich was beginning, however consciously, to work through her family and its cherished people and stories toward the idea that would become *A Lantern in Her Hand*. She knew she would write something about a woman like her pioneer mother and originally had thought it would be a short story.[13] She touched on it in *Rim* when she has Field, after talking to old Jud Moore and with the encouragement of Nancy Moore, begin writing again, creating the book that is accepted for publication. The material about which Aldrich chose to have Warner write is that of the early pioneering into Nebraska, the tracklessness of the prairie, the courage of the individuals, and the struggles they faced. These are, of course, the themes found in many pioneer tales, as Aldrich was aware, and she has random thoughts course through Field's mind: "What matter that other people had written it? What matter that it was only one more approach to the romantic history of the building of the mid-west? No one had written *his* story. Each one sees life differently. No one had felt the same sympathy with the adventure of the man in the prairie-schooner who was to wrestle with the land" (144). The idea that is taking hold in her imagination is of writing a tribute to these early plains settlers.

For now (1925), however, it was enough that she had been able to write her first full-length novel. Aldrich had sent the first draft, which was accepted, to Appleton's in New York; the rewriting was done, and the final draft was on its way. And then Cap died.

here

Is Nothing to Do

but Go On"

The headlines in the *Elmwood Leader-Echo* read:
C. S. ALDRICH PASSED AWAY VERY SUDDENLY, DIED WHILE
LISTENING TO SERVICE SUNDAY MORNING AT 11:45 AT M.E.
CHURCH. PASSING ALMOST INSTANTANEOUS.[1] The newspapers of the time declared the cause of death was a heart
attack; however, Cap, fifty-three years old, had had a cerebral hemorrhage.

In Elmwood in the mid-1920s, funeral rites occurred at home; thus, Cap Aldrich's body was returned for
two days to the new house into which the family had
recently moved. The *Leader-Echo* reported that "short services were conducted from the residence at two o'clock
Tuesday afternoon [May 5, 1925] after which services
were conducted from the Methodist Church at 2:30 . . .
which would not hold all who had come." The newspaper
noted that all business in town was suspended from 2 until 4 P.M., and the schools were closed for the afternoon.[2]

Cap's death took from the community one of its

most willing and active residents. At the time of his death, Cap was in his second term as president of the school board, served on the city board, on his church board, as a teacher and the superintendent of his church's Sunday school, as an organizer and treasurer of the Chautauqua, as vice-president of the state bankers division of the Nebraska Bankers' Association, and as a member of the Spanish-American War Veterans, the Odd Fellows, the Modern Woodmen, and the Masonic Lodge. He had been asked to run for governor, but had declined to do so.

Cap's death left a gap in Elmwood's community life, and it left an irreparable void in his family. He had loved to have Mary play the piano, and the Friday evening before his death had asked her to play "especially for him" from a hymnal he had accidentally brought home with other books from church.[3]

For the boys, there would be no more long walks with him. For the family in general, no more of his voice reading in the evenings, which he had done during the week from a wide variety of books and on Sundays nights from the Bible. For Bess, it seemed the end of her world, for he gave her encouragement, support, love, and friendship. Her sense of loss was immense. On Wednesday they had attended a county bankers' convention together; Thursday they had gone to Lincoln with two of the boys to buy shoes, and Cap also bought some commercial paper for the bank; Friday evening he gave a talk at the Odd Fellows session in Elmwood. Saturday Cap worked at the bank until almost 6 P.M., and on "Sunday morning at ten left for Sunday School with three of the children. . . . It all seems like a horrible nightmare. . . . I have had moments of extreme bitterness in wondering why it had to be a busy, useful, lovable man to whom everyone looked for help and advice when the town is full of men leaning against the store buildings wasting hour after hour. Our home was extremely happy,—and everywhere people are breaking up homes for their own selfish desires."[4]

In the days after the funeral, Bess Aldrich wrote notes to those friends who had helped, for she knew she could not retain her poise if she tried to thank them in person. To her close friend and neighbor Della Greene, she expressed appreciation "for all the things you did, for I'm in better shape to do it here alone at my desk."

One of the ways in which Della Greene had helped was to sing a solo at the funeral, "although I know it was hard for you because I've heard you say so before, but I just wanted you so badly that I had them ask you." She also spoke of the song Doris Cole Clapp sang, "Crossing the Bar," which had been a favorite song and poem of Cap's:

> We didn't know of course that the "one clear call for me" was going to be so sudden and distinct. I know [knew— line through the o] his deepest desires so well—that there should be "no moaning of the bar" when he put out to sea, that I would not let myself nor the children go to pieces. I just made myself an *iron* house and lived in it, but, Dell, it just seems as though the very foundation of things had crumpled.
>
> I'll tell you as I told Inez that Death has only one meaning to me now. When Cap came out here and bought the bank and I stayed six weeks in Iowa and took care of the baby until he sent for me, I lived as busily and cheerfully as I could until that time. That's the only signif- icance that Death has for me now, —to live as cheerfully and busily as I can and take care of the children—until I'm sent for. I'm no more afraid of it than I was of the short journey from Iowa to Nebraska.[5]

Bess responded to a letter of sympathy from her friend Grace Simpson Bailey in Cedar Falls. Grace had written, saying she had wondered what she—Grace—had done to deserve having her healthy, close family when others had been so hurt. Bess Aldrich answered that she didn't know "anyone else had ever had that same feeling," adding,

> I've often felt that I really had more than my share of things coming my way. Cap, always so kind to me and so

well-liked and prominent out here in Nebraska, the four children all well and healthy, my own health, a lovely new home and a small place in the writing world with a good income of my own from it. I used to tell myself that some day I'd have to have my share of trouble because other people had them, and things had gone a little too well for me. Well, I've had it. I know what trouble is now.

I've gone over in my mind a hundred times all the conversation of that morning. It seems so trivial to think it was the last talk we had, just the most ordinary little things. He started away with Bob and Mary and Charles down the walk. And that is the last I saw him alive. . . . As bad as the days of his death and the services were, they weren't as bad as these lonely weeks since. I think we were unusually happy. . . . That Sunday before the men brought him home from the church I got home in time to have a talk with the children. And I just *made* them take it bravely. I wouldn't let myself give way at any time because I knew my actions would largely determine theirs. We've gone right back to church and sat in our own pew where he died, and I went right back to the missionary society and the kensingtons. I knew if I stayed at home and mourned it would just be that much harder. And I've just taken up my life as best I could. We've had company and we're having a little party today for Bob on his birthday. It's the way Cap would want us to be. . . . I have my children to live for and I'm not going to allow their lives to be unhappy.

I'm mighty glad I have my little talent for writing because it's going to be bread and butter for us. There must have been a guiding hand in my taking it up while the children were little. . . . [Cap] was proud of my writing . . . but there is nothing to do but go on.

She closed the letter with the wistful "I wish you could come out and visit me."

The following morning, Bess glanced over the letter before taking it uptown to the post office and added a postscript in which she worried that her comments had made it sound as though Cap had not provided "in any way for them." She wrote that he had insurance and some stock; "but of course with four children, and especially that I want them to go to college, it is going to take some faithful work on my part." She wished now that instead of the large new house they had a small bungalow, "for it would do nicely for us." However, she knew she would have to take a loss if she sold, so they would continue to live in the new house "and try to get what pleasure out of it we can."[6]

The next few months were difficult for many reasons, and finances were among them. Always careful about recording monthly her income from her writing, Aldrich now also recorded other income. Her ledger indicates that because of Cap's services in the Spanish-American War, the family began receiving a $32 per month pension; she also recorded the sale of Cap's law books to Judge Beeson for $86. Bess Aldrich may have faltered in her financial recording or may have written a bitter comment, for here are the only torn edges in the book, indicating she must have removed the pages on which she had written the original figures for 1925 and begun anew. These two fresh pages indicate that she made no new sales in 1925 but did have royalties from *Mother Mason*, from syndications, and from a British publication sale, which, along with the pension, provided the family with an income somewhat under $2,000 for the year.[7]

The personal "iron house" into which Bess Streeter Aldrich retreated those first difficult months did not become permanent, and she drew strength from her strong religious faith, from her children, her friends, and the challenges of her added responsibilities. The poised and gracious exterior that she had maintained during this period merged again with the inner woman, but to the end of her life she never missed noting in her daybook the anniversary of Cap's death.[8]

The Rim of the Prairie was due for publication in August or September, which, along with the insurance money, would ease some of the more immediate financial concern. Publication date may have been somewhat later, however, for she did not record any royalties from it in November 1925 (Appleton's royalty checks were sent out in May and November).

Aldrich had said her writing would now be the family bread and butter, but she was not as sure as she sounded or as she would like to have believed. She had been able to write saleable material while Cap was alive. She questioned her abilities: could she still write to sell now that he was gone? The problem worried her, but it also seemed impossible to sit down and write freely. Not until a little over a year after Cap's death did she complete another short story, "He Whom a Dream Hath Possest," and sent it off in July to the *American Magazine.*

Aldrich allowed time for the manuscript to reach New York, and for it to be read and accepted or rejected; when she felt it was time to have a response, she told Mary of her concern and of her hopes to hear soon from the magazine. That summer, Mary, rather than her mother, made the twice-a-day trip to the post office, and Mary, too, began to feel the strain. Finally an envelope from the *American Magazine* came. "He Whom a Dream Hath Possest" had sold (for $600), and an excited Mary ran all the way through town. As she turned the corner to home, now waving the precious envelope above her head, she could see her mother standing at the window, waiting. Both knew that author Bess Streeter Aldrich was on her way again.[9]

The story focuses on the two elderly grandmothers of a young couple about to marry. The bridegroom's Grandma Burnham is a warm, kindly woman, grown old and stout, who lives in a small town. The bride's Grandma Jeffers is an urban sophisticate who has tried to retain her youth by staying thin, dyeing her hair, and wearing youthful clothing, but she has become brittle in her subterfuge. Grandma Burnham is the archetypal grandmother, stout because she has shared with others through the years not only food for the body but also nourishment of the soul. Grandma Jeffers, in contrast, has shared neither. She has self-centeredly spent her life guarding the secret that she has tried to stay young because she was possessed by the dream of meeting again the man with whom she had fallen in love as a young woman and with whom she has continued to believe she could have been happy. She carries also a strong sense of guilt that she has never loved the man she married.

The story underscores another Aldrich theme: how often individuals misunderstand one another because of life's hidden secrets and agendas. In "He Whom a Dream Hath Possest," Grandma Burnham is the friendly individual, yet she "took an intuitive and unreasoning dislike to [Mrs. Jeffers]," whom she regarded as "kittenish," and a "painted old butterfly," but whom she also recognized as "sophisticated, modern." Such negative reaction is not typical of Grandma Burnham, but, because of Mrs. Jeffers's sophistication, Mrs. Burnham feels painfully that "her [own] best black silk . . . was not right," nor were her "red, needle-pricked hands" (hurt in the process of making the young couple's wedding quilt), nor, even, were her "face and neck whose skin had been burned caring for the garden"; thus she felt "timid . . . frightened . . . ill at ease" (50ff).

In another story, "The Woman Nell Cutter Was Afraid Of," Aldrich suggests the similar response of a small-town woman confronted by a wealthy, citified woman. In both stories, Aldrich pits the rural woman against the sophisticated urbanite. In both "Dream" and the Nell Cutter story, first the city woman and then the rural woman admits to a heretofore hidden secret. Aldrich illustrates how each human being hides fears, hides sins both of omission and commission, shows that people are all very much alike, but that individuals must occasionally break through their facades. She does not, however, indicate that facades are unnecessary, for her characters tend to resume them as armor against the dangers in their worlds. This armoring was an Aldrich personal trait, and people did not ask her questions that were impertinent or improper. One of her sons described her as Victorian in some ways, retaining her privacy by a wall of courtesy so powerful it demanded courtesy from interviewers and questioners.[10]

As late as 1925, there was only one radio in Elmwood,

typifying the East's belief that the Midwest was backward. Aldrich was well aware of the differences between how the Midwest was and how the East regarded the Midwest, but the message in her fiction was that people share the basic human qualities. One of few comments that could arouse her ire was an aspersion on her part of the country. In a talk she gave in December 1925, she responded to the perception that Midwesterners were considered as in a "no-man's land between the effete east and what has seemingly grown to be the equally effete west": "I, for one, resent it," she declared. Aldrich continued by discussing a New York newspaper reviewer who "seemed to have nothing against the writing [in *Mother Mason* but] took out his criticism on Nebraska people in general. . . . The review was headed 'Nebraska Folks.' He said the type of people here were either morosely or jocosely boring." Aldrich added that she had had "the childish satisfaction of seeing my answer . . . syndicated in many newspapers."[11] For their part, Midwesterners and rural dwellers looked with distrust at the "city slickers."

As noted earlier, Aldrich defended rural values and people in her stories as well as in comments in articles and speeches. In a talk in 1923, she had said that writers whose work denigrated rural citizens were wrong, because such writers "almost hopelessly misrepresented" the small town. In a 1923 story, she accused modern authors of having "just two types of people in their small-town writings: the discontented kind, or the dull, stolid kind who are too dumb to know enough to *be* discontented."[12] As in "Nell Cutter" and "Dream," she emphasized the basic sameness of people regardless of place or position.

When Aldrich found a writer who agreed with her stand on village and rural life, she was inclined to savor the agreement. She clipped or tore from newspapers and magazines many poems, story possibilities, and articles that she felt expressed a sympathetic viewpoint. One she saved concerned an essay in the *Atlantic Monthly* in which Dr. S. M. Crothers, the author, wrote that "the small town is treated as if it were a disease." The article addressed particularly Sinclair Lewis's *Main Street*, and suggested that Lewis saw the community about which he wrote as "too bad! No art, no manners, no spontaneity, no free intelligence, no cosmopolitan culture—just Main Street." Crothers concluded with an attack on such authors, claiming that they reflected their own weaknesses inasmuch as "a novelist can't put more into a book than he has in himself."[13] Aldrich welcomed such comments.

Nebraska's small towns have been home to such writers as Willa Cather, Loren Eisley, Wright Morris, John Neihardt, and Mari Sandoz, among others. The state of Nebraska honors its writers. For Aldrich, the first major event of this sort came on 1 December 1925, when various "literary and semi-literary clubs" honored her at a Lincoln hotel with a dinner—arranged impromptu—to celebrate publication of *The Rim of the Prairie*. A few phone calls were made. A. E. Sheldon, superintendent of the Nebraska State Historical Society, was appointed master of ceremonies, and Aldrich was feted. She had spent the day in Lincoln, after taking the early-morning train from Elmwood. At noon, she spoke to a group of manufacturers; in the afternoon she autographed books; in the evening, she attended the dinner and returned to Elmwood. The close-knit community of the Midwest recognized and honored one of its own.[14]

Despite her affection for the small town, Aldrich briefly considered moving elsewhere. With Cap no longer living and working in Elmwood, a move to either coast would put her in closer contact with the moneyed areas of her profession. New York, for example, would give her the opportunities to talk directly to her editors and the large publishing houses; Hollywood would present access to the producers and directors she needed to have her stories made into movies, a powerful temptation. As her son Charles put it, "she had stars in her eyes." However, Bess Aldrich the mother decided to remain and rear her children in the small-town environment. It was home. The decision was inevitable and reasonable: she explained, "The handprints of my four children are in the sidewalk at the door. Such small and yet important bonds are what create a home, and once one has gone to the task of construction, why destroy it and move away?"[15]

Publication of her magazine stories continued, and the money from the sales of new short stories, as well as syndication, continued to come in. In late 1925 she was under contract to both the *American Magazine* and *McCall's* for short stories, and, while she was not writing as much short fiction as previously, her payments had increased substantially. In February 1926, the *Delineator* took "A Romance in G Minor" for $750, the largest sum she had up to that time received for a story. One reason for Aldrich's fewer magazine pieces was that she had been busy putting together *The Cutters,* the collection of stories published by Appleton early in 1926, most of which had appeared in 1922 and 1923 in the *American Magazine.* Later that year, D. Appleton brought out *Rim* in London, where her magazine stories were popular with British readers.

The Cutters, who live in Meadows, are reminiscent of the Masons; the characters, however, bear more resemblance, including the childrens' ages, to the Aldrich family than did the Masons.[16] The mother, Nell Cutter, is more slim than Molly Mason, as was Aldrich herself; the father, Ed Cutter, is an attorney; the children—Josephine, twelve, Craig, nine, Nicholas, seven, and the baby, Leonard—form the same mix as the Aldriches: a firstborn daughter and three sons. Gramma Cutter lives with the family, which was also true with the Aldrich family, where Bess's mother divided her time between living with them and with Clara and John Cobb. Opal Peterson, who in the story works in the Cutter household, occupies a position similar to Aldrich's Gussie.

In *The Cutters,* as so often, Aldrich drew on activities in her own family.[17] For example, a parallel can be seen in "The Home-Coming." All six of Gramma Cutter's sons return home at the same time to visit her: one is the state's governor; another is a doctor; the others are a farmer, a university professor, a surgeon, and a pastor. She thinks about her successful children and admits she doesn't know why they all turned out so well, for she knew only that she had used "work . . . common sense . . . love . . . prayer" (158). Aldrich's mother, too, was proud of her grown children, and the Cutter recipe was the same as that by which they were reared.

While these Cutter stories remained basically as they first appeared, Aldrich rewrote the beginnings of most of them to provide transitions. The rewriting provided greater continuity, as in a novel, rather than individual stories loosely joined, as the Masons had been. Some of the tales had minor changes in title. The only story not originally in the *American Magazine* is "Easy Money," which appeared under the same name in *McCall's* in September 1925. This was a tale of the traditional U.S. home and family and their money problems that Mrs. Newsome, the mother, decides to solve. It describes the attempts she makes and the results that involve her children and husband. With name changes, the story fits in well with the Cutter style.

In "Meadows Entertains a Celebrity," the Cutters's hometown will entertain "one of the nation's big writers" (180). The women plan a dinner party for the whole town, with food and flowers arriving on the local afternoon train. However, the expected supplies are not on the train. Nell Cutter is horrified; Ed Cutter thinks it a great joke and cries out, " 'We are lost,' the captain shouted, as he staggered down the stairs!' " (194). Nell is not amused. The people rally to provide a hometown feast rather than an imitation city extravaganza, and here again Aldrich speaks out for the good qualities of the small town (183–84).

In *The Cutters*, Aldrich also points out the cyclic nature of the challenges faced by youth groping toward maturity. A visiting niece delights the children and shocks the elders with her "flippant" ways. Ed Cutter understands, however: "[T]he present generation . . . says a great many things to hear itself talk—and then it goes ahead and does just about like folks have been doing for a couple of thousand years" (251, 252). Aldrich despaired of reformers, and she pilloried them in "The White Elephant Sale." In this story, a newcomer to Meadows, Mrs. Ramsey, possesses such reforming zeal that she "gave one the sensation of seeing a funnel-shaped cloud coming one's way" (55). Life was real and it was earnest for Mrs. Ramsey; Aldrich notes that she has never seen a reformer who possesses "a sense of humor, that third eye which sees whimsy behind the reality, and the fun along with the earnestness."

Reviews of *The Cutters* were generally good. The *Literary Review* noted that "it is pitched in a light, pleasant key, and in the list of summer fiction comes as a welcome relief from adventure yarns and tales of mooncalf love"; the *Star* (Washington DC) called it "a splendidly real story to take away the bitter taste of so many other 'real' stories"; the *New York Evening Post* commented on the "genuine pleasure [the family has] in each other's society. . . . A good story for family reading"; and the *New York Times*, approving of the book, said "Mrs. Aldrich tells the stor[ies] . . . with such humor, such spirit, such understanding, and such unobtrusive recognition of the essential of happiness . . . that they offer a pleasant antidote to readers who grow weary of depictions of the drab and bedraggled aspects of society."[18] An occasional reviewer faulted Aldrich for the book's being too similar to her previous family book, *The Masons*; nonetheless, the new book modestly outsold the well-received *Masons*.

With Cap so suddenly gone, Aldrich probably welcomed the opportunity to rework these stories, a task less stressful than beginning new work. And Aldrich needed to be busy. Further, a book provided a steadier income than short stories, and the time for Mary to go to college was rapidly approaching.

During this time, Aldrich continued with the activities of her children, her church work, kensingtons, the Women's Club, and the Darners. The Darners were a group of eight Elmwood friends who gathered casually to sew, to chat, and to enjoy one another's company—a close-knit group that provided Aldrich with essential female camaraderie as did no other organization. In addition to her Elmwood affiliations, she was an honorary member of Chi Delta Phi, the national literary fraternity, Theta Sigma Phi, the national sorority for women journalists, the Omaha Women's Press Club, and, in Lincoln, the Quill, P.E.O., and Altrusa. She also lectured to various groups, although she disliked lecturing, and kept up with the fan mail that continued to pour in. Her ability to turn out substantial amounts of work remained extraordinary.

On 27 November 1927, Aldrich completed a sale that, although it brought relatively little money ($175) was particularly gratifying. This sale ended the manuscript odyssey of "The Man Who Caught the Weather." It had gone to twenty-eight magazines before the twenty-ninth—*Century Magazine*—bought it. Aldrich noted in 1949 that "*Century* [was] at that time one of the 'big four' literary magazines, [and] the story was later chosen for the O. Henry Award Memorial volume, has been read on the radio several times recently, and resold in other countries." This is one of the pieces to which she referred when she commented that she "had enough rejection slips to fill an old-fashioned bedtick" (HIMS 32). She responded to a reviewer who had corresponded with her, "That's one for all the young writers who turn pale at the sight of a rejection slip or two."[19]

"The Man Who Caught the Weather" is the story of elderly Mr. Parline, whose main activities were to bring gifts of homegrown vegetables to the doors of neighbors, to care for his feeble wife, and to make accurate notes of the temperature and the weather. The story appeared eight months after its November sale, in the July 1928 *Century*. This story is unquestionably the best evidence of her persistence. Aldrich, who had childhood memories of a similar man, believed in this story. In Cedar Falls her family had had a neighbor very like Mr. Parline, with his love of gardening and his interest in the weather.[20] Another reason for Aldrich's desire to find a publisher for "The Man" can no doubt be seen in her own interest in the weather. Her daily journal, which has very short entries, almost without fail records something about the weather conditions, temperatures, or both.

The same month that "The Man" sold (November 1927) Aldrich was elected president of the Nebraska Writers Guild. Shortly thereafter the *Omaha World-Herald* asked her to write a descriptive sketch of her work and herself for a Sunday edition. She responded that she was not sure what to write in the "bit about myself," but she assumed that they wanted information about her writing. She said she "had sold over one hundred short stories . . . many [of which] have been resold to British magazines and as syndicated material in this country," and that her publishers say her books have become "regular sellers . . . that is, there are constant reorders" and that "the books have all gone into Braille type for the blind." She added that a favorite sport was "getting over the ground as fast as I can to a theater where there is good spoken drama." She touched on the fact that she was working on a new novel about which she could say very little other than that it would be set in southeastern Nebraska and that she expected it to be ready for publication in the fall of 1928. That novel would be *A Lantern in Her Hand.*

During this time, Aldrich continued to vacation in Minnesota, where fishing was her favorite pastime and where the world of the Roaring Twenties was remote. The McClintocks, owners of the bank equipment company and publishers of a trade journal, *McClintock's Magazine,* in which she occasionally published, had invited her to spend time at their private Bonnie Lake Farms resort at Cross Lake, Minnesota. The families became friends, and later the McClintocks gave her land on which to build a summer home. Her two older boys, James and Charles, built the cabin, allotting to young Robert the gofer role, one that he did not find particularly challenging.[21] The cottage sat on a steep bank, covered with white birch and pine, at the edge of the lake. It was eighteen by thirty feet, with the thirty-foot side being a solid bank of windows facing the lake—an invaluable retreat, where Aldrich could relax and restore her energies, even though she generally took her typewriter and work with her.

When she was not out on the lake fishing or in the cottage writing or proofreading, she sewed. Often she worked at cross-stitching table cloths and napkins that she gave to friends. Aldrich enjoyed her fishing and working trips so much that, as she wrote to Grace Simpson Bailey, she realized she was going to Minnesota earlier each year and returning home at the latest possible date in August to get the family ready for school. She vacationed at the lake in the late 1920s and early 1930s, but during the later years of the depression and World War II did not make the trip. She had resumed her trips to Cross Lake by 1950.[22]

In the late 1920s, Aldrich continued to give occasional talks in Omaha and Lincoln, for which she was paid, and to give interviews throughout Nebraska. In 1929, Aldrich wrote "Nebraska History in Nebraska Novels" for the *Omaha World-Herald.* As an ardent Nebraska booster, she urged writers to write about the rapidly vanishing times of early settlement in the state and so help to preserve them. She praised the art of Willa Cather, "whose novels with their settings of the windswept prairies gave the reading public its first and closest contact with the state," and wrote of John G. Neihardt, "whose epics will no doubt be living when most of the present day fiction shall have gone the way of all forgotten stories." She strongly believed in the variety of stories that must be written, for "the founding of a village by Nebraska Bohemians is not the story of Fort Kearney. The story of the cattle ranches is not the story of the young capital city. The story of the beet fields is not the story of . . . Omaha with its industrial and social development." Specifically she urged the young writers to use their talents and write these novels as a tribute to those who had settled the state, for they were the people by whom such "novels were lived, not written."[23] She practiced these precepts, and all of her novels would bear the Midwest imprint.

Lantern

in Her

Hand

Aldrich's first novel, *The Rim of the Prairie*, was doing well; the collection of stories for *The Cutters* was at the publishers, and she was considering her next work, a long narrative using all pioneer material. The genesis of the story went back years to a discussion with her mother, who "had the faculty of describing the scenes so merrily and with such fascination for me that I used to wish I had been born in an earlier and what seemed a far more enchanting time of the world."[1]

Aldrich recounted an occasion when her mother, in her eighties, was living at the Aldrich home. Mrs. Streeter had described an early experience in her life, telling how the snow sifted through the chinks of their cabin and onto the bed, making strange patterns. Bess, in a rush of sympathy, had said that she was sorry her mother's life had "been cast in such hard places and strenuous times. [Mother turned to] me with a mixture of surprise, amusement, and pity and said: 'Why, don't feel *sorry* for us. In with the hard times, we had the best time in the world.' " The look and the accompanying words were a recurring memory for Aldrich, at times causing her to consider writing a short story of the woman pioneer. However, a short work seemed inadequate for this theme, and the pioneer couple of *Rim* did not constitute the definitive story she wanted to tell. During this period of indecision, she read of a statue being erected in another state to honor pioneer mothers; she reasoned that as others could create with stone so she could create with pen. She would honor her own pioneer mother and all such mothers with a book devoted to them.[2]

In 1925, the editor of the *Nebraska State Journal* asked Aldrich to give a talk about "The Pioneer in Fiction" over the fairly new medium of radio. She did not realize the importance or the effects of radio and afterward admitted that the idea of giving a talk on the air made her feel rather like a pioneer herself. The only receiver in Elmwood at that time was owned by the town physician, Dr. Liston, and the Aldrich children went to his home to hear their slightly nervous mother address her invisible audience.

Aldrich discussed her topic, after which she said that she was under contract for a book the following year and that she was considering "something more with the pioneer idea, perhaps make it the main theme of the book." She then requested that

> any of you who were in the midwest in an early day and who feel that you can take time to do so, write me at my home in Elmwood, Nebraska . . . a few anecdotes concerning those early years. I do not so much need a full life sketch as little detailed enlightening anecdotes,—some dramatic thing which happened to you and which you recall vividly,—or some humorous thing which still brings forth a smile as you remember. I can do nothing to repay you for this trouble, but if the anecdote you send proves to have fictional value, you might have the satisfaction

later of seeing it worked into a novel, and you would feel that *you* had helped to preserve the old pioneer days of fiction.[3]

She later said that she had hoped for possibly a "half dozen or so responses" and "was amazed to see the letters, newspaper clippings, scrapbooks, and diaries which almost swamped me." Word of mouth augmented the radio request, and the material sent deluged the Elmwood post office as well. To this richness of information, she added primary material gained through her interviews with many of the early settlers still living in Cass County, Nebraska, who remembered the 1860s and 1870s. And, of course, there were the pioneering stories with which Bess had grown up, which she had confessed were sometimes boring to her as a child. Aldrich would later say that so great was the response from the radio talk that the resulting book had seemed like a joint authorship and that the work was more of an "assembling of a story rather than the construction of one. . . . It was my intention to make some reference in the book to the fact that [so many had contributed], but my publisher vetoed the idea."[4]

However, simply wanting to write a narrative emphasizing the female pioneer, even gathering the materials for it, did not automatically remove problems and answer questions about whether or not such a work was feasible. While Aldrich struggled with several decisions before making the final commitment, she was most concerned about three specific points.[5]

First, she worried that the reading public might be surfeited with pioneer and farm novels.[6] In fact, however, authors of the 1920s had produced only about ten such works; they wrote more of urban life, indicating the interest in the faster pace of larger town and city. Sales in the following decade would also reflect the times, for in the 1930s prople in the United States needed to reestablish their ties to a more secure past and to revive interest in the nation's cultural heritage. In the years of drought, dust, and depression, the number of farm novels tripled.

Second, Aldrich felt she was "audacious" to attempt such

work when, as she would comment, many other well known and respected "writers . . . had pictured these midwest women of the soil. We had had all of Hamlin Garland's and Herbert Quick's splendid work . . . *Wild Geese* [Ostenso], and *Giants in the Earth* [Rölvaag] . . . all with women of the soil. Who was I to follow in the footsteps of these artists?"[7]

And third, she knew the kinds of women about whom she would write were not the same kinds portrayed in many of the frontier stories. Of one thing she was sure: she would write a realistic work. In the United States of the 1920s, there was a dual perception of the "Westward Movement." In part, people saw it as the push of thousands into areas of cheap land; in part, they believed in the unchallenged stereotypes of the Natty Bumppos, Mike Finks, and Ned Buntlines—these were the people of "the West." Frontiering was seen as a male enterprise, and the Western women of the time were either Calamity Janes or prostitutes, "caricatured as 'coarse,' 'crude,' 'unlettered,' drudges who were both 'slovenly' and 'unfeminine.'" Through the years, the male Westerners continued with little change, but the female picture softened to allow women to become either the self-effacing Madonnas of the Prairie, or, at the other end of the spectrum and equally inaccurate, the heroic pioneer mother, combating white- or red-skinned marauders, standing and conquering with rifle or pistol. These changes were made in order to sell penny dreadfuls (whose authors were often women), as well as novels, radio scripts, and movies. Reality was between the two extremes. However, women still had few champions to refute the belief that women "were physically, as well as socially and emotionally, unable to take advantage of the opportunities offered by the frontier."[8] Because of her childhood, Aldrich had an accurate vision of what those days had been.

Aldrich knew her idea was sound and that she could write her story after she spent time thinking about her mother, her mother's sense of humor, and her love of family. When Aldrich decided that she would write this book of the pioneers she set two goals she believed were essential: "My first desire was to get the spirit of a woman caught in the pages of a manuscript—the second, historical accuracy."[9] Aldrich had spent years of apprenticeship learning to portray on paper the people and stories of her childhood. In Elmwood, through the simple act of walking uptown for the daily mail, she also was in contact with the area's elderly survivors of pioneering days. Therefore, she would base her characters' physical and emotional reactions to the new land on firsthand accounts told to her by her parents, aunts, uncles, numerous visitors to the Streeter home, and local Elmwood residents.

By 1 September 1925, Aldrich was sorting through the mountain of materials sent as the result of the radio request, a job that had to be accomplished before she could begin to shape the story. Aldrich later admitted somewhat ruefully: "It seems a matter for apologetic explanation that a book which finished reads as simply as a child's primer should take one nineteen months to do. Fourteen months were spent in getting material together, sorting, eliminating, blocking out chapters. All the mechanical procedure which is necessary in the making of a book. Only five months were spent in the actual writing after all the preliminary work was done." However, the "rambling nature of those letters and interviews, as they jumped blithely from one subject to another and the sequence of events making one huge jigsaw puzzle," did not allow for speed, so "it took that long to prepare anecdotes and events in their correct succession of time." The information was sorted "into containers for each year of the story [so] that when the actual writing began I could pick up any chapter and work on it, be it fourteen, five or eleven."[10]

Some years after *Lantern*'s publication, Aldrich remarked that, so far as she could determine, the book was "historically correct," adding:

> I reasoned that if it were worth doing at all it was worth doing accurately in point of time and places. There are some discrepancies. Shakespeare causes one of his characters to say 'If to do were as easy as to know what were good

to do, chapels had been churches and poor men's cottages princes' palaces.' So there are mistakes. Col. McCullough tells me that I have called tomatoes love apples in 1865, some years after they were known as tomatoes. But please set that down to poetic license. Col. McCullough will agree with me that it was much more picturesque to say 'A long row of love apples stood in the window' the night of the wedding, than to have said 'A long row of tomato cans stood in the window.' I am very much ashamed of a mistake in the first editions. In speaking of the town springing forth from the brow of the prairie, I have said Diana-like the town had sprung forth from the brow of the prairie. I had my mythology mixed. It was Minerva who was supposed to have done that rather acrobatic feat. Later editions corrected this.[11]

Such inaccuracies are rare, and educators throughout the nation, struck by *Lantern*'s fidelity to fact, used it as a teaching text or supplement in social studies and history classes in junior high schools, high schools, and universities. It is still used.

Before Aldrich had the outline for this work, she had named her protagonist Abbie Deal, "a name which seemed from the first to fit her." She also had picked the locale for the story, which Aldrich felt could have been "anywhere." Abbie, she wrote, "might have traveled down into the Mohawk Valley. She might have gone with her husband to the wheatlands of Canada, onto a Montana sheep ranch . . . into the orange groves of Florida. But the natural thing for me, living where the historical background was familiar, was to choose this same background."[12] Determining Abbie's name provided Aldrich with a real person who must now have her own life and time frame. This time frame compassed eighty years, the span that Abbie would live.

Aldrich described the "mechanical limitations" that would affect the book:

Getting a full-life portrait of a woman into the scope of eighty or eighty-five thousand words necessitated that the tempo of the book be swift. There could be no long descriptions, no lengthy word pictures or prolonged conversations. Time had to move rapidly through the chapters. Abbie Deal had to feel the quick passage of time in order that the reader might sense it. And so you who have lived this will remember countless picturesque events of those early days which are unmentioned. Also if your criticism should be that there is little in the book of the economic and political life of the state, remember that the whole hard fight for existence is seen through the eyes of the woman, which took a slightly different angle than if it had been observed through the eyes of the man. The era of The League Of Women Voters had not arrived.[13]

Aldrich planned meticulously before she began the actual writing. Her short stories she worked out in her head but, for this longer fiction, she made detailed schema, listing, by chapter, in dense, chart form, events, chronology, and even denouments. She sketched out geneologies and tracked her characters through the years to keep their lives in step, one with the other. Her files, complete with dates and details, would follow Abbie Mackenzie from her childhood to maturity in eastern Iowa, her marriage to Will Deal, their pioneering into southeastern Nebraska, and the events of her approximately sixty years there.

Filled with both anticipation and humility, Aldrich sat at her desk. She later would recall the moments spent in focusing and tightening her concentration before she began. Remembering, she wrote on the back of a piece of notebook paper:

I began my work at 10:30 on a sunshiny morning of Nov. 1—1926. The first thing I did was to pray for strength, guidance, and a little of the divine spirit without which I would be nothing.

I prayed that if possible all those I love who have gone on might be allowed to bend over me for a moment with words of encouragement.

Then I opened *Daily Food* and read what was set

apart for Nov. 1st and it said: "Thou, Lord, wilt bless the righteous; with favor wilt thou compass him as with a shield" and "He that walketh uprightly, walketh surely."

It is in this spirit that I begin my book.[14]

She began by writing the conclusion, incorporating it at the end of the Introduction, in which she describes the principal locale of the story, Cedartown, Nebraska. Aldrich opens in her favorite mode, that of the oral storyteller, to establish place and time before moving into the body of the work:

> Cedartown sits beside a great highway which was once a buffalo trail. . . . [It] is beautiful only in the eyes of those who live here and in the memories of the Nebraska-born [who have moved elsewhere]. The paved streets of Cedartown lie primly parallel over the obliterated tracks of the buffalo. The substantial buildings of Cedartown stand smartly over the dead ashes of Indian campfires. There are very few people left now in the community who have seen the transition, witnessed the westward trek of the last buffalo, the flicker of the last burnt-out ember.
> Old Abbie Deal was one of these. (1–2)

Old Abbie Deal has just died, and her five grown children and several grandchildren are mourning her having died alone. Having written the end of Abbie Mackenzie Deal's life, Aldrich moves back to 1854. Abbie, her mother, two sisters, and three brothers are on the final evening of their trek into Iowa. The story that unfolds from here concentrates on Abbie and her life. As she grows, Abbie acquires as much education as is available in the frontier of eastern Iowa, develops her talents for music and art, and teaches at a rural school. She falls in love with and marries childhood friend Will Deal after he returns from the Civil War; two years later they use money he saved during the war to purchase land in eastern Nebraska, where they migrate with three other families and settle in an area very like the Elmwood area of today.

Abbie and Will together endure the problems and enjoy the pleasures of pioneering in this new and sparsely settled land. Will dies quite suddenly, much as Cap Aldrich did, leaving Abbie with five children. Aldrich later commented how much of her own loss she had reprised in Will's death. After Will's death, Aldrich demonstrates Abbie's previously untested strength and initiative as she sells off or rents parts of the land to help pay for the children's education. She remains on the land.

At eighty, Abbie still lives in the same house where she has been for sixty years. A frequent visitor is her granddaughter, Laura Deal, who shares much of Abbie's emotional and artistic make-up, and who lives nearby with her parents. Through the years, Abbie has told Laura many stories of the old days, as Aldrich's mother had told them to Bess, and has encouraged the girl to write stories, as Abbie herself had wanted to do. From her own experience, Abbie can assure Laura that at times "realities seem dreams . . . but the dreams . . . are all real" (282).

Late on a July afternoon, Abbie Deal's heart wears out, and she dies alone in her home, as she had wished to do. Because of the circularity Aldrich used, the novel thus returns to the scene of the Introduction.

With Abbie's death, Aldrich carried the story into July 1927, in accordance with her worksheets; however, she finished the actual writing of *A Lantern in Her Hand* in April 1927. She had become so intensely a part of her characters' lives that she may have written faster than she anticipated, and she was also deeply interested in the Deals. She would later say "that after I was well into the writing, I would have finished the story even though I had known not a copy would be sold . . . [for I was] so interested . . . in the characters and in the early Nebraska setting."[15]

Aldrich used a great deal of family history in this work, basing the trip into Nebraska on her own mother's trip into Iowa (although Aldrich's mother, Mary Wilson Anderson, was ten years older than Abbie at the time of the move). Another fact-to-fiction link can be seen in Abbie's Irish mother, Maggie O'Connor

Mackenzie, who is modeled on Bess's Cinderella grandmother, Scotswoman Margaret Stevens Anderson.

Because this book is a tribute to her mother, Aldrich draws on a great many of the stories she heard from her mother. She also adopts artifacts, mixing the generations as she does so: the strand of pearls that is frequently mentioned was inspired by a strand of blue beads purchased by Margaret Anderson's family at the roup sale—one of the few reminders of her home in Scotland that Aldrich's grandmother carried with her to the United States. A white silk shawl in the story represents Bess's mother's wedding shawl from the day she married James Streeter; a stone doll and acorn dishes also match Bess's mother's keepsakes—items with which Bess had played (21, 27–28).

In *Lantern*, son John's education, law degree, typhoid fever in the Spanish-American War, and experiences as U.S. Commissioner in Alaska parallel Cap Aldrich's life. Abbie receives letters from John when the winter's ice melts enough to allow the mail to come south. These letters describe Christmas dinner delicacies such as fishballs, egg sauce, and ptarmigan pot roast, as well as gold strikes and the swift claim-staking of rivers and benches. This information was contained in Charles Aldrich's diary and in letters to Bess from Cap when he was in Alaska.[16]

Aldrich also used historical facts other than her own family's. Women not uncommonly worked alongside men in the fields, and, although Abbie Deal does not do so, Christine Reinmuller performs field labor. Among Aldrich's observations was the truth of many a pioneering woman: like many others, Abbie was never financially able to return to her Eastern home, or did so only because of a death. Aldrich also pointed out through Abbie's realization in an Iowa cemetery that "a trail of graves" marked the westering path of her family (189). Historic fact woven throughout *Lantern* as a part of the story gives this work a dimension beyond fiction. Thus, in 1902, when Abbie was to see her first magic-lantern show (forerunner of moving pictures), she reflects the attitude of her times. She was suspicious, sure it was some kind of trick: there was a "catch in it somewhere." But the characters, "unbelievable as it was. . . waved and jerked and twitched. . . . The advertisement had not lied. Across the sheet the people moved" (213–14). On another occasion, when Abbie plants her first, small sowing of winter wheat in 1894 and alfalfa the following year, Aldrich is providing data about the changing farming practices from the corn-crop basics of previous years to the tentative beginnings of diversified farming. For Abbie, these experiments and farming on shares with two neighbors help financially, although "one year of drought followed another, so that a share in a poor crop was sometimes next to nothing" (191). Aldrich writes that Abbie spends nothing on herself, makes and sells butter in town, and trades chickens and eggs for staples at the town store, for every cent possible must be used to pay for schooling for John and Isabelle. In the late part of the 1800s and into the 1900s, many a rural homemaker followed a similar pattern. "Egg money" was often the only cash that came into the home.

Aldrich fuses material from diverse sources. One scene includes local Elmwood history, her grandmother, and information sent in response to her radio request. This was to describe a 1925 "old settlers' " picnic on the Chautauqua grounds near Stove Creek. Abbie is seventy-eight and Aldrich describes her as "shriveled as . . . when the frost comes on. Her O'Connor body was shaped like her mother's had been,—a pudding bag tied in the middle" (243). The reader listens in on the story of the Mormon women pulling their carts across the prairie; hears of a child crying because his shoe was laced too loosely, but whose mother was afraid she would lose their place if she stopped to fix it; empathizes with the woman settler who saw and heard the event, and who tells of having nightmares for years afterward because she didn't help the little boy. Another conversational scrap is a discussion of how much the Indians liked watermelon; another is about making syrup by boiling down watermelon juice (244). The last three elements were taken from materials sent in response to the radio program.[17]

The book was published in September 1928, and reviews

soon appeared. The *New York City Times* began its review, "With real sympathy, beauty of expression and apparent intuitive accuracy, Bess Streeter Aldrich has infused *A Lantern in Her Hand* with some of the rugged spirit of the earlier West." Following a synopsis, the reviewer concluded that "this novel may be considered as a contribution to a literature that is pecularly American." Another mewspaper called *Lantern* "a splendid tribute to the pioneer woman, whose part in the growth of the country can not be measured." A review syndicated in more than forty papers noted "the writer seemingly made no effort to inject drama . . . beyond that which came into the lives of every family . . . [fighting] nature for possession of the rich soil." Aldrich specifically commented that there was neither sophistication nor diversity of scene, for Abbie was a woman of the soil, a homemaker who did not go far from home, a mother who devoted her life to loving and rearing her family. The same review added that "one likes the Plains states better, and has more faith in the United States, for reading the book. . . . But chiefly I like to boost this book because it is so true, so natural and so American." Earl A. Aldrich (no relation), of the *Saturday Review of Literature,* struggled against wanting to like *Lantern*: "Some ruthless person should review Mrs. Aldrich's last novel, someone who would treat it with the callous injustice that it richly deserves, someone who would not mind ignoring its merits and who would call it canned soup and be done with it." Grumbling, he admits that the pioneer hardships, the mother's sacrifices, and the Christmas parties all seem "real," just as the "pioneer accomplishments are heroic." Finally, he acknowledges that "she does make the settlement of the West seem an epic accomplishment. That just men and women could have brought it about and borne children and educated them and built cities and so on passes belief. . . . [She] makes it seem worth doing." The *St. Louis Times* wrote that *Lantern* was "a picture as thrilling and joyously fresh as the prairie sky. A most welcome addition to those . . . documents that recount the development of our national consciousness."[18]

In a talk in Tucson, Arizona, after *Lantern* came out, Appleton editor and vice president Rutger Bleeker Jewett expressed his delight with the book and called it "one of the epics of the day depicting pioneer life," adding that "each book done by Mrs. Aldrich is richer than the preceding." *Lantern* became one of the most popular books of the Christmas season. Appleton had so many orders from booksellers that during the week of 7 December 1928 the company ran "three large printings" and the following week ran two more. A delighted Aldrich wrote her friend Bess Furman that *Lantern* went into its seventh printing in January, adding "it grieves me not."[19]

March 1929 saw *Lantern* reach the best-seller list for the first time. It appeared on at least five such lists and "was still there in April, 1931." In May 1930, "sales [were] running between 1,500 and 4,000 weekly. The *Bookman* ranked it as one of most popular books in libraries throughout the country by June 1930, a ranking that remained into 1931. In December 1929, sixteen months after publication, sales doubled those of the previous Christmas season.[20] Columnist Harry Carr, in the *Los Angeles Times*, pronounced that "[Aldrich's] novel ranks with *The Good Earth* as one of the most remarkable and genuine of these ten years." *Publishers' Weekly* reported in January 1932 that "perhaps the most amazing sale is that of *A Lantern in Her Hand* which was published in September, 1928. It sold more than 1500 copies this January" (on this clipping, Bess Aldrich added in pen: "4 years after publication"). Aldrich, in 1930, responding to a "very gracious letter" from Herma Naomi Clark, wrote that "Bowker, who gets out the list of the twenty-five best sellers each month, report[ed] that it [was] the oldest title now of the twenty-five." A 1936 listing of "Weekly News of Books, a Check List of Old Favorites for New Readers" includes *Lantern,* noting that the work was in its sixty-third printing. In this page-length old favorites listing, only three novels had gone into more printings: *David Harum, Uncle Remus: His Songs and His Sayings,* and *Mrs. Wiggs of the Cabbage Patch.* Bess Aldrich noted at the top of this clipping that the others had all been in print much longer than *Lantern.* Bessie Rowe, field editor of *Farmer's Wife Magazine,* credited *Lantern* with beginning a great change of attitude toward frontier women. Rowe noted that Aldrich had shown women could "love the soil" as much as men were purported to do, adding that the author had also demonstrated women possessed a great "spirit of hopefulness" rather than the usual "dullness and steady decline of spirit." In a March 1939 radio program on Station KDKA Pittsburgh it was reported that "*A Lantern in Her Hand,* written ten years ago, was listed recently in a Gallup poll as one of the ten books most read by American women," and "last year it was among the first ten in point of sales to women readers"; it had "gone into seventy printings by that time."[21]

As a portrait of an era, the popularity of this work did not diminish. In 1942, Aldrich was asked for permission, which she granted, that it be added to other classics for classroom use in the Modern Literature Series, which included such works as Steven Crane's *Red Badge of Courage* and Edith Wharton's *The Age of Innocence.* In 1947, it went into the Pocket Books, series making Aldrich "one of the first Nebraska writers to have a pocketbook edition. About 250,000 pocket editions of *Lantern* have been sold."[22] As with all of her books, she gave permission to have it set in braille shortly after publication.

What made this book so popular? One factor was partisan readership. In the late 1920s and early 1930s there were wrenching disagreements among readers. Some rejected works that were "not clean" (i.e., books that used obscenities or graphically depicted the grim aspects of living); other readers viewed works that did not contain these darker aspects, which they felt reflected the truth of life, as "Pollyana" or sweetly sentimental works. Aldrich disagreed with the latter view, feeling that "sentiment . . . lies in the hearts of people. Wherever there are folk who live and work and love and die, there is the stuff of which stories are made." Because Aldrich stressed such basic values as home, love, and family, *Lantern* was used often as a text for those arguing to keep and strengthen those values. During the Roosevelt presidency, a woman in Washington DC wrote Aldrich to tell her that President Roosevelt's pastor, when Roosevelt was in attendance, had referred to *A Lantern in Her Hand* in the sermon. Aldrich wrote to an Oregon publisher, who included some Aldrich stories in an anthology, that she, too, had heard at least two such sermons, and, over the years, many others reported *Lantern*-based sermons. Reviews often noted its "decency." In a speech, Aldrich referred to *Lantern* by quoting from a *New York Times* review:

> The success of a book as *A Lantern in Her Hand* shows that the American people are inherently decent. Here is a book without a single vulgar word in it, characterized by the finest qualities of cleanliness and decency that has remained consistently upon the best seller lists. While many shake their heads over present day looseness of language and subject matter in so much of the fiction published, there is evidence to hand that the American people can take to heart a clean and decent novel.[23]

Another factor was that, even while understanding that what the characters accomplished was extraordinary, readers could imagine themselves as these characters. In a talk, Aldrich noted that "the pioneers wrote no novels, you know. They lived them. Heroes never seem heroic to themselves. When they do they cease to be heroes. So it is only in looking backward that the things they did appear to take on heroic proportions." She gave credit to others: "I've been fortunate in my contact with people who gave me an immense amount of first hand knowledge."[24]

Adding to the reality of the characters was the reality of setting. Again, Aldrich used family history as well as her own sense of writing: her "own people talked pioneer days a great deal when I was a child." In a draft for a talk, she described elements that were important for authors to add to novels: "a myriad of small deft touches compose its [the book's] fabric. The things seen and felt, smelled and tasted and heard. Those hundreds of references which quicken the reader's senses and which bring him a feeling of living in the story almost unrealized to him. Characters protrude themselves, atmosphere surrounds them. It is the writer's achievement when the reader is unconscious of the two and knows only the effect blending." People wrote to her from everywhere, and there were times when the large tapestry-bag she carried over her arm could scarcely hold all the mail she received when she went on her twice-daily uptown trips to the post office.[25] Aldrich responded, answering questions and thanking the individual for writing.

One of Aldrich's hopes was that *Lantern* would be made into a movie. In 1944 she wrote in a letter that "Frank Lloyd so nearly took it for pictures that we had luncheon together over it at the studio. He couldn't get the star he wanted [Helen Hayes] and dropped the idea. . . . When I had tea at the Oscar Hammersteins they said that Irene Dunne's husband had wanted her to do it." One studio assured her that it would be filmed sometime, "for it's on the way to becoming a classic." Mary Pickford wrote Aldrich that "I can't tell you how many people have suggested your novel LANTERN IN HER HAND to me, and I have a copy on my desk now waiting for me to read it. It is a pleasure I have long promised myself."[26]

The book achieved international readership. In England, the *Times Library Supplement* wrote, "There is imaginative power in this story of pioneering days in Iowa and Nebraska, and even the most homely and trivial happenings in the eighty years of Abbie Deal's life are so dramatically treated as to give the chronicle of her struggle against an adverse destiny an absorbing interest." Another English review, in the *Dundee Courier,* stated that "if not actually the best, certainly one of the best novels to come from America. A story told with beauty and distinction that has in it the ring of real literature. As a story of womanhood there is something epic about the novel."[27]

A Japanese girl said she rejected her contemplated suicide after reading *Lantern* and gaining insight into her own troubles; a Los Angeles newspaper headlined, CHINA TURNS CURIOUS, MIDWEST NOVEL INTERESTS ORIENT, adding that as Americans had read Pearl S. Buck's best-selling novel about China, *The Good Earth,* "China became aroused by an equally stirring book, *A Lantern in Her Hand.*" Aldrich wrote to her publishers asking them to help get copies of *Lantern* to "an English class for Chinese girls in Shanghai . . . for they could only scrape together 12 loaned copies . . . and [the teacher] has decided she wants each senior class to study it." Reflecting further interest in China, *Lantern* "was made into a serial for publication in a Chinese magazine."[28] In 1939, it was serialized in Belfast, in the *Irish Christian Advocate*. *Lantern* was translated into most of the languages of Europe, including Latvian and Greek, into Thai, and, in 1953, into Arabic.

In a letter Aldrich wrote to author Mari Sandoz congratulating her on a recent book, Aldrich mentioned being surprised at the request for permission to have *Lantern* translated into Arabic and expressed regret that she had made Abbie fearful of Native Americans. Now, she said, she understood better. Sandoz replied that "I don't see why the Arabs wouldn't like Abbie's story. There is a lot of remote living among them now, since the nomadic hunting patterns have broken up, and much that can pass as pioneering is taking place." About Abbie and Native Americans she added, "Don't regret the fact that Abbie Deal was afraid of Indians. The propaganda that made it possible to expropriate the Indian convinced people with much more time and sophistication. . . . Besides there were bad Indians just as there were bad whites . . . often heightened by the white man's firewater."[29]

Lantern has remained in print continuously since its first publication in 1928. In 1950 it was selected as one of the ten "best books to be recommended to foreigners and newcomers-to-America, because of its accurate portrayal of this country." Inspired by Aldrich's portrait of her mother, the Lincoln Women's Club commissioned a statue honoring "early comers to this region," which was erected in 1935. It still stands.[30] Thus, Aldrich's desire to pay homage to her own and other pioneering mothers ultimately resulted in both a book and a statue, and her pen was responsible for both.

Aldrich was "thoroughly surprised as well as gratified" with the response to her book, particularly as she had worried because previously "not one [author] has done my kind of mother." People wrote her from everywhere, and she summed up the importance of these letters in an article: "There have been many gracious reviews. But nothing any clever critic has said meant so much to me as the commendations of the children of the prairie. No New York or Boston or London review has pleased me as have the letters from the pioneers' sons and daughters which said 'You have written the story of my own mother,' or 'Abbie Deal was just like my grandmother.'"[31] The results of her book were more rewarding than she could possibly have hoped.

7

White Bird

Flying

After the publication of *A Lantern in Her Hand*, Aldrich could ease her writing schedule for the remainder of 1928, except for answering the great number of readers' letters. She also corresponded with editors at Doubleday, Doran about a series of short stories. However, in early January, Doubleday wrote, rejecting her suggestion of the short story series because "the fact is that sales of such stories are not apt to be profitable unless they are included in a series such as the O. Henry Prize list."[1]

In 1929, Aldrich sold little new work, placing only one short story, one short short story, and one article. She planned to work as she had previously; that is, following publication of a novel she would spend the next year writing short pieces. Alternating long and short fiction gave her a change of pace.

Although she was doing relatively little creative work, she found time after *Lantern* to write "Pie," a story about Miriam Foster, an assistant supervisor at a teachers college (Aldrich had been an assistant supervisor while she worked on her second degree at Iowa State Normal School). Miriam sees a bleak future because the training she is receiving will prepare her only to teach other young women to be primary grade teachers. They will then instill in their students the three Rs and such incidentals as knowing about healthful foods. Miriam jokes to a young man, Barton Jones, that nutrition lessons instruct children to "eschew pie and chew prunes," confessing, "I know that's an awfully low type humor" (78). Jones is a young attorney to whom Miriam later explains that she will eat pie if she ever, for any reason including marriage, leaves teaching at the college, where there is a rule that "every woman teacher who marries must leave the faculty" (78). As the reader anticipates, Aldrich has Jones persuade Miriam that they should marry, and, at a dinner watched over by her shocked students, Miriam orders the gloriously rich "chocolate pie with the whipped cream and marshmallow icing" (85). After completing the lighthearted "Pie," Aldrich sent it to *Ladies' Home Journal.* They rejected it on 3 January 1929 and she then sent it to the *Saturday Evening Post.*

On New Year's Day, Aldrich had answered a letter from the managing editor of the McClure Newspaper Syndicate, wanting to syndicate "The Man Who Caught the Weather." She told him she had refused a similar offer from another syndicate but would sign with him. Pleased, he wrote a few days later thanking her and enclosing a contract that gave her 50 percent of the net proceeds of syndication in the United States and Canada. For the year, this came to a little less than $50, but Bess Aldrich welcomed the small as well as the large sums, including the occasional $10 from the Northwestern Speech College of Minneapolis for "dramatic rights" to some of her stories.[2] As a good businesswoman, she wanted her name and material in the public eye.

Later that January she responded to a letter from Rutger Bleeker Jewett, editor in chief of Appleton, admitting that she was discouraged and had no new creative ideas. He disputed this, telling her of others who had felt the same and who had then gone on to write more successful works. Jewett also encouraged her by pointing out that *Lantern* was making more sales in January "than any of the novels carried over from last year's list." He sent her some books that he thought she might enjoy.[3]

The *Saturday Evening Post* returned "Pie" in February; *Red Book* and *Smart Set* rejected it in May. Generally, they felt that the work was too slight but invariably asked her to send more material, saying they were sure the next one would be just what they wanted. At last, the *Country Gentleman*, "The Oldest Agricultural Journal in the World," accepted it on 3 July 1929. Editor H. C. Paxton's letter indicates they were pleased with their purchase and willing to pay whatever she asked. He asked, "What price are you getting for your fiction now?" They sent her a check for $1,000.[4] She was pleased finally to have made this sale.

Because Aldrich was a persistent advocate of small towns and rural life and an opponent of the superior attitude of Eastern city dwellers, Paxton asked her to

> write a series on the up-to-dateness of the small towner. There are a lot of people here in the East who still think the farmer is a hick who goes to town in overalls and chews a straw. It seems impossible to get that idea out of their minds and I want to attack that belief through a series of fiction stories. . . . In recent trips that I have made out through that country I find the girls wear the same kind of clothes that they do on Fifth Avenue. They use lipstick as freely, they know the latest slang and about the same proportion of them are acquainted with hip flasks and all the other social accoutrements of the effete East. The sheiks are just as smart and their hair just as slick in the West as they are in the East. . . . [M]y idea is not to moralize nor to play up bootlegging, highjacking or the vices of the young folks, but I would like a rather accurate picture of life just as it is lived. I should [like] to show that little towns have stepped ahead . . . and that the old-time slow hayseed town that may have existed twenty-five or thirty years ago is no longer to be found in America.

The terms *hick* and *effete East* indicate the continuing deep opposition between the two segments of the country in the pre–World War II era; Aldrich and many other Midwesterners chafed against the belittling attitude they believed Easterners ascribed to the people of the Midwest. Aldrich could not accept this project, for Paxton was not seeing the kind of young people her children were, the young people they knew and with whom they associated, or the rural family life she knew so well.[5]

Aldrich's children were a great source of joy to her, full of laughter and fun and rarely causing her concern. Aldrich and Mary shared a close mother-daughter relationship. Aldrich often discussed her writing with Mary, frequently having Mary critique a story before it was sent to a publisher. Mary was now in college, attending the University of Nebraska in Lincoln and coming home often on weekends, which delighted Aldrich. After graduation, Mary taught for a year before marrying her college sweetheart.

Aldrich enjoyed her sons, too. At the age of fifteen, Jim had built a large backyard roller-coaster that brought youth from many parts of the county for the wild ride. By the age of seventeen, he had abandoned such engineering and had become engrossed in art, drawing in every spare moment. Jim was perhaps the quietest and most introverted of the Aldrich sons. As he became more proficient as an artist, he hung pictures of nudes in his bedroom and practiced drawing them. Despite her Victorian upbringing, Aldrich did not fuss or have him take them down, for she recognized his talent and his insatiable desire to learn. Everything was a subject for his sketching pencil, and one of his cartoons remained on a basement door in the Aldrich home for many years. He would later provide dust jackets for some of his mother's books, the illustrations for some, and illustrations and dust jackets for many other writers.[6]

Chuck, twenty months younger than Jim, always active, worked on farms during the summer to build muscle for the football season. Football-playing ended for him in his senior year of high school when he severely damaged a knee. The farmwork had another purpose for Chuck also. When he was thirteen, he saved his summer wages and bought a motorcycle without telling his mother. The first day he rode it home, he did so with both pride and trepidation. He knew his mother wouldn't like it. She didn't. But he also knew he would "bring her around." And he did. The motorcycle also brought around the neighborhood youngsters, clamoring for a ride. Chuck told them he would take whoever "could yell the loudest, and [they] yelled as hard as [they] could until he finally chose one." When he entered the University of Nebraska, Aldrich bought him a baby-blue convertible as a special gift, because, he claimed, he was the best driver in the family. A few years later, after graduating from college and getting a job in aeronautical engineering, he bought a small Piper Coupe and flew it to Lincoln, where he met his mother and Mary. Aldrich's reaction was much as it had been to the motorcycle.[7]

Bob was the youngest, seven years separating him from Chuck. Bob had the advantage of having older siblings and learning from them; and, like them, he developed his own field of expertise. His mother's skill with words, as well as her youthful writing activities, manifested themselves in Bob. From childhood, he wrote stories that he proudly showed his mother, demonstrating early the signs of the writer and newpaperman he would become.

The youngsters generally got along well together, yet they were a collection of different personalities. Mary had a gentle humor, and even though she teased her brothers, she "being the oldest and a girl, was respected." Jim got along well with both his sister and his brothers. He could irritate Chuck with his habitual slowness to get started at chores or jobs they were to do, but there was more grumbling than physical disagreement among the boys. Chuck was the family tease: he enjoyed trying to provoke his brothers, particularly his younger brother. Sometimes he pushed too far, and the other brothers would go after him, but their infrequent fights were quickly ended. Occasionally, Bob's brothers would not take him to out-of-town basketball games, which disappointed him, but only when he felt "put-upon" by them did he lose his temper—and because he was so much younger than his brothers, he did not worry them too much. Their mother's high expectations of the boys kept them from getting into serious disagreements with one another, for it was simply not done in their family. Jim died in 1972, but the remaining children have stayed close by visits, telephone, and letters through the years.[8]

Being an Aldrich in Elmwood was not always easy for the youngsters, for they well knew that, as Mrs. Aldrich's children, their activities were noted by the townspeople. This did not keep them from enjoying themselves, however. Aldrich did not lecture the youngsters about morals or proper behavior, but when others erred would take the occasion to comment to the children that she knew "none of you would do anything like that." Such comments reflected "the Victorian way she herself was raised." Aldrich "trusted [her children] to behave, so [they] felt they had to"; these were the expectations held by their friends' parents as well. As their mother made and retained lifelong friendships in Cedar Falls, the Aldrich children made and have retained lifelong friendships in Elmwood.[9]

To be a member of Bess Aldrich's household meant pancakes or waffles on a cold winter's morning; meant dinner of baked or fried chicken or the family favorite, meatloaf, which the children all agreed they could never have often enough; meant conversations about national as well as local events; and meant attending Sunday school and church. It also meant reading. Aldrich had continued the practice she and Cap had begun of reading to the children each evening, from children's books at first, and as they grew older from such books as Booth Tarkington's *Penrod* and *Sam*, from James Thurber and Robert Benchley, and from magazines. Family bookshelves contained both American and European classics, a set of the *Encyclopedia Brittanica*, Carl Sandberg's *Lincoln*, several Barrie and Dickens volumes, and many others. Aldrich was an avid reader until she became a book reviewer for the *Christian Herald*; thereafter, she had little time for pursuing her own reading choices. In the winter, after supper, their evening meal, the family read and listened to the radio or records. Aldrich often had a basket of sewing to work on. If she were behind on a book or story, she sometimes went into her bedroom to work with the door closed. Summer evenings, similarly peaceful, were spent on the big front porch, although then the youngsters were more often out with other young people. As twilight came, Aldrich would put away her reading or handwork and water her many flowers or go across the street to visit with Marie Clements or Inez Greene.[10]

Aldrich did not curse or use strong language, nor do any of her characters. Her children, too, "never got away with any cuss words." Her occasional "land o' Goshen" echoed her own mother's strongest language. A term she used and believed in was *gumption;* Bob, for example, recalled hearing such directions as, "show a little gumption and get the lawn mowed!" He knew he'd better do it. When two of the sons later discussed their childhood, they "both agreed that it was remarkable that neither of us could remember Mother once getting annoyed when we interrupted in her writing. . . . Somehow she could deal with the problem and go right back to her work."[11]

Aldrich enjoyed having friends in her home, and she entertained when it was her turn to have the Women's Club, kensington, the Darners, or some other event or organization. In Elmwood, her closest friends were the women of the Darners (mentioned above). The group had no officers, rules, or set meeting dates. They got together when one of them would decide she hadn't had the others over for a while and would call and tell each to bring her darning and come. These women, Doris Cole Clapp, Marie Clements, Emma Clements, Opal Clements, Della Greene, Inez Greene, Mary Hazel Liston, and Naomi Totman were friends Aldrich would remain in contact with and cherish for life. Her P.E.O. group from Lincoln came down in a bus once a year for a meeting at the Aldrich home. At such times, as would any mother, she reminded the children not to "sample the sandwiches or cake." Gussie Rosenkoetter would make the children a pie for themselves, just in case there were no leftovers. Aldrich also enjoyed the young people who came in with her children to play or to study or to eat. For Aldrich, life in Elmwood was family and home and work. It was good.[12]

The mail brought the outside world to her. In June 1929, an editor at Little, Brown sent Aldrich a complimentary copy of Mazo de la Roche's forthcoming novel, *Whiteoaks of Jalna*. The accompanying letter noted that "it seemed to many readers, when they finished JALNA [an earlier novel, published in 1927], that there still existed, between the various members of the Whiteoaks family, almost unlimited possibilities of dramatic, even explosive[,] developments. These . . . are traced in WHITEOAKS OF JALNA—and we feel that Miss de la Roche has performed the rare feat of producing a new story that, while it is in a sense a sequel, stands on its own feet as a novel."[13] This idea may have dropped into Aldrich's subconscious and become a part of the impetus for *A White Bird Flying*.

Also in June, O. B. McClintock wrote, telling Aldrich that they were going to reactivate the company house organ, *McClintock's Magazine*, which had not been published for some time, adding that they would print an Aldrich story they had had in their files prior to discontinuing publication. "The Cashier and the Business Woman" underscored the cashier's patience with customers and was calculated to amuse the patrons of McClintock's Minneapolis banking-supply business. As in Aldrich's other stories for *McClintock's*, the cashier was the bank representative providing the same services as had Cap in Elmwood. With the letter announcing the renewal of their publication, McClintock enclosed a booklet describing Bonnie Lake Farms, "a private place used for the benefit of our families, friends and people who are connected with us in business."[14]

His letter contained an invitation for Aldrich and her family to visit his Bonnie Lakes Farm on Cross Lake. Aldrich accepted with pleasure, for she loved to fish. She was ready, too, to get away for a while from Elmwood, where she continued to be a bank director and had her other activities. Charles (Chuck) Aldrich described his mother as "super busy"—although she was never too busy to stop and talk with them about whatever was on their minds.[15] The family had rarely taken vacations farther than Lincoln, and they were growing up: Mary was twenty; Jim, seventeen; Chuck, sixteen; and Bob, almost ten. A trip to the lake was a good way to end the summer together.

McClintock added to his June letter that "when I wept over the prologue or first chapter of *A Lantern*, I thought how wonderful it would have been could that chapter have been published in [our] magazine." Aldrich realized that if McClintock had liked *Lantern*, he and his readers might also like to know the background of the book; shortly thereafter she sent him "The Story Behind *A Lantern in Her Hand*," which was the only article she wrote in 1929. Here she described, for the first time in depth, her thoughts and expectations behind that novel. Later, she would expand parts of these ideas for talks, and in 1952 she would again expand the article for the *Christian Herald*. On 2 July, McClintock wrote accepting the story, sight unseen; it appeared in the October issue.[16]

Aldrich never asked for or received more than $50 for the short short stories in *McClintock's*, but McClintock and his wife later furnished the land at Cross Lake, Minnesota, on which—as noted earlier—the Aldrich family built their cottage.

There were royalties and syndication fees in 1929, but no more sales. The summer vacation had been helpful and had bolstered the Aldrich persistence. Now she wrote "Will the Romance Be the Same?" The story concerns Mary and Sam Wakely, their twenty-fifth wedding anniversary preparations and party, and the discovery that one of their daughters and her young man are on the same path to romance that Mary and Sam had walked in their early years. Aldrich sent "Will the Romance Be the Same?" to the *American Magazine*, but they rejected it with the comment that they remembered her success ten years earlier with the two Mason and Cutter series and suggested another such series. She may have been considering this work as such, which she mentioned in a subsequent letter to the *American Magazine*. They responded that had they been aware of that possibility they would have read it in a different light, but they did not ask to see it again.

In June, *McCall's* returned "Will the Romance be the Same?" *Country Gentleman* returned it in August; the *Saturday Evening Post* returned it in September. The *Post* wrote that "there is scarcely enough action, so little in fact that the story is nearly a sketch. If you ever try your hand at something more robust or complex, I wish you would give us a look at it." The fact that Bess and Charles Aldrich had not been married long enough to celebrate a twenty-fifth anniversary may have been the reason she could not provide greater depth. *Ladies' Home Journal* returned it with the hope that she would "continue to direct your work our way," and *Colliers* sent it back in October. The discomfort felt by those who rejected an Aldrich story is clear in the *Colliers'* message: "It is hardly necessary to tell you that I regret the necessity of giving you such a verdict." *Good Housekeeping* rejected it 30 November.[17]

Aldrich continued to feel frustrated with her inability to start a new novel, and perhaps frustrated also by the constant queries from New York. From early January, letters had been arriving from Appleton editors: Rutger Bleeker Jewett wrote on 18 January with "at the risk of being considered an Oliver Twist, I pass my plate for more, eager to know what next. Have you another novel in mind?" She could only reply that she was "written out."[18] Aldrich was disheartened by her inability to begin a long fiction and her inability to sell quickly the small amounts of material she did write. While money was less of a problem now, she remained cautious about spending, even though scarcely a month passed during 1929 that she did not receive a check for foreign reprints, a speaking engagement, for the dramatic or speech rights for an earlier story, or for syndication. Substantial royalties on her four books arrived on schedule in May and November.

John L. B. Williams, Jewett's associate editor, also queried her about the new novel, and her response to him was the same as to Jewett, that she was "written out." He rejected that as a possibility and suggested that she consider as a theme the importance of the small-town banker. He concluded that "perhaps there might be a suggestion in this, for a new novel, providing it all chimes in with any idea of yours."[19]

Jewett continued his letter-writing barrage, and he too tried to suggest characters and ideas for her to explore. Almost every month, in 1929, either Jewett or Williams, and sometimes both, had written with variations of "What about the new novel?" "Are you resting?" and "I am wondering what has happened?" Eleven months after Jewett had urged Aldrich not to believe that she was written out, she still had been unable to start the next book of the three for which she was under contract to Appleton, and Jewett was asking if "the theme for the new book [has] crystalized in your mind?" He reminded her that, "from a business point of view, it will be wise to follow the LANTERN IN HER HAND with a novel in 1930. I hope you can create in the new book another pioneer character, preferably a man with a mellow, shrewd, wise, philosophy of life."[20]

In November 1929, Aldrich received peer recognition by being asked to join the Society of Midland Authors, an organization of some of the best Midwest writers and a group that could be joined only by invitation. After a name was put forward, the proposed member was required to have a seconding letter submitted, and Aldrich asked Rutger Bleeker Jewett to write such a letter for her. She later became the Nebraska vice-president, as, for example, in Kansas, was William Allen White.[21] On this positive note her professional year ended, while Aldrich and her family looked forward to the joys of Thanksgiving and, especially, Christmas.

The following year, 1930, continued to bring revenue from syndications, royalties, personal appearances to autograph books, and—finally—four magazine sales. In March and April, Aldrich sent two short stories to *McClintock's*; "The Cashier and the Children" appeared in their March issue and "The Cashier and the Old Man" in the April/May issue. However, she was not

Bessie Genevra Streeter, aged five or so, is standing between her parents, James and Mary Streeter. She later dropped the *ie* and became *Bess*. Clara is probably the seated woman at left. Cedar Falls Historical Society.

This picture of Bess was taken around 1891 when she would have been ten years old. NSHS, A365-25.

Training Department graduation picture from Iowa State Normal School, 1907. Rod Library, University Archives, University of Northern Iowa.

Charles S. "Cap" Aldrich in his Spanish-American War uniform. Charles was one of the youngest captains in that war. Mary Aldrich Beechner.

The Aldrich family, c. 1920. From l. to r. Jim, Cap, Chuck, and Mary. Bob is in Bess's arms. They rented this house before building "The Elms." Mary Aldrich Beechner.

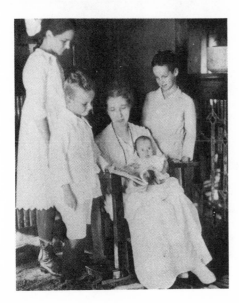

Bess Aldrich and children, also c. 1920. From l. to r. Mary, Chuck, Bess with Bob on her lap, and Jim. At this time Bess had been working seriously on her writing for about ten years. Mary Aldrich Beechner.

Cap Aldrich, probably around 1924. Mary Aldrich Beechner.

First honorary member, News Press Association, Hastings NE, February 1926. NSHS, A365:1-2.

"The Elms," the home that Charles and Bess built about a year before he died. Mary Aldrich Beechner.

Bess Streeter Aldrich, mid- to late 1920s. NSHS, A365:1-4.

Mary Eleanor Aldrich, high-school graduation portrait, 1926. Later, after graduating from the university, Mary became a teacher before marrying. Elmwood–Murdock School Board.

James Whitson Aldrich, high-school graduation portrait, 1929. Jim went on to art school in New York, became a commercial artist, and provided artwork for some of his mother's short stories and book jackets. Elmwood–Murdock School Board.

Charles S. Aldrich, high-school graduation portrait, 1930. Chuck, later getting a degree in engineering, became a pilot and aeronautical engineer. Elmwood–Murdock School Board.

Robert S. Aldrich, high-school graduation portrait, 1937. Bob became a writer, selling many short stories and writing for the *Los Gatos Gazette,* a California newspaper. Elmwood–Murdock School Board.

Bess Streeter Aldrich as she appeared on the dust jacket of her 1942 *The Lieutenant's Lady.* NSHS, A365:1-9.

The house Aldrich built in Lincoln NE in 1945–46. The street at that time was known as 52nd Street. After her death, neighbors petitioned to have it renamed Aldrich Road. Mary Aldrich Beechner.

making big-money sales and was struggling. She revised "Will the Romance Be the Same?" for *Country Gentleman*, but they turned it down in March. The revised version went from them to *Ladies' Home Journal, Cosmopolitan,* the *American Magazine,* the *Christian Herald,* and *Farmer's Wife*. Not until February 1931 was it purchased, when *Physical Culture Magazine* paid $750 for it.[22] She had been trying to place the story for twenty months.

In the meantime, Aldrich was also trying with little success to sell "Rose Leaves in a Jar." The story involves an old farmwoman, recently widowed, who, early in her marriage, had picked roses and put the petals in a jar where they dried. She spent the following thirty-nine years of married life in penury and fear, believing her husband in his insistence that they were barely able to pay taxes and were in constant danger of losing the land for which she had slaved and saved. After her husband's death, she learns the truth from the banker, which is that they have substantial investments and income. In retrospect, she understands that she has been as closed in a jar as the rose leaves, and with similar withering results. She goes on a brief and enjoyable spending-spree before returning to her habitual, spartan ways. *Good Housekeeping, Ladies' Home Journal, McCall's,* the *Saturday Evening Post, McCall's* (a revised version), the *American Magazine,* and *Country Gentleman* all returned it. Finally, in May 1930, the *Delineator* purchased it for $800 and changed the story's name to "It's Never Too Late to Live."[23] The *Delineator* still had the reputation of accepting only high quality stories.

Aldrich's hopes for *Lantern's* sale to Hollywood continued. She wrote Universal Pictures, MGM, and R.K.O., asking them to reread *Lantern*. They did, and all replied in a similar pattern: "The story covers too big a span of time, during which the heroine lives to be a great-grandmother. And, naturally a life so long and rich in incident and detail would require too large a canvas, much larger than the ordinary size of picture [film] requires."[24] A movie sale would have provided some sense of security, since the Depression, following the stock-market crash of 1929, was threatening all facets of the national economy; no area was exempt.

None of the Aldrich children was through college yet. Jewett had earlier written that, because of the expenses of children in school and college, she could draw an advance on royalties if such would be useful. Aldrich, however, was deeply afraid of debt and had expressed that fear in an early Cutter story, "The Nicest House in Town," in which she described debt as "an animal that eats the trimming off your dress and the paint off the house."[25]

Neither Williams's book suggestion of the banker nor Jewett's of the old pioneer man had helped Aldrich to realize theme or characters for a new work, but the two men continued their letter-writing campaign. In January 1930, Jewett was still pushing Aldrich to write to him and relate "what you can about the next novel." She was at last able to answer with the idea she had been mentally stirring about. Aldrich suggested that perhaps the public might want to know more about the Deals, their continuing lives, and their roles in the rural community. She sent Jewett some preliminary pages in which a young girl was the main character. He agreed that the public remained interested in the family, but he was not enthusiastic. He warned that modern agriculture was not as popular as pioneering and again stressed the importance he perceived of using, as a thread running through the work, the philosophy of an old man. Aldrich had asked his opinion of the title she was considering, *A White Bird Flying*, which Jewett approved, "if it is true to your story." Aldrich was not completely comfortable with it and wrote again, this time suggesting *Old Man of the Prairie*. Jewett liked that and asked if she would have the book finished so that he could include *Old Man of the Prairie* in Appleton's 1930 list of autumn publications. However, no new Aldrich title would appear on the autumn list. In July, Jewett wrote that "next spring is the psychological moment to strike hard with another novel. . . . When (with good fortune) will the manuscript be complete and ready to come to my desk from yours?"[26] Aldrich did not know.

With Jewett not enthusiastic about the young girl as protagonist and Aldrich not satisfied with the story of an old man as a major character, she turned again to short pieces. In May, Aldrich sold "Wild Critics I Have Known" to the *Bookman*. In this work, Aldrich lumps all critics into one persona, "The Critic," and finds him contradicting himself on books and short stories. Her humor surfaces often as she places together comments critics had made about her writing, always pairing the same works, giving their opposing reviews. Among the examples she uses are these two headlines leading into reviews of an earlier book: "CHARMING ROMANCE BEAUTIFULLY TOLD" and "AUTHOR TRIES TO PROVE CABBAGES ARE BEAUTIFUL." The result, she concludes, is that a writer must do her or his best, "then neither the criticism nor the commendation seems very significant. What is written, is written. And the next task lies before him."[27] One task that pleased Aldrich that year came about because President Hoover had named 1930 as Centennial Year to commemorate the Westward movement, and the *Christian Herald* commissioned Aldrich to write an article. The Centennial Year celebrated the one-hundredth anniversary of Captain William Sublette's leading the first wagon train from St. Louis to Wyoming on the route that became known as the Oregon Trail. In requesting the article, the editor gave Aldrich free rein on whatever she might choose to do with the idea. She wrote "The Faith that Rode with the Covered Wagon," discussing pioneers in general and her pioneering family in particular. It was published as a two-part work in the 9 August and 16 August issues.

Aldrich had enjoyed writing these articles, but work on the new book would not go well. Aldrich wrote Jewett in July that she had "not been able to dig in, close the mouth of the cave and concentrate on the novel."[28] At this point, she did not know if she could, or even wanted to, use the characters from *Lantern*, nor was she sure what time frame she wanted to use. Jewett answered that

> [I believe] you will have greater freedom and less restraint if you forget the individual characters in The Lantern [*sic*] but keep the period in mind. It is unimportant whether the family of The Lantern is mentioned or not in the new book provided you can create a new group headed by The Old Man of the Prairies. The period, the historic back-

ground, are particularly good for you . . . but I am inclined to agree with you that it would be a mistake to have the connection between the two books close enough so that one would seem like a sequel to the other, because of the characters described.

Do not despair. . . . You have not exhausted the mine of either history or legend in The Lantern. I do not share your apprehension.[29]

Aldrich was at probably the lowest point in her career. *Lantern* had been such a great and surprising success that the pressure to write up to its stature seems to have been taking its toll. Late in 1930, Aldrich wrote Jewett that she wanted to forget about a novel for a while and bring out a book of short stories. Jewett responded in December to what he called her "period of discouragement and distrust that is the fate of each and every artist." He said, however, he felt the short stories should be postponed a "few years" because "such a volume is not popular with the booksellers and [is] difficult to sell." He argued that "you must not . . . ruin the big chance you have made for yourself with The Lantern by bringing the short stories out now. In a year or two . . . select the cream of them and send them on to me." He concluded with the hope that she would soon have a good progress report to send him on the new book.[30]

Three personality traits pushed Aldrich harder even than the relentless stream of letters from New York. One was her honesty: she had the Appleton contract obligation to fulfill, and one did not renege on one's word; second was her pragmatism: only she could write her book; third was her "gumption": she needed to, as she told her sons, "show a little gumption" and get her work done. These, and the fact that a new year, 1931, was beginning, made the time ripe for the new work. Aldrich believed strongly that people were still interested in the Deal family, and she had decided that Abbie's granddaughter would be the personna to carry the story. Thus, in January she settled into the preparation and then into the writing, having determined the title would be *A*

White Bird Flying. When Aldrich wrote the final chapter of the book, her concerns over the economy and her own slow sales become apparent. In the story, a drought has made money scarce, and Aldrich has Laura, the protagonist, comment that "I've written a few stories and sold them . . . when I didn't need the money . . . and now, that I want cash so badly . . . genius won't burn. I'm nervous and tense, thinking about the money all the time I write." (328).

By early June, she could tell Jewett that the completed novel was on its way. He sent his congratulations, and, acknowledging that he realized how frustrated she had at times been, added that he was "glad the burden has dropped from your shoulders." He also told her that her son's [James's] sketch had been chosen for the jacket and cover design for the forthcoming work.[31]

Jewett read the manuscript and was delighted. Although the national economy continued to move deeper into the Depression, and sales in many industries, including book sales, were in decline, Jewett could assure Aldrich that "in spite of bad business conditions I believe [*A White Bird Flying*] will also prove a successful one, that the sales will gratify us both." He added that he "love[d] Laura all the way through your chapters" as he did all of the individuals. One character particulary amused him, and he recognized "what fun you must have had painting Eloise! How typical she is of the efficient, fussy bromide! I believe every large family knows an Eloise well."[32] Appleton moved quickly, and the new Aldrich book went out to the public in late August.

A White Bird Flying opens with two neighbors having a conversation much like an antiphonal duet as they watch twelve-year-old Laura Deal, granddaughter of Abbie Deal of *A Lantern in Her Hand,* going into her grandmother's former home. Old Abbie's funeral has taken place two days earlier, but Laura has not yet assimilated the death. She is enjoying the dramatic sense of being young and alone where someone has died, and she is imagining how she will write this into a story and then read it to her grandmother, the only person who shares and understands her pleasure in writing. She suddenly realizes that her grandmother will never be there again: that death is final.

After this introduction, the story moves with Laura into young womanhood, touching also on the lives of her parents, aunts, uncles, and cousins, all children or grandchildren of Abbie Deal. Among the nonfamily characters are Oscar Lutz and Christine Reinmueller, whose name has now been Americanized to Rinemiller.

Laura's schooling takes her through college, after which her mother, the "efficient, fussy bromide Eloise" about whom Jewett commented, arranges for Laura to become a surrogate daughter to some of Eloise's wealthy relatives. Laura is tempted, for this would give her opportunity to see the world as well as time to devote to her writing. Laura is ready to agree to her mother's plan, when events make her realize that she would rather marry her hometown and college sweetheart, Allen Rinemiller.

The final chapter of *A White Bird Flying,* rather like an epilogue, takes place eight or ten years later. Laura and Allen are married and have four children, the youngest of whom is a toddler. They are living on the land Abbie sold to Oscar, who after many years sold it to the Rinemillers, and which Christine later gave to Allen. Times are difficult, and Laura, who has sold some stories, is struggling to write and sell more, for they need the money. One day, rather than write, she takes the children to the pasture to have a picnic. Telling them not to look, she tosses a coin into the field, saying she is throwing out there "one of the most valuable things in the world" (333). Laura then sends them off to find whatever they believe is the most valuable item in the field. The treasures they return with remind Laura that other objects of life and living have much greater intrinsic value than does money, something Laura had temporarily forgotten.

The Aldrich name and the Aldrich pen were magic. Even though the Depression and the days of drought and blowing dust were taking a heavy toll on the economy, the new book sold so quickly that within two weeks of its 4 August publication it appeared on the nation's best-seller lists. Critics liked *White Bird,* writing such positive reviews as that in the *New York Times*: "Miss [*sic*] Aldrich has re-created the spirit of the descendants of the early Scotch and German settlers of the great Nebraska plains, the spirit of healthy morality and calm contentment that is a characteristic of these people." Other reviews included the *Boston Transcript*: "It is an interesting and valuable cross section of American life still in the making that is presented here with no little ability"; *Good Housekeeping*: "The secret of this popular writer's success in getting close to her readers' hearts lies in her ability to appeal to our deeper instincts"; the *Philadelphia Public Ledger*: "Written with the fresh wholesomeness and inspiration of Mrs. Aldrich's former triumph, *A Lantern in Her Hand*"; *America*: "Nice characterization, brisk and arresting conversation, and perhaps best of all in our pseudo-realistic age, a tale of the heart, well told"; and the *Cincinnati Post*: "Always the Nebraska landscape, dominant and compelling, with the splendid heritage of American endeavor and ideals."[33] A few reviewers called the book sentimental, a charge Aldrich had heard before about other of her works, and, as noted in "Wild Critics I Have Known," about which she felt little concern.

Some of the problems current in the 1930s Midwest, such as banking issues on both state and personal levels, are traced in *White Bird.* Here Aldrich demonstrates how they touch on individuals, and, indeed, how they can set brothers, one a banker and one an attorney, against each other. Descriptions of college life in the late 1920s and early 1930s also appear. The reader learns of life in the United States immediately after the pioneering era. *White Bird* is another of the Aldrich books that has never gone out of print and is read anew by succeeding generations for its literary content as well as its social and historical accuracy.

Although *A White Bird Flying* fulfills the terms of a sequel in that its chronology continues the Deal family in *A Lantern in Her Hand,* it is not necessary to have read *Lantern* to follow the lives of *White Bird.* Appleton, however, was willing to sell the two as a boxed set for their top novel price of $4 ($2 apiece), and this symbiotic arrangement enhanced sales of both. By the end of the year, only four months after it arrived at bookstores, *A White Bird Flying* was closing in on Pearl S. Buck's *The Good Earth* and Willa Cather's *Shadows on the Rock* for top sales of the year. Buck, Cather, and Aldrich's 1931 sales finished first, second, and third respectively for the year.

8

Miss Bishop

and the

Early 1930s

A White Bird Flying was in bookstores by early August 1931, and only two weeks after publication it reached best-seller lists. The book's acceptance proved that Aldrich was correct in believing that the public was still interested in the Deal family. Sales were also rewarding to Aldrich emotionally, for they proved to her that she was not written-out as she had feared, and gave her confidence that new commissions would relieve some of her worries about money.

The Depression was growing steadily worse; financial concerns deepened. Fewer people could afford book purchases, and the actual numbers of sales were less than previous works. Sales from the last months of 1931 were included in her commission check for May 1932; together, they totaled a little over $19,000. Sales then slowed considerably, as Aldrich anticipated. In November she received only $1,850. Aldrich did not discuss these concerns in Elmwood but wrote Jewett in mid-August that she was considering selling some bonds, which she hated to do at current sacrifice prices. Jewett responded immediately, first by wire and then by confirming letter on 20 August 1931, telling her to keep them, that Appleton would advance her money on the royalties she would receive in November and more if she needed it, for "I cannot endure the idea of your selling your hard-earned securities at a loss when there is absolutely no reason for it." He acknowledged that "at present fear and pessimism sweep the land, rattle the stock market and drive down good stocks and bonds," and that "advance sales on books is about 50% less than it was in the optimistic years." At the same time, however, "reorders on good books is cheering." While urging her to keep her bonds, he urged that "equipping the children with shoes, clothes and books for the fall term . . . not eat up the result[s] of your hard work."[1]

His words reassured Aldrich. However, clothes and books were only part of her worries, for she felt she needed a solid financial reserve and also wanted to have enough to provide Mary and future son-in-law Milton with the beautiful wedding Aldrich felt Mary deserved. Through the years since Cap's death, Bess Aldrich had discussed stories with Mary, who was reader, critic, and enthusiast for her mother and was the only person other than Aldrich to read the complete manuscript of *A Lantern in Her Hand* prior to its going to the editors and on to publication. The formal wedding that she provided in the Elmwood church late in November was Bess Aldrich's opportunity to thank her deeply loved daughter; the gift of a baby grand piano to the young couple was another acknowledgment of Bess's affection and appreciation. The two older Aldrich sons, James and Charles, ushered, "and looked pretty nice to their mother," as Bess, trying to be modest, later wrote a friend.[2] However, with all the prenuptial parties and activities, it was an exhausting period, and, after the wedding and the usual excitement of Christmas, Aldrich admitted that she was "nearly all in" and felt she needed to take a vacation.

Teacher Bess Streeter had been as far west as Salt Lake City; author and mother Bess Streeter Aldrich had not been west of Nebraska, so in 1932 Aldrich found several reasons to go to California: she wanted to give Bob, who was too young to be given an active role in the wedding, a special treat; she needed a vacation; she decided she could afford the trip; and she could push her novels as motion picture vehicles. Thus, on 24 January 1932, Aldrich and eleven-year-old Bob boarded the train for California, planning to stay four weeks; however, there was so much to see and do that they were gone for eleven weeks, two of which they spent in Laguna Beach, away from crowds and work. On their return trip they visited in San Francisco, Salt Lake City, and Denver. Later, on 26 April, she explained in a letter to Grace Simpson Bailey that she had wanted to go to California in order to give "Bob a good chance to see his country, [and] he learned more than a whole year of school." Aldrich, always the teacher, added, "However, I made him do arithmetic twice a day when we were at the beach."[3]

While in the Los Angeles and Hollywood areas, Aldrich visited studios, met producers, actors, and actresses, and addressed many organizations, including the Southern California Press Club, the Hollywood Women's Club, three P.E.O. chapters, and a chapter of the Daughters of the American Revolution (DAR). Many other organizations also requested her to give talks, but most surprising to her were the number of DAR invitations. Only later did she discover that a newspaper article before she arrived had incorrectly stated that Aldrich was a member. Amused, she described the DAR luncheon in the letter to Grace Bailey:

> Picture me at the luncheon sitting gaily at [the state regent's] right, in the midst of my soup, and she asking me which chapter in Nebraska I belonged to, and me having to choke and say I wasn't a member. I didn't know whether I'd be thrown out before I could finish the soup. Imagine, I hadn't known why I was deluged with DAR invitations. . . . I had to ride in on [sisters] Annie's and Clara's connections, having the same ancestors as I do.[4]

These luncheons and meetings were reported in Los Angeles newspapers and were important for book sales; thus Appleton urged her to attend as many as she could work into her schedule.

Aldrich was never eager to give talks, but she had determined to do all she could to promote awareness of her work in hopes that the movie industry would pick up at least one of her books.

Aldrich, a great fan of the movie industry, particularly wanted to have *Lantern* made into a film; she also believed in *Mother Mason* as a movie. Ivan Kahn, for a while her Hollywood agent, wrote her that Paramount was going to take *Lantern,* but that if they didn't, he believed that, with Frank Lloyd of Fox Studios directing, Helen Hayes would play Abbie Deal. Kahn told her he had quoted Lloyd a price of $50,000 for the purchase of the movie. Kahn was encouraging in his expectations and worked with several studios to promote Aldrich's work. He persuaded the president of R.K.O., B. B. Kahane, to read *The Rim of the Prairie* and, at Aldrich's suggestion, tried to place May Robson in the role of Mother Mason. Appleton's movie agents worked on industry moguls, too, and many times she expected *Lantern*'s options would be picked up. However, for the industrious Aldrich, neither agent nor Appleton was sufficient, and she worked for the sales in person. In March, she wrote son Chuck in great excitement, "*Prospects good.* Have been in Universal, MGM, Warners, First National and Fox. . . . Two best prospects are RKO for Ann Harding and MGM for Helen Hayes. Frank Lloyd, the director, put his ok on *Lantern* for Ann Harding and sent the book to Le Baron, the RKO producer, to read. His word is final." In 1935, Aldrich would take matters into her own hands and write a personal note to Mary Pickford, one of Hollywood's mature greats of the 1930s, suggesting that she play the role of Mother Mason. Miss Pickford responded that she would read the book immediately and, in a postscript, asked when she and Aldrich could meet.[5]

While on the 1932 California trip, Aldrich wrote Jewett about the overabundance of invitations and the lavish foods at the affairs she attended. On 18 March, he replied that "the great American public has a passion for killing its victims with kindness [much as] the witch in the old German fairy tale who stuffed her victims with sugar plums." His letter ended with the query about the new book. By May he could tell her that "THE LANTERN

AND THE WHITE BIRD have stood up amazingly well against the universal depression, but, of course, they like all other books are suffering from our psychological panic." As usual, Jewett had begun his campaign pushing Aldrich to write the next book shortly after publication of the previous one, and he urged her to consider the story of the country banker while she was in California. However, Aldrich did not yet want to write another book. By the time she was back in Elmwood in mid-April, she was firmly commited to her earlier suggestion of putting some of her short stories together in one volume. Jewett acceded and told her to send all that she currently had, that he would read them at his leisure, and they could later decide which to include, which to omit. He was still not enthusiastic about such a volume in the near future, feeling that "it would be bad policy to bring out anything until we [have] given A WHITE BIRD a free track a little longer." He agreed, however, that they should plan the stories so that they would be ready for publication.

During 1932, Aldrich added two more short stories to her list of publications, selling "The Old Judge Sits by Marathon" to *Ladies' Home Journal,* who changed its name to "The Runaway Judge" in their July issue, and placing "The Silent Stars Go By" in June with *Cosmopolitan* for their Christmas issue.[6] "Stars" is about a dying woman who regains her life through a dream-sequence experience that blends generations, much as in the earlier "Across the Smiling Meadow." This story would, many years later, become a television Christmas special (under the title "The Gift of Love"), appearing almost yearly on Public Broadcasting stations throughout the country, with Lee Remick and Angela Landsbury as stars.

Aldrich received frequent letters from Jewett, invariably closing with questions about the next book. In October 1932, she wrote that she had a title for the next novel: *Spring Came On Forever.* This particular phrase in Vachel Lindsay's poem, "The Chinese Nightingale," had touched her, and she wrote Jewett that she was considering using it, but that she had not yet shaped the story. Not until February would she write Jewett with a firm suggestion for the new novel—that it be based on her earlier story of the schoolteacher, "The Woman Who Was Forgotten." Aldrich told Jewett that several magazines were making overtures about serializing her next long fiction, and in her letter she discussed these possibilities. He recommended sending *Cosmopolitan* the opening chapters and a rough synopsis of her progress thus far. While she had been trying to pull together the characters and events for a new long work, she had also been thinking about the differences between her Hollywood experiences and her life in Elmwood, and the latter seemed very good. She wrote a reflective piece, "Why I Live in a Small Town," and sent it to the *Ladies' Home Journal*, where it was published in June 1933. Aldrich wrote that, of the past twelve months, she had spent five away from Elmwood but that she returned from trips aware of "that warmhearted hospitality, loyal friendship and deep sympathy of the small town . . . [which she] tried to stress in [her] short stories and books." On another occasion she would comment that her objective in writing was "sometimes sheer entertainment, but always to stress the happiness and contentment to be found in normal life."[7]

Writing about Elmwood was a change of pace from working on the new book, for which, at this point, Aldrich was still using the title of *Spring Came On Forever*, even though she was not comfortable with it. Near the end of March 1933, she thought perhaps she should change the title to either *Miss Bishop* or *Miss Ella Bishop*. To Jewett, she worried about being unsure of the title and was now considering *I Carry a Torch*, but felt it too long. He replied that it could be shortened to *The Torch*. By May, still trying to get the title just right, she suggested *Fifty-two Commencements*. Jewett answered that he preferred *Miss Bishop*, which was the name she, too, had finally settled upon.[8]

Aldrich may have been fretting about the title of this next book to offset the deeper concerns she was feeling during that spring. As a totally committed Republican, Aldrich had voted for Hoover, believing that the programs he had already set in motion would pull the country out of the Depression; and, as did most

Republicans of the time, she distrusted Roosevelt and the New Deal. Roosevelt, of course, was elected president. Following his inauguration in January 1933, in March he ordered the nation's banks to close for a week. None of the banks whose reserves were depleted would reopen. The American Exchange Bank of Elmwood had some South American paper they had bought in good faith, but it had become virtually worthless and had seriously eroded the bank's reserves. Aldrich was deeply distressed over the likelihood of the bank closing, for not only was she one of the three stockholders, she also understood how much pain and grief this would cause her sister and brother-in-law, the Cobbs, as well as her Elmwood community of neighbors and friends. Aldrich realized she was probably the one person who could prevent this imminent financial disaster, in which every depositor would lose money. Those who had mortgages could lose farms or homes. Aldrich's understanding and empathy about the financial losses was made even more acute because of the problems she was describing for her character Miss Bishop, subject of the novel she was then writing. She later shaped Miss Bishop's gravest financial reverses around the bank holiday.

Aldrich determined what she must do to save her bank and community and went to Lincoln to see George W. Woods, the state banking department chief from 1929 to 1934. Woods later described their meeting to Ted Landale of the *Omaha World-Herald*, telling him Aldrich said,

> "At present I am trying to write a book, but I cannot go on with it. . . . You do not know the amount of income and savings I have had; I suspect they are larger than you suppose. But if it takes all, to the last cent I have, I shall not permit that bank to close. If you will state the amount of cash necessary to keep the bank open at this time, I will have it ready for you within a few days. If more shall be required later, I will furnish it."

Aldrich then went to her "tin box," as she called it, and cashed in sufficient securities and jewelry to cover the deficit. The bank did not fail. Her only stipulation was that her assistance not be made public during her lifetime, a request both Woods and the newspaper honored.[9]

With the bank secure, Aldrich was able to finish the book, and by the middle of June had it in the Appleton-Century offices. On 25 August 1933 *Miss Bishop* was published. However, the money expended in keeping the bank solvent had cost Aldrich dearly. In November, she was forced to write for an advance of her next royalties check: never before had she had to request such help. In her letter, she explained to Jewett that she was one of the three owners of the bank. He responded that this information "staggered" him, and he wondered, "Should I send you sympathy or congratulations? . . . My prudent nature would make me hesitate a long time before committing myself too heavily with any bank east or west, north or south."[10] For Aldrich there was no such hesitation.

Miss Bishop is the story of Ella Bishop, who, at the age of sixteen in 1876, is a member of the first class to attend the newly opened Midwestern College in Oak River. The college symbolizes in part the coming-of-age of this prairie town, which had been founded twenty years earlier. At the time of the story's opening, the college consists solely of Central Hall, sitting in the middle of a forty-acre pasture of college-owned prairie grasses.

The book follows Ella Bishop through the next fifty-some years of her life, examining first one then another of the choices that Ella makes and by which she creates her destiny. These choices are the Fate Aldrich saw shaping lives in her early short story, "The Victory of Connie Lee," and also in the longer *Rim of the Prairie.* Fate is a specific in *Miss Bishop* as well, for Aldrich describes it in one instance as "the old woman of the loom" (214).

Immediately before graduation, Ella, who had studied didactics [education], as did Aldrich, is offered a position teaching English at Midwestern and quickly accepts. Ella has several offers of marriage, but each opportunity is blighted. She does not marry but remains as a teacher at Midwestern for fifty-two years. During this time, she is close to many students, assisting them, financially or emotionally, as individual needs require; in their youthful ways, they recognize her dedication and warm support.

In 1933, Ella Bishop discovers during the bank holiday that her savings have been almost wiped out. She is now seventy-three years old, although she admits only to being "three score and ten" (303). She had been considering retirement, but her financial problems cause her to realize that she cannot quit for at least two more years. During this time she must exercise great thrift to recoup her lost savings so that she will have enough money to live out her life without becoming dependent. However, a new president has come to Midwestern and is making changes. He gives her the option of resigning immediately or accepting the alternative: dismissal. Miss Bishop resigns. Also at this time she learns that Old Central, which was the only building on the campus when she first attended, is to be torn down. Fear of impoverished old age, resentment at the fate that has urged her to help others financially rather than looking to her own future, and bitterness at the new college administration gnaw at her and add to her sense of being an object outworn and to be disposed of in a degree comparable to that of Old Central.

However, a surprise is planned for Miss Bishop at Old Central on the night of the commencement dinner—the last such dinner to be held there. Many of her former students, now successful senators, ministers, merchants, and mothers, arrive to pay tribute to this woman who taught them a variety of lessons, literally and by example. As she comprehends their respect for her as both a teacher and an individual, her anger and bitterness are "swept away," and she realizes she was right to close "her work before her faculties dimmed." She knew that tomorrow "she would be an old woman," but that night "she was ageless. . . . She feared nothing now . . . poverty or old age or death" (334).

The theme for *Miss Bishop* was originally worked out in Aldrich's story entitled "The Woman Who Was Forgotten," which appeared in the June 1926 *American Magazine*. Here the teacher was a Miss Miller, who was facing the fact that after the long years of service and the meager salary of the educator she was too old to teach, too young to die, and too poor to live long comfortably. As already noted, the editors of the *National Education Association Journal* asked for permission to reprint the story, which appeared in their February 1927 issue. Shortly thereafter the NEA bought the story rights and backed production of the Miss Miller story into a movie, which was released in 1931 under the same title, *The Woman Who Was Forgotten*. In the contract for the movie rights, Aldrich required that a percentage of the proceeds from nationwide showings be used to build a retirement home for teachers in Washington DC. Continuing the saga of "The Woman Who Was Forgotten," an insurance company purchased the story for advertising purposes.[11]

Ella Bishop was often seen as the outgrowth of the Miss Miller character. Aldrich, however, wrote that there was much similarity in longtime schoolteachers of the day and that the two were not the same. Further, she pointed out that when she had completed the Miss Miller story and was ready to send it to the *American Magazine,* a copy of that magazine arrived with a very similar story by another author. Aldrich immediately wrote that author and included a copy of that letter with her manuscript to the *American Magazine.* The editors bought "The Woman Who Was Forgotten" immediately but held it for a year before publication. She noted that both her teacher characters, one a highschool teacher and one a college teacher, lost their jobs, "but if all the schoolteachers who had lost their jobs were laid end to end. . . !" While it was loosely based on the old story, Aldrich said she felt in her own mind "that Miss Bishop had a brighter, keener outlook on life than the teacher of the short story, so that her personality differs rather definitely. By the side of the other's old faded worn-out personality, Miss Bishop is smart and snappy to the end."[12]

Miss Bishop was another of Aldrich's composite personalities, for she included many of the strong qualities of educators she had known through the years. Several possibilities have been suggested regarding the identity of the original Miss Bishop, including Sarah Findlay Rice, instructor of history at Iowa State

Normal School, who was teaching at the college when Aldrich was a student there; Grace Norton, of the high-school Shakespeare class, whom Aldrich described as "a favorite of everyone"; and Louise P. Barrett, Bess's first cousin, graduate of Iowa State Normal and teacher at Whittier School in Brainerd, Minnesota, until her retirement in June 1932. While there are traits of Rice and others in the Miss Miller and Miss Bishop characters, Louise Barrett, an educator for fifty-two years, is the most identifiable model. She was twenty-five years older than Aldrich and had returned to Cedar Falls and ISNS to work on her master's degree while Aldrich was a student there. Barrett received her master's the year that Aldrich received her bachelor's. She would have been able to provide insight into the lives and problems of teachers who had survived for many years on their small salaries and who faced retirement with little income.[13] The number of years that Barrett taught, fifty-two, corresponded with those of Miss Bishop's.

Aldrich paid tribute to this teaching cousin through the frequent use of Whittier School in various short stories and as the school in which Nancy Moore taught in *The Rim of the Prairie*. Both "The Woman Who Was Forgotten" (1926) and the later *Miss Bishop* end with a testimonial dinner and financial donations for the retiring educator. On Barrett's retirement in 1932, a similar testimonial dinner was given in her honor—an example of Aldrich's fiction preceding fact.

Aldrich carefully avoided naming an actual place or school, and, because she wanted the book to honor all teachers, she told her publisher she did not want any specific reference concerning the locale of the story. Aldrich commented some years later that she "used anecdotes from Iowa State Teachers College, Ames (Iowa State University), the University of Iowa, and Nebraska University" because "what school in the midwest did not begin with a few acres of prairie grass, four or five teachers, one building and a handful of students? The history of one in its essence is the history of them all."[14]

Aldrich's portrayal of real people and real situations continued in *Miss Bishop*. In December 1932 a New Hampshire man had sent Aldrich a letter and biographical sketch of Professor Laurence Fossler, of the University of Nebraska, who had been a student at that university in its early days and who later returned to teach. Paralleling Fossler in *Miss Bishop* is George Schroeder, a penniless German student in that first year of classes at Midwestern, who would later return as a professor to his alma mater.[15] While Fossler may have served as a prototype, Aldrich's understanding of the pleasure the foreign-born had in their language of origin and the pain of the German American during World War I made her Schroeder live. She had seen some of this situation in Elmwood during that war, although the problems there had been minimal.

As do other authors, Aldrich introduced ideas or characters in earlier writings, then polished and transferred them into novels, where they added richness of detail. Several incidents in *Miss Bishop* appeared in previous Aldrich stories. One of these involves neighbors who live across the street from the Bishop house, Judge and Mrs. Peters and their two sons, the handsome, brilliant Chester and the homely, uninspired but steady, Sam. Chester, the pride of his father, has been away at school and has come home one spring to become the conquest of a flirtatious young woman. She marries another, Chester leaves town, and word later comes that he has fallen off a Mississippi River boat and drowned. Nearly twenty years pass, then one August evening Sam asks Miss Bishop for help. Chester has returned: he did not drown years earlier, but, to recover from his brief love, had "slipped out to see the world," had lived in the orient much of the intervening time, and had seen the "*under* side" of life (182–83). Aldrich has used in this episode the theme of one of her stories published in 1925, "The Weakling."[16] The pompous father/judge, the negligible wife, the loved son, the weak son, all appeared in the earlier story. In both instances, the beloved son returns home a derelict and dies in the company of his brother, who does not divulge the transient's identity to their father to protect the father from the pain of reality.

Here also from earlier Aldrich stories is the reunion of old college friends on the twenty-fifth anniversary of their graduation. She had written two similar versions, "A Few Fagots for the Fire," published in 1924, and the *Mother Mason* story "Mother Renews Her Youth." In *Miss Bishop*, Aldrich brings the first graduating class of Midwestern College together, and they become reacquainted and relive memories. While Aldrich was not able to return to Iowa State Normal School for her twenty-fifth reunion because it was her daughter Mary's high-school graduation weekend, she did visit Cedar Falls often. Shortly after Mary's graduation, Aldrich created her own reunion of school friends and relatives by taking Mary on a trip of several weeks. They went first to Cedar Falls and then on to Tipton, Marshalltown, Iowa City, and Janesville. In a 1921 letter printed in her college newspaper, she wrote: "I love the old town, the old school and all the old memories that cling round them both . . . [where the days] seem unbelievably carefree, magically golden . . . and [those] who were my close friends in those days have remained the close friends of my womanhood."[17]

The story "Pie" that had been on such a long odyssey in 1928–29 and was finally accepted by the *Country Gentleman* is another published work to make an appearance in *Miss Bishop*. Here the young woman who is to "eschew pie and chew prunes" (229) is Hope, the "niece" whom Ella Bishop has reared from infancy.

Aldrich liked the Vachel Lindsay poem, "The Chinese Nightingale," but she was an inveterate poetic parodist, and this poem lent itself to her sense of fun. When Hope's daughter, Gretchen, is living at Miss Bishop's and attending Midwestern, Gretchen and some friends make fudge one evening and leave the house while the candy is cooling. Aldrich, through Miss Bishop, cannot resist, and Miss Bishop leaves a poem for the young women burlesquing "The Chinese Nightingale" (274–75).

The Aldrich humor, often mentioned in reviews, was unquestionably among the reasons for the immediate strong sales of *Miss Bishop*, for humor is one of the threads. More than any other specific reason for good sales in hard times was the fact that an Aldrich book was by now an icon for clean and readable stories, and by 25 September, one month after its publication, Jewett could write that *Miss Bishop* was on best-seller lists in cities across the country. Reviews, as usual, were generally excellent, but, again as usual, some were negative. The newsweekly *Time* concluded its review by focusing on the author: "Aldrich writes with feminine gusto, human warmth." The *Houston Post* stated that the Ella Bishop character is "rare, [but] she actually lives and breathes. . . . Every time school bells ring the Ella Bishops of the world answer the summons. To them Mrs. Aldrich has written a beautiful tribute. *Miss Bishop* is not so modern as the average run-of-the-mill modern fiction goes; yet, it is not old-fashioned unless character and courage are dated." The St. Louis *Post Dispatch* remarked that Aldrich had won her following "through genuine understanding of the common life and a warm human sympathy. *Miss Bishop* is undoubtedly one of her best novels." And in Boston the *Christian Science Monitor* called the book "a sincere tribute to real teachers the world over," adding that "it is also a history of the development of a midwestern college from a glorified high school with its one Central Hall to a great institution." In contrast, the Montreal, Quebec, *Daily Star* saw the book as "the story of Ella Bishop working off a frustrated maternal instinct on her college class."[18]

Miss Bishop continued to sell strongly for the times, making the Baker and Taylor list of six best-selling novels for 1933. Sales in January 1934 of over one thousand copies were good, although less so if compared with *A White Bird Flying* at a similar time after publication. Jewett urged Aldrich not to be discouraged that it had not sold as well as *White Bird*, noting that *Miss Bishop* was a "relatively greater success in the trade." He added, "We thought we had hit the bottom of the depression the previous years but 1933 marked the lowest level of all."[19] *Miss Bishop*, like many of the Aldrich books, would also become a success overseas. The novel has remained in publication since its 1933 debut, becoming yet another Bess Streeter Aldrich book that has never been out of print.

In September 1933, Edward L. Smith wrote Aldrich that Metro-Goldwyn-Mayer was paying $1,000 down on a sixty-day option for the movie rights to *Miss Bishop*, the selling price for which would be $25,000. In October, Louella Parsons's newspaper column carried the information that MGM had purchased it as a vehicle for Myrna Loy, who would play Miss Bishop. On the strength of this good news, in October Aldrich took Bob to the Chicago World's Fair, billed as "The Century of Progress Exposition," which had begun in May. However, in November Jewett sent her the disappointing news that the option was relinquished. A few months later (January 1934), Smith wrote that Appleton had again quoted a sale price of $25,000 for movie rights of *Miss Bishop*, with a thirty-day option for $2,500. He noted that Katherine Hepburn was reading the story, that he was trying to go through Helen Hayes to approach MGM again, and that one of the editors at Fox was "really interested in its picture possibilities."[20] No action came about from any of these avenues, and again her hopes for a movie from one of her books were dashed.

9

The

Mid-1930s

and

Spring Came

On Forever

If Hollywood rejected her work, others did not. The name Aldrich was synonymous with wide readership and sales; thus, agents and publishing houses were eager to have her as a client. Many agents wrote and asked to handle her material, both for the Hollywood movies and for Eastern publications. Because Appleton-Century had its own motion picture department, and due to Aldrich's disenchantment over Hollywood, she had little contact with Hollywood agents. However, publishing houses as, for example, Houghton Mifflin, Alfred Knopf, Knight, and Macmillan, and New York literary agents (authors' representatives) sent a steady succession of mail to her

Elmwood home, all assuring her they could secure much more money for her book contracts or magazine stories than she currently received. Aldrich, always courteous, replied even to such as these. The belief that they could get her more money for her work may have been correct; Chesla G. Sherlock, former managing editor of *Ladies' Home Journal*, wrote her in 1934 that he believed she was selling her stories at too low a price and said she should ask *Cosmopolitan* for at least $3,500, adding that in pre-Depression days he would have recommended that she ask for and expect $5,000. He reminded her that magazine publishers wanted "big names"; he listed "Aldrich, Ferber, Tarkington, Alice [Roosevelt] Longworth, and Harold Bell Wright"; furthermore, he wrote, "you have another talking point. You live in the middle west and you are writing a type of story no other writer can touch; you have a following already made; and your type of merchandise is necessary to appeal to a large sector of the reading public."[1]

Frank Hanighen and Paul R. Reynolds, both of whom were authors as well as agents, F. M. Holly, book reviewer as well as agent, and Jean Wick, who was Faith Baldwin's agent, were among those who offered their services. Hanighen was one of the more persistent, even visiting Aldrich in Nebraska. Because Aldrich had been unable to sell "Soap Kettle," a story she liked and believed in, she sent it to him in January 1934. In "Soap Kettle," a woman now old and shriveled recalls her love of an earlier time, a time before she and a young man had to part and take different paths into the new state. The marriage and life together of which they had dreamed becomes a kind of reality when her great-grandson and the granddaughter of her former beau meet and marry. This was a story that Aldrich indicated she knew as fact, although she did not divulge her source.[2]

Although Hanighen tried diligently and talked to many editors, including Thomas B. Costain of the *Saturday Evening Post*, he could not find a purchaser for it and returned the piece. She then wrote what was for her a strongly worded letter to Costain, which she mentioned to Hanighen; Hanighen thanked her for her letter and said, "The best thing in it for me was that you wrote Costain and let him feel that he was an egregious ass for turning down 'Soap Kettle.' A wholesome hint like that to editors that they are not omniscient creatures is all to the good. You must have impressed him or he would not have suggested the change," which Hanighen did not describe. Hanighen's language was undoubtedly much stronger than that in Aldrich's letter. Aldrich was an excellent letter writer, but her language was never coarse. Hanighen continued to try to work for her, and at one point assured her that he was "not discouraged" by her refusals to send him stories to try to sell, advised her "to haggle with editors," and hoped that her decision to refuse his services would not "remain final," for he would "help if she became dissatisfied with her current arrangements."[3] Neither Hanighen nor any of the others ever became a full-time agent for her.

Meanwhile, book publishers continued to pressure Aldrich to change to their houses. She considered changing, for example, to Alfred Knopf, whom she recommended as an excellent firm to a young poet whose work she regarded highly. She wrote that Knopf "doesn't have as mammoth a business as one of the older concerns, [but] is very *choosy,* and pushes his authors for all he is worth. He asked me to leave Appleton and come with him but I can't quite see myself doing it after the Appleton people publishing three books for me and contracting for the fourth." Jewett, responding to a letter from her late in 1932 in which she told him of a suggestion from Houghton Mifflin that she join their firm, wrote that he appreciated her loyalty.[4]

Agent Paul R. Reynolds also tried to lure Aldrich from Appleton. In a 1971 memoir he wrote that a Doubleday editor told him "Doubleday would advance $20,000 against a royalty of 15 percent for a new novel by Mrs. Aldrich." Appleton, wrote Reynolds, "at that time had the reputation of being a sleepy house that seldom paid large dollar advances or high royalties to authors. Doubleday . . . was considered one of the best publishers in the country, and . . . their offer was probably way in excess of what Appleton was paying." Reynolds told of taking the train the long distance from New York to Elmwood to make this offer. He wrote,

"Mrs. Aldrich seemed amazed at the Doubleday offer. She admitted that Appleton paid her a small dollar advance against a straight 10 percent royalty. She said she would like to go to her study alone and think about the matter." When she returned in some twenty minutes, she told him that Appleton had published her first novel and every novel thereafter and that, " 'I have used the same doctor all my life, the same dentist all my life, and the same lawyer all my life, and I have decided I shall use the same publisher.' " Moreover, she would not allow him to negotiate higher fees for her with Appleton, because, she said, Appleton did not like agents. Reynolds added, "There was nothing more for me to say. I took the weary trip back to New York. Mrs. Aldrich meant what she said. . . . I admire her loyalty in comparison with the avarice of so many writers."[5]

The number of agents that approached her indicates the trade's regard for her and her work. The agents were not alone; many reflected other interests. E. A. Burnett, chancellor of the University of Nebraska, wrote to Aldrich in April inviting her to accept an honorary Doctor of Letters degree at the June commencement. Her son Charles was to receive his bachelor's degree the same day. On the big day, as Chuck let her out of the car, he teased that he had " 'to drudge away five years for my Engineer's degree and you get one handed to you on a silver platter. Pretty soft, Mother, pretty soft.' " And Aldrich, as she wrote Grace Simpson Bailey about the incident, "had to laugh."[6]

Aldrich found the university recognition gratifying, as was receiving the Lincoln (Nebraska) Kiwanis Club Medal in 1929 and the prestigious Iowa Authors Outstanding Contribution to Literature Award in 1949. She noted of the Kiwanis medal that "from a sheer sense of justice, as well as gratitude, I feel that I must share this great honor today with some of those who have been responsible in helping me." She named her mother and father; her sister and brother-in-law, Clara and John Cobb; her husband and their four children. She also credited three editors for their importance to her—John Siddall of the *American Magazine* and Rutger Bleeker Jewett and John L. B. Williams of Appleton, and concluded, "Had any one of these contributing factors been withdrawn,—or had any one or two failed to function,—another, and not I, would be standing here today." The medal was awarded for "distinguished service to the State of Nebraska as homemaker, citizen, and author."[7]

The year 1934 also saw Appleton's sale of *Mother Mason* for yet another translation, this time into Hungarian. "So," her editor wrote, "your circle of readers widens." Aldrich also gave herself "a graduation present"—a trip with Bob and Chuck to the Chicago World's Fair, then on to New York, where Aldrich visited Williams and others at Appleton. Son Jim, who lived in New York, joined the family, and together they toured New England. History buff Aldrich was in her element. She especially enjoyed seeing and showing her sons the Old North Church (Christ Church, the oldest church in Boston) in which the warning lantern had been placed in Revolutionary times, for family legend held that it was a Streeter who placed the lantern in the tower. From there the family went to West Point, Philadelphia, and Washington, returning to New York with Jim before traveling home. Later, Aldrich and Bob left for the lake cottage in Minnesota where they stayed well into August.[8]

While Aldrich was disappointed that *Miss Bishop* did not sell as well as she had wished, she took satisfaction in the fact that it "was included in the small list of best sellers of the year [1933]."[9] Aldrich was not one who dwelt on negatives and she continued to work. In 1933–34 she kept to her overall plan of following book publication with a period of a year or so devoted to writing short stories. The stories Aldrich completed between release of *Miss Bishop* and her next long fiction—utilizing the discarded title—*Spring Came On Forever*, in 1935, are examples of Aldrich near the peak of her versatility as a short story writer; later years would bring proportionately more Christmas stories and fewer general fiction pieces.

In November 1933, less than three months after publication of *Miss Bishop*, she had completed and sent to *Cosmopolitan* "Low Lies His Bed," a Christmas story, for which she received

$2,500. Because she was under contract for five of six story sub-mission and because she would not receive her first royalties from *Miss Bishop* until the following May, this sale was welcome.[10]

"Low Lies His Bed" is the story of the formerly wealthy Mrs. Parker, whose husband and son are dead, and who is now impoverished because of the Depression. This bitter, aloof woman has returned to the town her family founded generations earlier and where she must live in an "old folks home" on funds supplied by a local philanthropist. The same philanthropist has also provided a portion of the money for Mrs. Parker's former washlady to live in the home. This thrifty old German, in contrast to her former employer, lives in the belief that the home and her world are joyous and lively places. On Christmas Eve she goes to Mrs. Parker's assistance, an act that causes Mrs. Parker to under-stand she does not suffer alone and that she has, indeed, had a good life.

In March, Aldrich sold "Alma, Meaning to Cherish," to *Good Housekeeping*; in April, "How Far Is It to Hollywood?" to *Cosmopolitan* and, also in April, "Welcome Home, Hal," to the *Ladies' Home Journal*. By August she had completed "Juno's Swans," which went to *Cosmopolitan,* and near the end of September she sent "Bid the Tapers Twinkle" to *Ladies' Home Journal.*[11]

"Alma" is the story of a girl in a small town who lives with a childhood crush on the wealthy boy across the alley, who, six years older than she, doesn't even know her name. His house is the largest in town, with manicured lawns and a garden with a pool, in which squats a "green iron frog [that] spouted water impudently at an iron bird that was either a heron or a stork" (28). The youngsters grow up, graduate from college, and, as with most people in the United States in that period, are affected by the reverses of the Depression. Alma borrows for an hour his parents' now empty house to entertain some college friends who are drop-ping by on their way to a distant city. The young man, having recently taken a position in the town bank, unexpectedly returns, finds the house in use but doesn't announce his ownership. After the guests leave, the young man asks what the name *Alma* means, and she tells him it means "to cherish, to hold dear." The story concludes by reverting to the garden pool where, through Depression-caused years of neglect, the frog and bird have fallen into disrepair: "And the green frog leered impudently with his one good eye at the heron that probably *was* a stork" (232).

"How Far Is It to Hollywood?" introduces Angie Bryson and Emma-Jo Thomas. Angie is relatively unfettered by parental authority and not too concerned with school. In contrast, Emma-Jo, whose mother and father believe strongly in parental authority, works hard at school, especially on arithmetic. In the story, Emma-Jo is faced with needing to solve by Monday the arithmetic problem of how far it is to Hollywood if there are 68,742 telegraph poles set 100 feet apart between here and there. On this particular Thursday afternoon, the two little girls perch on the back fence, overjoyed that there will be no school on Friday. They are movie and movie-magazine fans, and as they fence-sit above the milkweeds and old tomato cans they are transmuted into Hollywood's Greta Garbo and Mae West. Indeed, so completely are they immersed in their changes that they address one another as Greta and Mae, and by some ingenious rationalizations convince themselves that it would be in their respective families' best interests if Greta and Mae went to Hollywood and worked in movies so they could send home money. Inasmuch as neither of the girls has any money, they decide to walk to California, a solution that will also solve Emma-Jo's arithmetic problem, for she can count the telegraph poles en route. They start west. However, only two towns away they find themselves in difficulties and are ignominiously returned to their homes. Angie receives money to go the movies, but Emma-Jo must stay in her room all day and do her arithmetic. She concludes that she does not need to figure the solution to the problem because if one were to go by train or plane the conductor or pilot would know the distance, and if one were to drive, the odometer would show it. "And if you were not going at all, you didn't need to know. *And she was not going*" (165).

Cosmopolitan liked this story so well they asked for more and suggested that this might be the beginning of another series such as the Mason and Cutter families. In August, *Cosmopolitan* purchased the subsequent Emma-Jo and Angie story, "Juno's Swans," but Aldrich wrote no others about the pair. In "Juno's Swans," the title of which alludes to Shakespeare's *As You Like It*, the two girls take part in an operetta at the closing of the school year, and shy Emma-Jo steps forward at a crucial moment to allow Angie to sing the solo another has almost denied her. These two Emma-Jo/Angie stories helped to fulfill her contract obligations to *Cosmopolitan*.

"Welcome Home, Hal" brought great response from *Ladies' Home Journal* readers. One wrote that she had just finished reading "Hal" and was delighted by Aldrich's understanding of small towns and their inhabitants. A Texas correspondent told Aldrich that she had enjoyed this story more than any she had ever read, adding that it was the best picture of life in a small town that she had seen. This reader lived in a small town, and she said the people of the story were as real as those on her Main Street.[12]

"Welcome Home, Hal" is the story of a local boy who has gone to New York, where his childhood drawing talents mature and he becomes a successful national cartoonist. Hal is stopping briefly in his hometown on his way to the West Coast. His school friend, now a teacher, Judith Marsh, who is unwed and twenty-nine, is looking forward to his imminent arrival until she finds that someone named Grace will be with him, All assume that Grace is his fiancée. Judith tries to hide her disappointment from local people while helping them prepare an area-wide public dinner to honor their returning native son. The woman who accompanies Hal is Gran, his grandmother, the mistake in the name coming from a misreading of his poor handwriting, and he confesses to Judith that she, Judith, is the reason for his return. He proposes marriage to her.

"Bid the Tapers Twinkle" is a Christmas story. It shows Aldrich's skill at portraying old people and household help. She also blends family activities, such as the traditional Aldrich Christmas Eve supper, with the "inside" sayings that are a part of all family traditions. For Aldrich, Christmas was the magnet and magic of family unity, regardless of distance, and epitomized all that the word *home* encompasses. This is the enchantment of Christmas for elderly Sara Atkin, too, in "Bid the Tapers Twinkle." Here, Mrs. Atkin and her housekeeper, Jennie, prepare for the usual large and festive Christmas, only for Sara to find that none of the family will be able to attend. Sara cannot tell Jennie that she will be alone, so when Jennie offers to set the table for the traditional Christmas Eve oyster supper before she leaves for her own home, Sara tells her that the family will help when they arrive. Jennie leaves, and Sara dozes and reminisces until she realizes there are people at the door. Her family, all twenty-one of them, have come home. They had told her they would not come in an effort to save her the physical exertions they knew went into her holiday preparations.

Scarcely had Aldrich mailed "Bid the Tapers" in September when she received a wire followed by a letter from Appleton's John L. B. Williams. He wrote that, although plans were as yet confidential, there would be book fairs in "three of the biggest stores in the Central West—Halle Bros. in Cleveland, Horne, in Pittsburgh, and Hudson in Detroit" on successive days during the last week of October. The plan, wrote Williams, was that "about twenty-five of the most prominent authors" would appear at the fairs. "We are eager to have you as one of our representatives," he told her. The authors were to autograph books and fulfill speaking engagements; the stores stipulated that only under their auspices should the authors make appearances. Williams assured Aldrich that her expenses would all be paid and that the event would be worthwhile because "educational institutions and libraries, clubs, and club women and book reviewers" would be present. Further, there would be "wide newspaper advertising, many programs printed, abundant window displays, and a long list of invitations issued. . . . There may be broadcasting also," he said. Ever the editor, he concluded with: "I am hoping that you will tell me real progress has been made on your plan for the new novel."[13]

Aldrich agreed to make the trip. The national *P.E.O. Record* later reported that many members had gone to see her on tour and had had books autographed. The article described the fifty-three-year-old author as "a cameo type, with white hair, pink cheeks, orchids on her shoulder and corals at her throat and wrist." A newspaper article reported that

> the public blocked entrances outside the doors . . . and poured into the inside to buy [the writers'] books. . . . Despite the fact that [Mrs. Aldrich] was the only one of the group that had not authored a book very recently, she was kept incessantly busy autographing her earlier ones. Moreover, her publisher sent her an orchid or gardenia corsage every day, thereby arousing Irving Stone—author of . . . *Lust for Life*, to such a pitch of envy that he threatened to switch to her publisher.

Each writer spoke three times each day at a school, a luncheon, and the store. Among the twenty-five writers were Aldrich, Irving Stone, Alexander Woollcott, Dr. Henry S. Canby, editor of the *Saturday Review*, Sterling North, Carl Van Doren, Lloyd Douglas, and Arthur Pound. Aldrich returned home "very happy and exhilarated" over the event. She later sent her list of expenses to Appleton, regarding which Williams, enclosing her check, asked with some amazement, "Are you sure you sent me the complete amount you expended?"[14] She had. Thrift was not reserved for home.

October began with a request from Universal Pictures that she write a few words on her opinion about Charles Dickens's work, as they were soon to bring to the screen his *Great Expectations* and *The Mystery of Edwin Drood*. The month closed with a pleasant note from Williams that new printings of *A Lantern in Her Hand*, *The Rim of the Prairie*, and *The Cutters* had been ordered. "Isn't it splendid the way the books already issued keep on moving?" he commented.[15]

November brought a new challenge. Aldrich received a letter from Merritt Hulburd, the head of the scenario department of Paramount Pictures, enclosing the "outline for a picture to be called PIONEER WOMAN." Paramount had purchased the script from another writer and liked the outline but realized their "own inadequacy here to develop the character and situations to the point where, when transferred to the screen, they will be three dimensional and full-bodied. And in casting about for someone to do this development, it seemed to us you were most ideally suited for the job." Hulburd assured her she would not be writing the picture, only expanding and developing existing material. The people at Paramount, he told her, felt she could work best by coming to Hollywood where she would be under their "sympathetic eye." He noted that time and money could be discussed if she were interested in the proposal.[16]

Aldrich responded with courtesy and a mild reproof, which sent Hulburd to a quick response: "Thank you very much for your pleasant and exceedingly reasonable letter. It wasn't very tactful of me, was it, not to mention LANTERN IN HER HAND? Naturally, we wrote you because of that book and its fine and spiritual interpretation of the pioneer woman. As you so honestly put it, however, our pioneer woman story is preferable for pictures because of its more picturesque, exciting and motionful background." He went on to explain their proposed time schedule and payments to her: Aldrich would go to Hollywood soon after the first of the year and work for two weeks at $2,000 each week. If they mutually agreed, she would continue to work until the project was completed but with a guarantee of a minimum four more weeks at $1,500 per week. Hulburd felt it would not take her more than six weeks because of the amount of research material they would have for her and the assistance of the producer, Lloyd Sheldon.[17]

Aldrich agreed. Writing to Grace Bailey about the coming work she said she would receive "such a fat salary that I can't afford not to do it, even though I'm a little vague as to what I'm supposed to do." She felt, she added, rather like the man who was broke but even so someone asked for the loan of twenty dollars: " 'I haven't got the twenty but thanks for the compliment.' In other words, I'm not sure I can do what they want but thanks for the compliment, and I'm going to try anyway." A fee of $2,000 for a week was a substantial sum, and Paramount was willing to pay because Aldrich was good at the type of writing they needed. She was also acknowledged as "one of the highest-paid writers in the country." In 1935, the price of admission to a movie was 35¢, sugar about 5¢ a pound, and milk about 10¢ a quart. Wages without board for a farmhand were around $27 per month.[18]

Because Aldrich did not know how long she might be in Hollywood, she left Bob in Elmwood with John and Clara Cobb. On 7 January she was in California and ready to go to work. While there, Aldrich went to the Pantages Theater one evening to hear Upton Sinclair give a talk. She wrote home in some disgust that "he thinks everyone should be given a piece of land, a team of horses, and a plow. Well, as for some of the people . . . they'd feed the horses the wrong thing, trade off the plow for a radio, and lie down on the land to rest."[19]

During January, Aldrich, who was to remain in California until April, received an invitation to attend a celebrity luncheon, where she sat next to Lloyd Douglas, author of *Magnificent Obsession* and *The Robe*, and his wife. Obviously pleased, given her high regard for him, she wrote to her family that "he said he and his wife came purposely to meet me when they heard I was to be there." On the other side of her at the luncheon was "Mr. Hugh Matier, Englishman, [who] was going to England shortly to have a reunion with George Bernard Shaw, G. K. Chesterton, and James Matthew Barrie. Just like that,—as though it were Dell, Inez, and Marie." There was awe in this comment, for Barrie was one of her favorite authors, and the others were, of course, also internationally known. There was also the sense of the community of friendships. In the same letter, Aldrich reported receiving an invitation to be the guest of honor at the Authors' Club luncheon on 4 February. "This is the literary club in which an author is always guest of honor,—they've had Walpole and Alexander Woolcott and Irvin Cobb." During this California trip, Aldrich also received a letter from Dorothy Canfield Fisher inviting her to a dinner in honor of Jane Addams. The event would be in Washington DC with a reception at the White House.[20] Here she would see her good friend, and fellow Nebraskan, Bess Furman, the national wire service correspondent assigned to Eleanor Roosevelt; and would also meet Mrs. Roosevelt. Aldrich was not able to accept this invitation.

Aldrich had been in Hollywood about three weeks when she received a letter from John L. B. Williams informing her that Appleton-Century's Rutger Bleeker Jewett had died. As her editor for many years, Jewett had pushed, urged, and cajoled her in almost every letter about her current or next novel. In 1934, when she was contemplating her next long fiction and Jewett was urging her to write the story of a small-town banker or doctor, Aldrich had written him about "Soap Kettle," the story that she liked so much but that none of the magazine publishers would accept. As she told him, the work was based on fact, and Jewett had responded that "the story behind the fictionized version of The Soap Kettle is significant—too good to be lost. I trust you will be able to make something of it."[21] However, the work he was most anxious to have her write was that of the banker or doctor, characters he felt she was particularly adept at creating.

In telling Aldrich of Jewett's death, Williams added that "I had talked many times to Mr. Jewett about your new novel. He was keenly interested, always, to learn of its progress. I hope it is getting on well and that I'll soon hear from you about it." This was the banker or doctor story Jewett had wanted. A few days later, Aldrich received word from Williams that he was flying to California and would like to visit her while there. She knew his purpose in coming was, at least in part, to try to make her commit to writing a new long fiction, which she did not want to do, saying, "I just want to do some more shorts [short stories] and have a book another year, for coming this way cuts into the time just horribly. If a picture would just sell I would feel so free to let the book go a year."[22]

When Williams arrived, he took her to lunch and told of his flight from New York in which the passengers, because of bad weather, were landed in Pittsburgh, taken by train to Indianapolis, where they met the plane (that had flown through to pick them up), and continued their trip to the West Coast. Aldrich, who would not herself fly, much preferring the train, during this lunch meeting told Williams the soap kettle story. Perhaps it was because of Williams's telling Aldrich of the challenge of his flight; perhaps it was because her books were not selling for films; perhaps it was because he was "crazy about that title 'Spring Came On Forever' and thinks it fits in with old Amalia and the soap kettle and the meadow larks and all," that Aldrich agreed to complete a manuscript by fall: "Dear Children, . . . I am to start a new book and rush it through before September (Soft hearted Hannah.)." Soon after Aldrich admitted ruefully that "here when I wasn't going to do so, he ups and talks me into it, and I could have stood adamant if it hadn't been that he got enthusiastic about old Amalia and wanted me to go on with her."[23]

Thus, the truth of a real life again became the basis for a book, and from the story of "The Soap Kettle" Aldrich wrote a book of such interest that one reviewer's lament was that it should have "been twice as long—and of how few novels could this be said!"[24]

Aldrich spent two weeks working for Paramount on the "Pioneer Woman" film script. Within a few months the producer decided against making it into a movie, a not unusual occurrence in Hollywood. Aldrich remained in California after her work for Paramount Studio was completed, so she could continue to push some of her work for films. To do this she attended functions that were reported in newspapers and talked to promotors and studio executives. In the meantime she also began work on *Spring*. She saw the new novel as having four sequences, which she did not specifically name nor did she include obvious breaks. Broadly, the events are the early years in which the young Matthias and Amalia meet; the time of their marriages to others and their becoming middle-aged; the maturing of the next three generations; the resolution. Aldrich discussed the four-part organization with Williams, and he agreed. As noted, she had immediately determined the title, *Spring Came On Forever*, which she had discarded in favor of *Miss Bishop* for the earlier work. In March, Williams sent her a note to tell her that he was writing Mrs. Vachel Lindsay, the poet's widow, and the Macmillan Company for permission to use that as the title, for it had come from Lindsay's poem, "The Chinese Nightingale." By early April, Williams was requesting a plot synopsis and soon sent her a copy of the title page, again urging her to send the plot synopsis. He also addressed a problem she wrote about, that of voice. Aldrich began the story from Matthias's point of view, but Williams suggested that, inasmuch as it was more Amalia's story, it should be from her point of view.[25] The result was that Aldrich returned to her favorite voice, that of storyteller, weaving for the listener the history and fiction of different and distinct characters.

The Depression was still a factor, both nationally and in individual people's lives, but there were signs that it was easing. Aldrich, in a letter to her children and Tallie (Tallie was sister Clara's nickname) said to "Tell John thanks for the bank report, looks as though things are beginning to show NET. Hooray!" Aldrich was able to do some writing in California but found it difficult to work away from her Elmwood home. However, she knew that when she returned the summer temperatures would be almost unbearable for her. The coolest part of the Elmwood house was the basement, and, although she did not like working there, she told Mary that she might have to take her typewriter down to complete the book, which she did. The heat notwithstanding, Aldrich was growing anxious to get "back to [current typist] Ruth Fitch, [for I have] some things to look up and am beginning to think it has been a long time since I've seen you. I'll never start a book that late in the spring again and could even yet kick myself that I let Mr. Williams hornswaggle me into it. Should have done shorts the rest of the year."[26] Soon after writing this letter, Aldrich left for Elmwood.

Spring Came On Forever tells the tale of a young man, Matthias Meier, and a young woman, Amalia Stoltz, who meet on an early spring day in 1866 at Matthias's uncle's foundry in Illinois. Amalia's father is at the foundry to buy a large iron soap kettle. To Matthias's comment about the weather, Amalia replies in German that "Meadow larks are singing, and I smell spring" (5). The Stoltzes and other German-Lutheran immigrants are soon to move to Nebraska, where Amalia is to marry the man of her father's choice, an older man of their congregation. However, after a few secret meetings, the two young people, Amalia and Matthias, realize they want to marry, and they make plans to tell her father. Before they can do so, news comes from the advance party of Germans sent to locate good land that they have found what they sought, and the others are to travel west immediately, which they do. Floods keep Matthias from reaching Amalia before she leaves. He follows her to Nebraska Territory, but she has already been forced to marry Herman Holmsdorfer, and Matthias knows neither Amalia nor he would break the marriage vows. She moves on to the eastern Nebraska prairies with others of the German families, while Matthias, after a year shoeing horses in Nebraska City, goes to the new capital town of Lincoln, where he feels there is future and opportunity.

The story moves back and forth between Amalia and Matthias, in paralleling segments of time or activity. Amalia has a son, Emil; her husband dies in a blizzard, but he is not found until spring "at the head of a small canyon pocket, his gun by his side" (130). Her authoritarian father, too, dies as a result of that storm. Son Emil, at the age of twenty, marries into the German clan. He also has a son, Joe; however, when Joe marries it is to a city girl who will later talk him into anglicizing the Holmsdorfer name to Holms, mortgaging much of their land to buy a house in town, and moving there. Before that, however, they have a son, whom they name Neal, making Amalia (who has refused to change her name) a great-grandmother at the age of sixty-three.

In the meantime, Matthias has become a merchant in Lincoln and married Ida Carter. Seven years later they have a son, Carter. Matthias sells the business he had built up, buys into a Lincoln bank, and builds "a showy residence" (170). They become a part of the upper echelon of society in the booming little capital. Aldrich, through the lives and activities of Matthias and

Ida, tells some of the history of Lincoln, including such details as the advent of the telephone and the coming to town of Oscar Wilde, Edwin Booth, Lily Langtry, and Modjeska (168–72). The opening in 1889 of the new, four-story Lansing Theatre "was like a Chicago event. Culture had come to the prairie" (172–73). Later Matthias retires, Ida dies in the Spanish-flu epidemic of 1919, and Matthias moves to Cedar City to be near his son, Carter, Carter's wife, Lucille, and their daughter, Hazel. Carter has purchased controlling interest in the local bank, and Matthias enjoys their business conversations for the few years remaining to him. When the bank moratorium takes effect in 1933, Carter's bank cannot reopen; Matthias is by now gone, and Carter and Lucille move to Lincoln, where Hazel's trust fund will carry her through to her university degree.

During this same period, Joe Holms, Amalia's grandson, loses his house in town and the two eighties of land on which he can no longer pay the mortgages because he abandoned farming and acceded to his wife's desire to be a member of the local town society. Amalia's original 240 acres of family land remain, and, despite financial problems, Neal will be able to finish his last year of college. Neal and Hazel Meier become engaged, but when Neal decides to return to the land Amalia holds rather than become a lawyer, Hazel breaks the engagement, preferring to be a schoolteacher rather than a farm wife.

One of Aldrich's fine descriptions, often mentioned by critics for its excellence of detail, is of the mid-1930s Republican River flood. This flood brings Neal and Hazel together again and they marry, returning to Amalia's farm to live and work. The Depression continues, and one fall day, Hazel tells Amalia that she has decided to clean out the old soap kettle and use it for its original purpose once again. Seeing the kettle triggers thoughts of Matthias Meier in the old woman's rather uncertain memory, and she calls out the name. She then tells Hazel how she and Matthias met on Sundays in Illinois in the woods, by the old soap kettle, while her father slept. Hazel recognizes the story as the one her grandfather told of following his first sweetheart, whose name was Amalia, into Nebraska, only to find she was already married. Old Amalia, looking "as though the girl in Breton's *Song of the Lark* had grown wrinkled and feeble after eighty-six years of listening," on that autumn day declares happily that "Meadow-larks iss singin', and I smell spring" (333).

Aldrich had orginally told Williams that she would be done by September, but he later urged an earlier date because Appleton would prefer to have the manuscript by 1 July. She tried, but realized she could not be finished by then. She wrote to say she felt she was being crowded on the work and that Appleton was not allowing her sufficient time to authenticate information she wanted to use. She also reminded him how strongly she felt that every paragraph printed under her name be correct. Williams agreed that the work must be right because "we know that your honesty of authorship does not countenance anything else." Further, Aldrich was chafing under the weight of Nebraska's deep summer heat, was, in fact, working in the basement, and was distressed that she was having to postpone her annual July and August trip to the cool, lakeside Minnesota cottage. Williams assured her they appreciated her efforts to finish despite the trying conditions and also said that the response to prepublication advertising sales of *Spring* were "very gratifying, everywhere enthusiasm for the new novel."[27]

On 21 August the manuscript arrived in New York, and Aldrich headed for Minnesota, where, because of Appleton's fast work and their desire to have the book out for fall publication, she proofread the galleys. Williams suggested one change: that the opening two paragraphs be placed at the front of the book, on a separate page, to serve as an attention-getter. Chapter 1 would then begin on the following page, " 'Matthias Meir was twenty-one in the year 1866.' " Aldrich, as she did so often, argued for and won her point. They should, she felt, put the first two paragraphs in italics, to which Williams replied that such was "absolutely what should be done and we shall do it."[28] In September 1935, Williams informed her that the *Saturday Evening Post* could not use *Spring Came On Forever* for a serial; therefore, Appleton would publish the book on 28 September or 4 October. In fact, it came out 11 October.

By the week following publication, the new novel was in its third printing, a very good record "for these times," as Williams wrote her. He added that Don Gordon, of *American News,* had given it a 3-A rating, which was very high. Williams kept Aldrich informed of *Spring*'s progress up the charts: "In addition to the good news you already have about the lists in the *Chicago Tribune,* in Boston, and St. Louis, I know you will be interested in the fact that in next Sunday's *Tribune Spring Came On Forever* is seventh. Last Sunday it was eleventh. This list is based on a nationwide canvas. So the sales thermometer is rising in good shape." A week later he wrote that *Spring* was a best-seller in New York, Boston, Washington, Atlanta, and St. Louis; that it would be in fifth place in next Sunday's *Herald-Tribune;* and that in the important Baker and Taylor list of best-selling books, *Spring Came On Forever* was in fourth place. By 8 November he could report that "the American Library Association comes out strong for *Spring Came On Forever,* recommending it for adult readers and suggesting. . . [it be] included among the purchases of even smaller libraries." *Spring* rapidly made best-sellers' lists in towns and cities across the country.[29]

The reviews were good. An Illinois newspaper (the *News*) wrote that "both as an American chronicle, and as an entertaining novel, it is recommended"; The *Cleveland Plain Dealer* said, "Never has Mrs. Aldrich probed the depths of human hearts with such gentle comprehension and tender sympathy as in this book"; and the *St. Louis Globe Democrat* noted the "effective contrast of the pioneer life in the town and on the farm. As an epic story of pioneer life, *Spring Came On Forever* deserves to be ranked with *A Lantern in Her Hand*." The *New York Times* reviewer pointed out that one had to believe that the "families whose history is described here actually existed and were known to Mrs. Aldrich," and that the ending, with its "shirt-sleeves to shirt-sleeves cycle" of generations was "so true." The reviewer also noted that "as an American document it would be difficult to praise 'Spring Came

On Forever' too highly," but that there was room for criticism—
"though, in view of its manifold good qualities, these criticisms
may seem a little ungrateful." The problem, according to the
Times review, was "a compression which is sometimes unfortu-
nate." The most frequent criticism was that the chapters were too
short for fullest development: A San Jose, California, reviewer
said, "Perhaps if details were given it would make the book too
long for the publisher, but not for the reader"; another, in
Greensboro, North Carolina, wrote that the work "just misses
distinction" because the plot "is a bit too deliberate and too romantic," acknowledging that "there are, however, other qualities
to offset Mrs. Aldrich's intentional concessions to popular taste.
She has the gift of making her characters human."[30]

For Aldrich, life that autumn was moving at a pleasant
pace. With the book out of the way, she was having the white
woodwork at The Elms, her big home, freshly enameled. The
house had been thoroughly cleaned, and preparations were nearly
complete for the family Thanksgiving holiday. All the children
would be present. Then an event occurred that made the Aldrich
"blood flow hot."[31]

John L. B. Williams was out of town, and C. Gibson
Sheaffer, who was taking care of Williams's correspondence, sent
Aldrich a copy of a letter Appleton had just received and to which
they wanted Aldrich to respond. The letter contained a charge of
plagiarism, relating to incidents appearing in *A Lantern in Her
Hand* and *Spring Came On Forever*. The incidents, said the ac-
cuser, Mrs. Peggy Haskell Benjamin, reproduced stories her father
had told of a particularly cold winter, a sheepherding incident,
and a man frozen in a canyon.

A similar letter, repeating the allegations, had been sent to
George E. Grimes, the day telegraph editor and book reviewer of
the *Omaha World-Herald*. Grimes wrote to Aldrich and enclosed
a copy of the letter he had received. Aldrich wrote Appleton immediately. She then answered Grimes, before directly answering
the woman who accused her, letting "the reply to the lady simmer
until such time as I wouldn't have to put it into a . . . refrigerator

before mailing it." She waited, as Aldrich said, "partly that I might handle it without rancor or indignation," partly because of the press of autographing fifty copies of her books for Carson-Pirie-Scott (the Chicago department store), partly because she was working on a contract (for *Miss Bishop* to be made into a stage play) and preparing for the coming holiday.[32]

Aldrich told Grimes of her talk years earlier on the radio asking for items listeners might choose to share about early experiences in Nebraska, adding "time and again I have said '*A Lantern In Her Hand* is not all mine but the experiences of several hundred early Nebraskans.'" She continued that

> I turn to my filing-case and find the item concerning the cold winter and the fact that beans, flour and left-over army clothes were distributed by the government has these names by it: Bailey—Ferguson—Berger—Clapp—Haskell [the correspondent's father].—So I take it that it *was* a cold winter, that these articles were distributed and that several others besides her father knew about it.
>
> The item concerning the young men from Boston and the sheep they drove in was distinctly her father's own experience contributed by himself voluntarily.

Later, in her letter to the woman, Aldrich added that "Old Mr. Charley Bailey [Elmwood resident] who was one of my best sources of information, recalling his experiences one day, began to tell about some young men camping near his shack in this region . . . and had not gone very far into it until I recognized the experience of your father as written to me in one of those letters from pioneers, and told him of the coincidence. He agreed that they must have been the same chaps. So the item could also have been used from the Bailey standpoint."[33]

The last item the woman had written to protest appeared in *Spring Came On Forever*, the finding of a frozen body with a gun alongside of it in a canyon (130). Again, Aldrich commented to Grimes on Peggy Haskell Benjamin's letter to him, writing that Benjamin felt Aldrich should have written the story of Haskell rather than the Germans because Haskell had been a man who worked hard at being a booster and builder of Nebraska. However, according to Aldrich's knowledge of what Benjamin had written to Appleton, Haskell was also a man with no fondness for the German immigrants. He distrusted them, disliked their speaking together in their native tongue, was distressed that the men treated the women harshly, believed that they had been poor neighbors to him, having stolen his cattle, shot at his horses, and even shot at him. Because of her regard for her father, Benjamin protested what she felt was Aldrich's stealing of his stories. Aldrich wrote to Grimes:

> As the only paragraph which she has reported from this new book as belonging to her father is the one concerning finding of a body frozen in the canyon, and reported to me in two others of those old contributions of letters, it doesn't seem to me the terrible thing she states.
>
> Her letters are something of a shock to me for in all these years those who have recognized in the Lantern [*sic*] something distinctly from their own family have been rather *flattered*. Apparently it's good for me to have someone think it not such a nice thing.

Aldrich added that a bookdealer to whom she mentioned the accusations said that uncountable times people had boasted that it was "'their cousin's brother-in-law's step-sister [who] was the one who wore the hat with the jet buckle' or words to that effect." Aldrich noted that she had spent long days and months preparing and writing a composite picture of experiences so true to life that many people think "it is their own grandmother's life"; she concluded with the wry comment, "and that, of course, isn't worth anything in the eyes of the woman whose father told me some of his experiences by letter many years ago."[34]

In her response to Benjamin, Aldrich told her that she was sorry "you have been disturbed by those things in the book which your father with many other Nebraskans voluntarily wrote me. Because they all had so much in common in those days any story of its kind seems almost an authentic picture of each family. . . . And almost every page does contain an indirect reference to something someone has told me,—many of them reported several times, such as the government supplies to which you refer and the body in the canyon." Further, these incidents could have all been eliminated, for there were "hundreds of unused experiences from other persons, any one of which could have been used."[35]

The following month, Sheaffer, in a note to Aldrich, said that they had just received a letter from Benjamin, that she did not seem entirely satisfied, but that there was nothing more to be done at the present, for "she does not intend, apparently, to carry the correspondence any further and I am sure we shall not be troubled again with a thing of this kind."[36] Many times Aldrich had spoken and written of the help that pioneers had given her, and she knew that her sources had shared their stories in the hopes that she would use them. Because of Aldrich's devotion to honesty and accuracy, as well as her careful record-keeping, the charges were painful but not devastating.

Perhaps a letter to Aldrich from Mari Sandoz, native Nebraskan, author of *Old Jules* and many other books and short stories, sums up the reaction of most people to the writer from Elmwood. The Sandoz letter was written in December, about two weeks following the last Sheaffer letter above, and thanked "Dear Mrs. Aldrich" for a "kindness yesterday" that had so overwhelmed Sandoz that she forgot to mention "an earlier favor." The earlier favor was Aldrich's nominating Sandoz for membership in the Society of Midland Authors; Sandoz now wrote, "Thank you for this grand gesture, which is, after all, only an inkling of your own true nature."[37]

10

The

Late 1930s

and More

Best-sellers

January 1936 began with the good news that between 11 October 1935 and 25 January 1936, *Spring Came On Forever* had sold over 45,000 copies. John L. B. Williams of Appleton called it "a grand showing in times like these, or any other times. And the end is not yet," for every week saw more sales of *Lantern,* which, along with all the other Aldrich works, was having renewed activity because of *Spring*'s popularity.[1] In February, Blanche Colton Williams and her coauthor, Ernest Gray Keller, completed their dramatization of *Miss Bishop* and sent it for Aldrich's approval. Over the next two years, Williams and Keller tried hard to mount it as a stage play; however, despite all the high hopes, it never saw an opening night. Twice it was close to being a summer stock piece, but each time the producers demanded a percentage should the play later move to Broadway, and Appleton refused to agree to this condition.

In March, Appleton sent Aldrich a copy of a letter that accused her of making disparaging remarks about Luther and the Lutheran Church in *Spring Came On Forever*. The manager of the Concordia (Lutheran) Publishing House wrote that their reviewers recommended that they not carry *Spring* because of its anti-Lutheran slant. He added that he felt it unnecessary for a talented author to pick out people of any denomination, particularly, as far as they were concerned, the Lutheran denomination, and paint a negative picture of them. He felt that even those who were not of that church would be offended at the unfair picture she presented of the Lutherans. When Williams wrote to Aldrich about this latest problem, he admitted to being at a loss to understand where the difficulty lay, for he did not know of anything to which they might object. Aldrich wrote immediately, assuring them that her intent had not been in any way to denigrate either Luther or Lutherans but simply to show how one segment of people lived in the early days in Nebraska. Concordia continued to carry her other works.[2]

Shortly after Aldrich put that response in the mail, she received exciting news from Williams—a proposal for an Oscar Hammerstein II–Jerome Kern "musical play" based on *Spring Came On Forever*. If the play went well, she would receive royalties of 1 percent of the weekly box office receipts up to $20,000 and 1.5 percent of the weekly receipts above that, which might equal or surpass the $20,000. However, Williams warned Aldrich to consider the matter carefully; for if Hammerstein decided against making *Spring* into a musical and instead decided to sell their rights to a motion-picture producer, she would receive only $5,000, far less than her asking price for movie rights of $20,000.

The contract called for "Jerome Kern or other first class composer" to write the musical score, and the verbal agreement was that if Kern were not available then Sigmund Romberg or someone of similar stature would be the composer. She would also receive billing wherever the composer's names appeared. Aldrich was excited over these prospects, yet she tempered excitement with the memory that similar high hopes for various productions had not borne fruit and that these sorts of possibilities and plans moved very slowly. She also tempered her excitement with practicality and told Appleton that she was not quite willing to accept the proposals. She felt that if the musical did not materialize, the possibility of only a $5,000 sale to a film company was not enough; if the show did become a reality, the royalty percentage was insufficient.[3] Negotiations continued.

As always, Aldrich kept busy. She was planning the long-projected book of short stories. On 10 April Williams sent her a list of the eleven short-story manuscripts she had provided in 1935. Appleton also had "The Woman Who Was Forgotten," but Williams did not include it because he felt it had been sufficiently developed in *Miss Bishop* and should not at that time be re-published. The suggested length for the book was about 80,000 words, which would be in keeping with her usual 80,000 to 85,000 words. The list of stories held by Williams totaled only about 50,000 words; hence, she needed to find four or five more stories in her files to send him. Williams requested that she put these new stories in the mail in the next day or so, in order to get all the material immediately to the printer.[4]

However, Williams was now dealing with Grandmother Aldrich; the christening of her first grandson, David Aldrich Beechner, came before book publishing. She wrote Williams that she would not, therefore, have time for a week or so to prepare more manuscripts. He concurred that nothing should interfere with the upcoming big event and asked her to send the complete set early in May.[5]

Of the eleven stories listed by Appleton, Aldrich rejected four and sent seven previously published ones that he did not have. She also set out the order in which they were to appear. The works she decided against including were "He Whom a Dream Hath Possest," "A Long Distance Call from Jim," "Romance in G Minor," and "Ginger Cookies." Of the original eleven, this left "The Man Who Caught the Weather," "Trust the Irish for That,"

"Will the Romance Be the Same," "The Day of Retaliation," "It's Never Too Late to Live," "The Runaway Judge," and a Christmas story, "The Silent Stars Go By." Aldrich added three more Christmas stories, "Bid the Tapers Twinkle," "Low Lies His Bed," and "Another Brought Gifts." The four were spaced evenly throughout the work. Ultimately, this new book also contained "Alma, Meaning to Cherish," "How Far Is It to Hollywood?" "Juno's Swans," "Welcome Home, Hal!" and "The Runaway Judge" (which returned to its original title, "The Mountain Looks on Marathon").

Aldrich had signed a contract with Appleton for the book in February 1935, writing to her children with amusement over the title, *The Man Who Caught the Weather*, "from that old short story which would be the first in the volume. Some successful ending for an old story that was turned down" so many times. Both she and Williams agreed the book should carry the O. Henry Award winning story as the lead and carry on the cover the words *The Man Who Caught the Weather*. The title page would add *And Other Stories*. The book was released on 18 September to good reviews and sales, although, as Williams had indicated, a book of short stories would not prove as popular as her novels. Nevertheless, by 10 December *The Man Who Caught the Weather* had gone into its fourth printing; a good run for such a work with Christmas sales just getting under way.[6]

Before the book was published, Aldrich completed two other tasks. She had been asked to write an article about herself "to appeal to the thousands of members for the women's institutes of Great Britain and the English Colonies to whom such books as 'The Lantern' and 'Miss Bishop' have had such an unusual appeal." She had also been commissioned to write an article recommending *Reader's Digest* as a Christmas gift. For this she received $500. During this same period, Danish translation rights to *A Lantern in Her Hand* were sold.[7] A few months later, she gave permission for both *A White Bird Flying* and *Miss Bishop* to be set in braille.

In early May, Aldrich had company at Elmwood; John

L. B. Williams visited, meeting the Aldrich family. He and Aldrich discussed a new novel that Aldrich was considering about the growth of a city like Omaha. The protagonist would be a woman who had participated from the early years. They also considered plans to issue one of the *Cosmopolitan* Christmas stories in booklet form during a Christmas season when there was no new Aldrich book on the market and explored the possibilities of compiling another book of short stories at some future date. Williams urged Aldrich to consider writing more articles about her childhood because "I Remember" (*McCall's*, November 1926) had been so popular. Williams felt such articles gathered together would make a good book.[8]

Shortly after the Williams visit, Aldrich, Chuck, and Bob left for California. California was special to Aldrich, not only because of her hopes for sale to the motion-picture industry, but also because of family ties. In California she could visit both Streeter and Aldrich relatives, as well as John Cobb's brother and his family. She had also made a large number of social and professional friends in the Hollywood and Los Angeles areas on two previous visits, and many wanted her as guest or guest speaker. Such society or literary events were noteworthy and were reported in trade and daily newspapers, and the exposure kept her name and works in front of movie moguls.

John McCormick had replaced Ivan Kahn, representing Aldrich and Appleton in seeking screen sales. McCormick wrote Aldrich frequent, optimistic letters, indicating that he anticipated momentarily that this studio or that, this producer or that, this actress or that, would pick up *Lantern, Miss Bishop, The Masons, The Cutters,* or *Rim.* Soon after sending her several hopeful letters, he would write that pioneer stories were not in favor at the moment, or the anticipated director or actress was not available. Hopes were raised again when John McCormick's partner, George Landy, took proofs from the Angie and Emma-Jo stories in the forthcoming *Man Who Caught the Weather* to Sam Goldwyn, at whose studio there had been some interest. Landy told Goldwyn that Aldrich would "be available to help build up more of a sequence" if they wanted her.[9] Again, nothing came of it. McCormick wrote to Ed Smith of Appleton's finance department that part of the problem was due to the money Aldrich felt she should have, which made it difficult for them to convince a producer to buy one of her books with its leisurely pace and extended time period.

Aldrich was still looking for a Hollywood sale that would provide a financial cushion; however, her faith in her material was strong, and she would not give away her work. Aldrich fretted occasionally about the great fluctuations in her writing income, which ran from $393 in 1928 up to $33,000 in 1932, and down again to $14,000 in 1935. Generally she could look at her life philosophically; thus, she wrote brother-in-law John Cobb that "if, by any chance, the movie rights would be sold, I'll be sitting pretty, but I'm counting on absolutely nothing,—for many times they don't go over. . . . In the meantime, I'm just forgetting it, for these things are too uncertain and my business is the writing, not the screen."[10]

Aldrich had become sensitized to plagiarism because of her brush with Benjamin, and, while in California, read a book that seemed to her a "direct imitation of the *Lantern*." In July, she wrote as much to Williams, who replied that unless the words follow the actual order in which they first appeared, it is almost impossible to prove plagiarism. With her usual humor and aplomb, Aldrich wrote to her family that she couldn't argue, for "it's not a steal when one uses pioneer material,—the same blizzards blizzed and the same grasshoppers hopped, so what can you do about it?"[11]

In late August she was invited to tea at the Oscar Hammerstein home in the winding canyons above Hollywood to discuss the possibilities of turning *Spring Came On Forever* into a musical. Hammerstein's wife told Aldrich that she and her husband were both Aldrich fans. The problem with *Spring*, Hammerstein told her, was the time element. Knowing this might be discussed, Aldrich had taken with her for Hammerstein to read a copy of *The Rim of the Prairie*, which covers only eight months, telling him that "it had the same background and atmosphere." The episode seemed full of promise, but Aldrich did not allow herself more elation than to acknowledge in a letter that "anyway, I know he is interested."[12]

Aldrich returned to Elmwood shortly after the tea with the Hammersteins and the next months passed quickly but without the intended beginning of a new novel. Not until December did she "square off," as she called it, at her desk. She was not satisfied with the early results and wrote as much to Williams. She remained unwilling to write a pioneering novel, saying she had "hoped I was through with stories laid in an early day, largely because I did not want to overdo the setting." In a return letter, he suggested that she begin at the current time with a woman of sixty or sixty-five whose years had been witness to the growth of the area from small town to city and whose experiences could provide guidance to her family. He felt this would eliminate a lot of historical research.[13] Aldrich, reluctant to create another three-generation story, did little more with an Omaha setting at this time. Such a work would wait for five years.

By January 1937, Aldrich still had not established a satisfactory basis for the book. She continued to go through files, casting about for ideas, while Appleton pressed for another pioneer work. As Aldrich reflected on the possibilities, she recalled a brief meeting and subsequent exchange of correspondence of some seven years earlier. During a 1930 visit to Cedar Falls, Aldrich had chatted with seventy-year-old banker Roger Leavitt, whose family, like her own, were early settlers of the region. In November of that year, Leavitt had written Aldrich, congratulating her on *A Lantern in Her Hand* and telling her how much he had liked it and *The Rim of the Prairie*. He had suggested that she write a novel based on historically correct accounts of early Iowa history, much as she had written of Nebraska. Leavitt had assured her that he could supply a large amount of information, for he had been saving pioneer stories for many years. She had replied, in effect, that such a novel could not be "absolutely correct historically," that a novelist must use her imagination, and that she did not, therefore, feel she could write what he suggested, although she did appreciate his suggestion and offer of helpful materials. Leavitt's next letter explained that he did not expect the work to be exact in every detail and that conversations, for example, would have to be invented. He offered to show her the Iowa history room the next time she visited Cedar Falls. This series of letters closed with her telling him that to write such a work she "would have to have some special inspiration."[14]

Seven years later, the "special inspiration" arrived through Appleton's continued urging that she write another book. On 29 January 1937, Aldrich wrote Leavitt that she had thought she was "through with stories laid in an early day, largely because I did not want to overdo the setting, but the publishers are anxious that I bring forth another one, and I am beginning to go over various clippings and articles with this in mind." She inquired what sorts of materials he had that might be useful in writing a story of early Iowa. Knowing he felt that the story should be accurate, she pointed out that

> the great stumbling block in the way of using material from some specific source is that it is an impossibility for a writer to use it in its honest entirety if it is in the form of fiction.[15]
>
> One has to fictionize the story element, for the plot often calls for drama where there was none in real life, and hence the finished product isn't at all the way it was in real life even though the setting and background may be authentic.
>
> All of which goes back to the question of whether you would want me to use anything and still fictionize it.

She pointed out to him that "as a matter of fact, thousands read a fictionized historical event where few read the truer but often less dramatic article."[16]

Leavitt was delighted at the possibility of Iowa receiving this kind of wide attention and hurried to provide information. Four days after she sent her letter, Aldrich received from him two letters and an eighteen-pound box of pages, loose leaves, from his seventy scrapbooks. Aldrich quickly wrote Leavitt that she was "both amazed and chagrined to think you sent so much and such important documents. I had in mind perhaps a single large envelope mailed out to me and think if I had realized the pains you were to take in getting all this together I wouldn't have had the courage to say anything about it." She added that the letters from his father were "simply splendid," for Leavitt's father had written to his own father in Massachusetts beginning in 1854 with explicit descriptions about conditions and the settlement of Iowa, particularly Black Hawk County. She also told Leavitt that she had not taken out all of the packets yet, as she had been so fascinated by the letters, adding that she was "not sure just what my outline will be, or what I shall do. There must be a story which will keep young people reading, and which of necessity will be concerning fictitious characters, for I haven't yet come to the point where I can drag real people and their foibles out into the open." Aldrich assured him that "I shall keep the setting and the customs and costumes of the times intact. After all—that is all that is required of us, I believe, that we do not distort the background."[17] She was particularly interested in having young people read her book to learn what their forebears had done.

Less than a week later, Aldrich wrote Leavitt again, this time to tell him that the second package of clippings had arrived. She had, she said, "been reading almost continuously . . . scarcely coming up for air." She commented that she was taking notes on the most dramatic events. One such event, she felt, was the "young man returning on foot to Dubuque [110 miles] to register his claim and getting there before the [men] in the buggy." The incident, she said, "lends itself very readily to a story."

Aldrich stressed again her concern about using this real material in a fictional form; she noted that, although it happened only once, she had been distressed by a person who "made life rather unpleasant" because of a true incident about which Aldrich had written. Hence, she queried, "do you feel that I can use everything you sent without criticism?" She explained further: "I imagine you understand exactly what I shall have to do. There will be a character called John Smith or Tom Brown who will do something which your father has done, something which Mr. Hanna did, and something which no one probably did. Jane or Mary might be something of my mother, something of Mrs. Joseph Chase, and something purely imaginary."[18]

During their continued correspondence, Aldrich asked Leavitt to discuss with the editor of the *Waterloo Courier,* from which many of the articles had come, what constraints would be placed upon her use of material from the newspaper. The editor assured Leavitt and Aldrich that she could use anything she wanted in her own way. Leavitt also gave unqualified consent to her using any of his materials in any way she chose. Aldrich then wove together the background of the story, using materials from the scrapbooks, the letters, and the clippings that Leavitt had sent, and letters written by her grandfather when he was a member of the 1858 and 1859 Iowa legislatures. She used also recollections of her older sister Clara and information and maps from her eighty-one-year-old cousin, Louise Barrett, the Minnesota educator, who had lived in the Cedar Falls area before the Civil War and witnessed many of the events. With all of these she added anecdotes from her childhood, for "I remember the tales my father and mother told so that I feel close to the days of their youth."[19]

By March, Aldrich had enough of an outline that she could write Appleton about the new work, and they were so delighted that the president, editor-in-chief, sales manager, and head of the dramatic department all sent wires of congratulations. That spring, she put the materials together, following a system similar to the one she had worked out with *Lantern,* "making it so correct as to time and events that it can be referred to as authentic." The time frame would be from 1854 through the spring of 1865. Aldrich told Leavitt that the title would come from an old patriotic song called "The Song of a Thousand Years," by Henry Clay Work, who also wrote "Marching Through Georgia." The book, she said, will be the love story of Suzanne Martin, one of the seven daughters of Jeremiah Martin, this latter character based somewhat upon the life of my own grandfather. While I have births and deaths and some serious events, together with the regulation early day blizzards and storms, there is a very light, cheerful and gay thread of laughter through the whole thing, as the seven sisters (as my seven aunts were known to be) are full of fun. You know my old contention that pioneer days were not all gloom, because not all pioneers were *gloomy*. I am not following anyone in the story to war, but remaining in the Valley there in eastern Iowa and picturing only the echoes of the war. I enter no one's mind in the telling excepting those of Suzanne, the young man she loves, and old Jeremiah. All other characters are subservient to these.

In later correspondence to a fellow native of Cedar Falls, Iowa, in 1949 Aldrich again described both Jeremiah and his wife as "pretty largely patterned after my grandparents, [and] my father really had the seven sisters, although I didn't try very hard to pattern each story girl exactly after one of them. I just knew the whole seven were lively and full of fun."[20]

On 11 May she wrote to Leavitt that she was "working on the manuscript every day and while it is very tiring and feel as though I had washed, ironed, swept and baked at the end of the day (and some people think [writing] is all checks, fame, and roses), it is still very interesting to arrange and rearrange the events and write of my fictitious family." Aldrich remained in Elmwood that summer in order to work on what was first to be titled *Song of a Thousand Years*. Williams, at Appleton, suggested that, while that was an arresting title, it would be enhanced by being shorter. He suggested *Song of the Years*. By July, she decided on simply, *Song of Years*. Williams wanted the manuscript by 15 October, a request she told him was impossible. As she later wrote to Leavitt, "It takes a full year to do a book such as I am doing . . .

[as I am] checking various events in the story with those old articles."[21]

The story opens with the narrator providing a broad panorama of the land and creeks and towns of the Red Cedar Valley in eastern Iowa. The time is the late 1930s. The focus then narrows to a paved road that runs past cornfields and turns at a sideroad. Following this road beside cornfields to a wire fence, through first one gate and then another, the narrator takes the reader to the place where "rest those first settlers," the area's early pioneers: "It is a place of utter peace" (2). The narrator speaks of the people whose names appear on the gravestones, pausing especially to discuss Suzanne, whose story this will be and on whose headstone only the words "Suzanne, Beloved Wife of" can be read, for woodbine and sweet william cover the lower part. The narrator points out that the telling of Suzanne's story must also include the stories of those named on surrounding markers, and the combination of these events "begins, perhaps, on a June day in 1854. . ." (3). Walking into this valley is a young pioneer, Wayne Lockwood, who occasionally consults a piece of paper that lists the unpatented and unsold lands in the vicinity. He finds several parcels that look good, but they are taken. Then, moving northwest, he finds a piece of land with creek, timber, and good soil that to him is beautiful. The quarter section meets all of his requirements. Turning to look around, he is amazed to see two men approaching in a buggy. They are landboomers, men who preempt land and require any potential purchaser to pay their prices. They tell him they are going back to Dubuque to file on the piece he has just chosen; because they are driving a pair of good horses, they will spend the night in nearby Sturgis Falls and still arrive at the land office before he can.

After they leave, Wayne realizes he has a chance of beating them if he can walk long enough and fast enough through the nights and the next two days. He turns east and begins the 110-mile trip, reaching Dubuque and the land office shortly after dawn of the third day, uncertain if the two men have arrived before closing the previous evening. He drops down on the steps to sleep and to await the office's opening. When the clerk opens the office, Lockwood finds that the boomers have not yet arrived; he files and pays his money. As he leaves, the two men appear, and he takes pleasure in telling them he already has the land. This early part of *Song of Years* is Aldrich's recreation of the true Jacob Hoffman story to which she had referred in one of her early letters to Leavitt.

After Wayne returns to his newly acquired land, he meets a neighboring landowner, Jeremiah Martin, and Suzanne, one of Martin's seven daughters, and is invited to their home for dinner. Here Aldrich paints pictures of the family and the settlement and the ways of living on the edge of white settlement. She portrays the importance of physical events in the molding of individual landholders into a community: the coming of the first schoolbell to the valley, the first bridge across the river, the first portion of the railroad. The early days of the Republican Party are described, and Jeremiah, whose life has become deeply entwined with politics, is elected to the state legislature and works to help get Lincoln elected. The Civil War begins; a few of the local men buy their way out of the draft, but some go off to fight; some return, and some do not; whatever the fate of each soldier, he is regarded as a son of all residents in the valley.

Paralleling the Jeremiah stories of farming and politics are the stories of the women, the courtships, weddings, births, deaths, and community growth. Throughout, there is emphasis on Suzanne's life and her growth to maturity with the subsequent realization that she loves Wayne but that his interest is in another woman. However, shortly before he leaves for the Civil War, he realizes it is Suzanne he wants to marry. When he is later reported to have been killed, Suzanne's zest for life is dulled, and she plans to teach school rather than marry. Landboomer and war profiteer Cady Bedson courts her, and because she now feels indifferent about everything she agrees to marry him and makes plans for the wedding. Wayne Lockwood returns the evening of the wedding. The other sisters and two brothers of the Martin family also mature, each facing and working through her or his own life. The entire Martin family bears close resemblance to the Streeter family, from Zimri and Lucinda to the seven daughters and the two sons, the quiet one of whom is patterned on Aldrich's father.

In 1864, Jeremiah, at the request of the Iowa governor, goes to Georgia to bring back the Iowa soldiers' votes cast in the election for president. With communications cut off to the north, he is forced to join Sherman's march to the sea. Jeremiah returns, not only with the votes but also with $3,000 to bank, the accumulated pay of some of the Iowa soldiers. Again, this reconstructs adventures of Zimri Streeter. The story of *Song of Years* concludes in the following year, 1865, with Lee's surrender, Lincoln's assassination, and Suzanne's wedding. It is also the end of the pioneering era of the Red Cedar Valley. The storyteller, who has been describing events of years past, returns the reader to the present.

In late March 1938, Aldrich sent *Song* to New York. Williams wrote that, because the book would be longer than five hundred pages, Appleton would issue it in a larger format and that it would retail for $2.50. He pointed out that "of course means more royalties to you on each copy sold since your 15% will be based on the $2.50 price instead of the $2.00 price." Publication was set for September 1938. Also in March, *The Man Who Caught the Weather* was purchased for publication in Sweden.[22]

Aldrich sent *Song*'s manuscript to the *Saturday Evening Post,* who had been urging her to let them see her next novel prior to book publication. On 18 April they asked if she would agree to postponement of *Song* in book form if it were serialized in the *Post,* although they felt some rewriting would strengthen the last half. She felt book publication could be delayed for a brief period, adding that she was willing to work with their suggestion about the last half of the story.[23]

Four days later the *Post* editors wired that *Song* was definitely a novel and that they might be able to use part of it in serial form; but they wanted a new opening. They offered to do the editing, cutting out some sections, but suggested Aldrich would have to reochestrate the story before they made a final decision.

She wired her response the next day, "Will rewrite, enforcing last half as suggested."[24]

On 28 April, Aldrich received an offer from the *Post* of $15,000 for the serial rights, payable when she had revised the story to their satisfaction. Erd Brandt, the *Post*'s editor, also said that while they would make great effort to schedule *Song* for fall publication, she could not safely count on it being free for book publication before spring. Both Aldrich and Appleton had counted on *Song*'s coming out as a book in time for the Christmas trade, and word that it might not was a serious problem. Williams's suggestion was that Aldrich make the changes as quickly as possible; however Aldrich did not like the uncertain publishing date and asked for more time in which to reach a decision. She wrote the *Post*'s Brandt: "Am rather upset about indefinite date of publication and am wondering now if we can carry the transaction through. I must have a few days to figure out just where this will leave me if I delay publication this way. I want just a very few days, if I may, to do a little figuring on the financial side as well as communicate with the publishers about the indefiniteness of the schedule."[25]

This led the *Post* to wire her that they would try to finish the serial so that it could come out in book form by 15 November, but since they could not give her a definite assurance, they would instead make the price $20,000 to compensate for possible delay. She wired, "Accept offer and will reconstruct story at once."[26] Aldrich did not anticipate that this would take a great amount of time, and she still planned on going to southern California early in June. Having acted as her own agent in this sale, she had saved $2,000 in commission, which pleased her.

In a letter to her friend Grace Simpson Bailey, Aldrich noted that those weeks had been a difficult period, for she had had "to come to some decision about whether to cut my book manuscript in two and let the SATEVEPOST use the latter half. They offered me such a fat sum and even raised it by telegraph (me wishing they hadn't let the village telegraph operator in on the secret) that I just couldn't afford not to take it. It means that, unlike the woman in the Bible when Solomon threatened to cut her child in two, I am allowing my brain child to be divided. . . . They are using just the Civil War years, which includes the love story." In a note to John McCormick in Hollywood, she added the good news of the Appleton book-price increase, hoping this would be useful for book-to-movie sales. He immediately sent his congratulations on the sale to the *Post,* noting that $20,000 for half a story was great.[27]

However, on 6 June Brandt wired that he liked her revisions but requested further changes, specifically, that she provide a new lead for the opening installment. Aldrich agreed, but she could not work with as much concentration or speed as she would have liked because of her brother-in-law John Cobb's illness and death. Further compounding her trials this summer was her concern over selling her bank stock. The bank had substantial losses, losses that were greater than her income for the entire year. Yet she was reluctant to sell, for she wanted to remain a part of the bank. Aldrich was hopeful that some items that had been turned over to her would help recoup the losses. The situation, as she wrote to Williams, worried her. He responded with sympathy and concern, warning her that "reinvesting [is] difficult in these days, for it seems to be mighty hard to find investments which present returns and security. Be sure to be careful in whatever you buy if you do sell the bank." Aldrich was also distressed that she was having to postpone her trip to California, which she did not want to do because being there, she felt, was important in trying to sell her books to the moviemakers. Williams agreed with her assessment that she could not go: "under the circumstances you cannot budge."[28]

On 19 July, Brandt wrote that there would have to be a greater delay than they had first anticipated, for "the serial list is heavily overloaded with Frontier stories, and it is essential that two such not run concurrently." Thus, the *Post* would probably run a "mystery or other strongly contrasting serial at this point. . . . The first opportunity of starting the Aldrich would be in the December tenth issue, following the [James] Boyd. This would not bring it to conclusion until the January twenty-first number."[29]

Aldrich was distressed about the resulting late dates, telling her Elmwood friend and neighbor Marie Clements that "life would be very pleasant if I didn't have this horrible blow about the book." Although the *Post* editors had warned that the book might not come out until mid-January, neither Aldrich nor Williams had taken it seriously. Aldrich added, "I have not heard from [the publishers] since, making me think they are too sore to write. It means a lot to them to have gone to the expense of building up a sale and then recalling it. Jim [her son] told me there were posters in the New York shops saying they were taking Xmas orders for the Aldrich novel. . . . Well, you can't have your cake and eat it, and I did get my big check from the POST." Undoubtedly Appleton had had large advertising expenditures, and Aldrich's following was wide indeed: one correspondent wrote Appleton "that the best book display he had seen was in a window of *Song of Years* in some town in South Africa."[30]

Williams was distinctly unhappy over the probability of missing the Christmas season sales, writing Aldrich that it was "most disconcerting not to obtain definite news from Philadelphia [the *Post*]." However, Brandt's tentative expectation of starting the serial on 10 December was accurate. In October, Brandt wrote to Aldrich again, this time asking for a two-hundred-word informal biography, a snapshot, and some interesting items about the writing of, or the gathering of information for, *Song of Years*. This material would appear on the *Post*'s "Keeping Posted" page.[31]

The McCormick agency, in Hollywood, knew that Aldrich would be popular with the *Post*'s readers; thus, the agency sent word of the serialization to all film studios, stating that "the editors of the *Post* held this particular story until the year's end as their choice of serials for the holdover for subscriptions between the old year and the new, which is about as high a compliment as could be paid to Mrs. Aldrich." Within a year, Brandt would be writing Aldrich almost monthly, urging her to send them another work to serialize because "you made so many friends among the *Post* readers with *Song* that it would be a shame not to follow it up."[32]

The artwork in the *Post* pleased Aldrich, and she wrote as much to Brandt. Shortly thereafter, she received a letter from one of Brandt's assistants saying that it was so rare for a writer to take note of the illustrator's work that they had passed on her comments to artist Harold von Schmidt; and Schmidt had sent one of the original paintings to Elmwood with his compliments. Unfortunately, the canvas never arrived. Aldrich appreciated the gesture.

An even greater pleasure to Aldrich was that Appleton had accepted her son James's painting for the *Song of Years* jacket. That both the outside and the inside were Aldrich family works was rather unusual and delighted Aldrich.

As Appleton prepared for early January publication and sent Aldrich the proofs, she read them and sent them on to Roger Leavitt, wanting to share with him the work in which he had played a vital part. As the *Post* had published less than half the novel, many readers were eager to read the whole story. Appleton's first printing was substantial, and they had expected to have enough copies for several months of sales; however, the first run was sold out a month prior to publication. The second printing also was sold out, and Appleton was racing through the third prepublication printing the week before the proposed 17 January release date. *Song* now had the largest advance sale to that time of any Aldrich novel.[33]

Song of Years quickly hit the best-seller lists, prompting Aldrich to comment to Brandt that the Martin girls would have laughed about its heading the best-seller lists. For the *Post*, he replied: "We were not surprised." Aldrich wrote to Roger Leavitt on 7 February that "new reviews come in constantly, nine out of ten being very good indeed. . . . In the last analysis, it is the reading public who decides the issue." Perhaps the popularity of all of the Aldrich works was best expressed shortly before *Song*'s publication by former managing editor of the *Ladies' Home Journal*, Chesla C. Sherlock, who had published some of her earlier stories. In an article discussing Aldrich's career, he wrote that "her strength has been in the fact that she has not lost contact at any time with *the real people in this land!*"[34] *Song of Years* sales indicated that that continued to be true.

In her letter to Leavitt, Aldrich mentioned that that morning's reports listed *Song* as one of the top six best-sellers in Chicago, Philadelphia, New York, and Boston, while "the Baker Taylor report lists it fourth for the entire country. A Copenhagen concern is negotiating for Scandinavian translation rights." This last note would please Leavitt and the heavily Danish population in Cedar Falls. Some people had felt that historical accuracy would have been better served if real names had been used; Leavitt, however, had a broad perspective, and he often pointed out that he was "thankful that Mrs. Aldrich has put many of the early day stories into dramatic form for our children's children. What difference does it make to us whether it was Jacob Hoffman or Wayne Lockwood who raced to Dubuque or whether J. T. Knapp or Tom Bostwick built the Cedar Falls Women's Club House [now home of the Cedar Falls Historical Society] where Suzanne planned to be married."[35]

Aldrich took a balanced approach in the writing, and reviewers singled out either the land or the people as the main interest. Wallace Stegner, in a piece in the *Saturday Review of Literature* under the headline "American Dream," described it as a chronicle of "the growth of the towns of Waterloo and Cedar Falls . . . from 1855 to the end of the Civil War." A California review, "Novel Pulses with Vitality of Pioneers," said *Song*'s substance lay in the "convincing manner in which its characters live and breathe and laugh and labor, finding great pleasure in small things and taking the large ones in their stride. Perhaps it is the story of any pioneers, yet it is given a touch that makes it seem to be the tale of ones you have known." The *New York Times* saw it as a "study of a locale and a period"; another reviewer described it as "epic in its sweep," adding, "Mrs. Aldrich has a fluid style of writing."[36] Reviewers applauded the care Aldrich took to present, factually, the history of both the time and the pioneer spirit. The

St. Louis Globe-Democrat called it Aldrich's "best novel since *A Lantern in Her Hand*." The Pittsburgh *Press* wrote that "it is an earthy, vibrant story of pioneer life." Another review said *Song* was "undoubtedly one of the best of the new novels. . . . Mrs. Aldrich has surpassed her previous works in this . . . the kind of a novel that will be read and reread for a long time to come. It is destined to hold a prominent place among novels of American background by reason of the historical material it contains." One columnist, while describing it as "unsensational," added that *Song* "nevertheless holds one in its spell because the reader shares with the individual personalities their poignant dramas, and above all because, as the author herself points out in her conclusion, it typifies something sturdily American, handed down from these early settlers, which has not yet been extinguished—a bit of the old pioneers: independence, practical philosophy, ingenuity and propensity to 'pull on through.'"[37]

Aldrich spent two months in California after finishing the book, visiting Hamlin Garland and Lloyd C. Douglas, among others, before returning to Elmwood. Soon after the New Year and publication of the book, Aldrich received a letter from Edward H. Dodd Jr. of Dodd, Mead telling her of their plans to publish a series of books, one based on each state of the union, and asking her to provide the Nebraska book. He said the plan included having H. L. Mencken write the book on Maryland, John Steinbeck the one on California, Carl Van Doren the one on Illinois, and so on. Their plan was to start in the Midwest, and they wanted her to be one of the first writers. Aldrich declined. Dodd, however, persisted, and was still urging this book on her in September. Aldrich recommended several other Nebraska writers, and a year later Dodd admitted defeat, thanking her for the names and adding that "somehow or other, none of their names fill me with nearly the enthusiasm that yours does. We have enough books scheduled for five years. For the present, I intend to postpone Nebraska, at least for a number of years."[38] Plans for the series were later dropped.

Early in 1939 Aldrich accepted an invitation to attend a

dinner in Washington DC honoring Mrs. Franklin D. Roosevelt. In a February letter to Roger Leavitt describing the event, Aldrich wrote that the list of people at the dinner "was composed of so many well known names that we mere garden variety of people were in the minority,—Mrs. Roosevelt and the elder Mrs. Roosevelt, Lady Lindsey, wife of the British ambassador, Mrs. Charles Evans Hughes [wife of the chief justice of the United States], Mrs. (Henry A.) Wallace [wife of the secretary of agriculture, who was later to be vice-president under Roosevelt], Mrs. (Harold L.) Ickes [wife of the secretary of the interior], Ruth Bryan Owen [minister to Denmark], Mrs. (Henry) Morganthau [wife of the secretary of the treasury], Dolly Gann [author], etc., etc."[39]

Less than a month after *Song*'s January publication, Williams notified Aldrich of an autographing tour beginning 1 March and lasting more than three weeks. She would be in Detroit, Cleveland, Chicago, Washington DC, New York, Boston, and Philadelphia. When the tour reached New York, Aldrich, her son James, and Williams dined at the Princeton Club and then attended Robert Sherwood's play, *Abe Lincoln in Illinois*, a play Aldrich described as "*grand—such* a grand play." Because Aldrich always had a passion for the theater, she found time to attend six more plays while in the city. Other events in New York included a National Booksellers dinner at which she, Carl Van Doren, Agnes Sligh Turnbull, and Marcia Davenport were the guests of honor, a Book and Author Luncheon at the Hotel Astor, a New York Press Association tea given by Margaret Widdemer (from one of whose poems came the title for *A White Bird Flying*), and an Authors' League party. She also met, talked with, or listened to other writers, including Pearl Buck, John Gunther, and Alexander Wolcott.[40]

From New York, Aldrich went to Boston, where she met friends from Cedar Falls days. In Boston, history fan Aldrich took over from author Aldrich. Writing of this part of her trip to her friend Bess Furman Armstrong, a Washington DC journalist, Aldrich said she and her friends had dinner at the old Wayside Inn, another evening dinner at Marblehead, "went through the Nathaniel Hawthorne home, crawled up the secret staircase in the House of the Seven Gables . . . followed the Paul Revere road, saw the steeple where the 'one if by land and two if by sea' lanterns were hung (the hanger being my own ancestor . . .) and a lot of other very interesting things."[41]

In June, Aldrich was traveling again, this time to California, for the long desired sale of one of her books to the movies. Richard Rowland purchased "motion picture, radio, and television rights" to *Miss Bishop*. Rowland had gone directly to Appleton and not to McCormick. Despite this, because McCormick had worked so hard on all of her books, Aldrich insisted that he must receive half of the agent's fees. Williams agreed, and Appleton split the commission with McCormick.[42]

That year—1939—for Aldrich and people the world over international concerns were hovering over their day-to-day lives. Europe was moving toward major war. On 1 September, Germany invaded Poland: it was the start of World War II. All parts of the U.S. economy were affected in one way or another, and the cinema was no exception. On 23 September, McCormick's partner, George Landy, wrote Aldrich that sales to producers had virtually halted because of the "war hysteria and resultant buying apathy." Erd Brandt, writing almost monthly, urged Aldrich to write a new book for serialization in the *Saturday Evening Post*, reminding her that "there is no telling how long this war will drag on, and people need a lot of pleasant reading to make up for what their newspapers bring them every day."[43]

Also in this 1939–40 period, the war, which had "not only upset editorial offices but writers as well," completely eliminated her hopes for *The Rim of the Prairie, Spring Came On Forever*, or *Song of Years* becoming a musical. When she knew the musical would remain only a dream, Aldrich admitted to mystery writer and fellow Nebraskan Mignon Eberhart, in a rare letter of discouragement, that she was deeply disappointed that none of those three books would be transformed into a Broadway production. Eberhart responded with, "Here is the shoulder and I know just how you feel and am awfully sorry about the Hammerstein deal . . . it *is* so disappointing for anything to be all set as that was, and then held up." While Aldrich acknowledged that she had "had high hopes of a Broadway musical," she later could point out to son Bob with a touch of both pride and amusement that "at least I came *that close* to having something of mine on Broadway." The next Hammerstein musical—staged three years later—was done in conjunction with Richard Rodgers. It was based on a 1931 book by Lynn Riggs entitled *Green Grow the Lilacs*, a work that has many parallels with *The Rim of the Prairie*. Hammerstein, when reading *Rim*, must have found many elements he was looking for.[44] *Lilacs* is set in a farm community in 1900, with such characters as Aunt Eller, Laurey, her orphaned niece, Jeeter Fry, passionate and vindictive, and Curly, the handsome cowboy who loves Laurey. *Rim* is set in a farm community in the early 1900s, with such characters as Aunt Biny, Nancy, her orphaned niece, Alice Rineland, cold and vindictive, and Warner Field, the handsome writer who loves Nancy. The Rodgers-Hammerstein adaptation arrived on Broadway in 1943 under the title of *Oklahoma!*

11

$\mathcal{T}$he 1940s,

A Movie at Last,

The Lieutenant's Lady,

and the 1950s

Christmas 1939 saw a typical Aldrich blaze of joy. Mary and family visited from Lincoln; Charles took a few days from his design work at United Aircraft to return to Elmwood; Robert returned from university; and artist James, visiting from New York for the holidays, stayed through January—during most of which time he and Bess were snowed in. As Aldrich wrote a friend, there was little that gave her more pleasure than having her family near: "That's all I care about now. If people knew how little I care about any publicity over me or my books they would think I was very much interested in my own work."[1] Family was increasingly important with the coming to Europe of war.

But business called. Among the first letters Aldrich received in the new decade was one from Williams with the news that Appleton's London office had sold Dutch translation rights for book versions of *Song of Years,* adding "in the face of war-time conditions, that shows what a fine novel you wrote. It is a real tribute to the perspicacity and good taste of the Dutch reading public." In this same letter, Williams also told her that he was planning the summer and fall fiction list and, as they had previously discussed, he wished to publish another book of her short stories. Williams asked that she send him a list of stories she wanted to include as well as the title for such a work.[2] Aldrich countered with questions about the possibility of a book of Christmas stories.

Occasional correspondence continued about either a short-story collection or a Christmas book, but no Aldrich work would come out in 1940. She was putting together ideas and plot for the book she planned to write as a sequel to *Song of Years,* and she was trying to accumulate enough factual material to create the frame for such a story. The superintendent of the State Historical Society of Iowa, at the request of Roger Leavitt, sent a pamphlet for her consideration entitled *Two Hundred Topics in Iowa History.* Leavitt also sent more of his materials.

Aldrich was not able to concentrate on the project, for the distress of the war in Europe was felt in this country, in the hamlets like Elmwood as well as in the cities. Reflecting the views of many people, she wrote a friend that "the war news is so horrible that life hasn't been happy for anyone. . . . It just sickens me to think of what the future might hold for our own country, but I'm hopeful that the defense measures will be all that's required of us. Three sons between 19 and 27 for me, —and you and all my friends have them about the same age. Queer how we used to think that as civilization advanced wars would become a thing of the past."[3]

Being unable to write was not an unusual problem for artists at that time. George Landy, of the McCormick agency in Hollywood, told Aldrich that "the whole prospect here looks very bleak—the town is completely hysterical over the foreign situation." And from the opposite side of the country, Erd Brandt of the *Post* said that "we are finding that the war has not only upset editorial offices but writers as well, so we can understand what has happened to your story." He continued, however, to urge her to send them whatever she wrote.[4]

Aldrich stayed in Elmwood throughout February, digging her way through a "huge accumulation of mail," then closed the house 1 March and left for the East. She went first to Washington DC. During her stay, she toured the White House, the Senate, and the House of Representatives, and went again to Mount Vernon, where she always responded to its "sensation of peace and solemnity. And that feeling of change." From there she went to Philadelphia, visiting historic sights she had missed on earlier trips, and on to New York. Always one of Aldrich's great pleasures was seeing stories transformed into actions; thus, during her time in New York she attended six Broadway plays and sixteen movies. Sometimes she went on her own in the afternoons, sometimes in the evening or on weekends she was accompanied by one or both of her sons who lived in the East. She also visited museums, watched the Easter parade, and had conferences with her publishers. The Aldrich interest in times past, evident in her choice of subjects for novels, showed also in her choice of activities when on vacation. In April she returned to the Washington DC area and took a three-day tour of historic colonial places and homes before going back to Elmwood, steeped in the past and admitting that "I am a pushover as a history worshipper. All one has to say to send shivers down my spine is 'This is the very spot on which so and so did so and so in 1789.' If I've never heard of so and so I still shiver with excitement."[5]

She was producing no new material at this time, but some of her old stories continued to make their way in new forms. Theodore Roosevelt Jr., head of Doubleday, Doran and an Aldrich fan, wrote in April 1940 that his company was preparing a new "Mothers' Anthology," and would be requesting permission from Appleton to use one of her works. Their lead piece would be "Mother [Mason] Gets Back on the Job" (1922).[6] A Father Mason story had appeared earlier in a father's anthology.

In 1939, United Artists decided they could work out the problems of the time span of *Miss Bishop* and bought the movie rights for Richard Rowland to produce. Barbara Stanwyck was originally to play Ella Bishop, but when the script was not ready in time, she could not change previous commitments. Margaret Sullavan was the next choice, but again, problems arose. Sullavan, too, could not make the film. Then Martha Scott was chosen; filming, however, was delayed until 1940. Word reached Aldrich in early September that Richard Rowland had secured Tay Garnett, then directing a Marlene Dietrich movie, as director for the film that would become *Cheers for Miss Bishop*. William Gargan played Sam Peters, and Edmund Gwenn, Sidney Blackmer, and Mary Anderson were featured. Rosemary DeCamp, who in later years would appear in many movies and television programs, played Minna Fields, one of Ella Bishop's early students. Stephen Vincent Benet adapted the novel for the screen.

Rowland wanted Aldrich in Hollywood as consultant, and she wanted to see her work recreated from print into film. She was in California by mid-September, staying again at the Knickerbocker and sending back to Elmwood a hotel menu indicating both kinds and prices of food: breakfast was 50¢; lunch (for example, fruit cocktail or juice, broiled double-rib spring lamb chop, salad, potatoes, vegetables, rolls and butter, dessert, and coffee) was 75¢; and dinner (for example, shrimp cocktail, soup, salad, "broiled thick juicy top sirloin steak with Bordelaise Sauce," potatoes, vegetable, dessert and coffee) was $1.[7]

When filming began, Aldrich found it "such a queer experience to see my characters come to life . . . [and] to see the Bishop house all built on the lots with a lawn in front,—the house is solid and substantial looking and yesterday when I was in it, the paper hangers were papering the rooms just as though it were to be lived in." As consultant, Aldrich was to verify that the cinematic portrayal of details was accurate, and for the most part it was. She wrote her friend Marie Clements of the typical script changes she suggested, such as scenes in which Amy was going "to the drug store for an ice-cream soda which they didn't have in those days,

—they had soda-water but not ice-cream sodas." In another, scene, the film people "were talking about caps and gowns on the graduating class away back in the eighties which weren't used, at least not in the middle-west." On another occasion, she commented with some amusement that she felt her "helpfulness could be summed up in the fact that I put ribbons on the diplomas." After the movie was screened in Lincoln, Aldrich received some "very abusive anonymous letters" because sherry was served in the teacher's home. In the days of Miss Bishop, many Midwest teachers would not only have scandalized the citizenry by having any form of alcohol; they would have been dismissed. In fact, Aldrich had been called home before the movie was completed. She had written the director, urging him to use other glasses, but her letter arrived after the scene was filmed and the wine glasses remained.[8]

Late in September, Aldrich had word from her good friend Marie Clements that Bess's sister in Elmwood, Clara (Tallie) Cobb, who had been ill, had suffered a setback. Aldrich did not know whether to leave at once for Elmwood or remain to work on the picture because "the vitality of our people makes it possible that she would go into a long invalidism"; yet "everything out here is secondary to being back there if I should be." She made plans to leave the following Monday; however, another letter from Marie arrived that Saturday saying the consensus was that Clara was not in immediate danger, and Aldrich decided to remain on a day-to-day basis. She canceled all her West Coast social activities: "after Tallie got so bad," she wrote, she "had no heart for them. . . . The studio and my own folks constitute my days." On 7 November, Aldrich received word that Clara needed her, and she left for Elmwood the next morning along with the brother and his wife who lived in the Los Angeles area. The remaining members of the Streeter clan gathered in Elmwood, a fact not lost on Clara, who announced to a neighbor, "Did you know we are having a nice family reunion?" Clara died in mid-December, five weeks after Bess returned home.[9]

Probably no death since Cap's had been so hard on Aldrich, for Clara had been not only Bess's older sister and "always such a stand-by," but also the only close woman and friend remaining who had shared much of Bess's youth and home and memories; she had also been the grandmotherly aunt to Bess's children.[10] Over a month later (in January 1941), Aldrich wrote Grace Bailey in Cedar Falls that the loss had been and was still difficult, that Tallie's house remained almost the way it was when Clara died except that she (Bess) had had the utilities turned off and brought some of Clara's personal items to her own home. But "dishes, furniture, kitchen utensils, everything, even books and pictures on the wall are just as they were. Sometimes I go up and go in just like little Laura did in A WHITE BIRD FLYING,—queer that I could write that long ago before I'd experienced the feeling."

In this same letter Bess said "I'm writing this blizzardy P.M. with no one to disturb me. But how I wish someone *would* disturb me. Oh, I tell you, Grace, when the kids were little and all home and making the most work and commotion was the happiest time." Christmas, that most special of holidays, had come and gone. Chuck did not come home, unable to leave his defense work; Jim was commissioned to do a painting for a new book jacket and could not return; Mary, Milton, and the children were going to be there, but the children came down with the measles; taken "altogether it was was about the most 'down' Christmas we've ever had with poor old Bob and me having a Christmas tree by ourselves, opening our packages alone. He's been my good old stand-by so many times."[11] That year, Aldrich lived not only scenes from *A White Bird Flying*, but also experienced some of the same emotions and loneliness she had ascribed to characters in Christmas stories. Again, fiction had preceded fact.

Aldrich was not one to allow herself to be down for long, however, and for her the business of life was to keep going. The world premiere of *Cheers for Miss Bishop* was to be held on 7 January 1941. Scenes were shot at the University of Nebraska's campus in Lincoln because the film company's publicity department wanted to have a specific school and place. It was a big event for the author and the entire area. Because of the numbers of people wanting to attend the premiere, two theaters, the Stuart and the Nebraska, were used, and fifteen thousand people gathered to see and take part in the excitement of Lincoln's first movie opening, which "lacked neither color nor enthusiasm."[12] The director and many actors and actresses who were in the movie, as well as many who were not, were in Lincoln for the event. State, city, and university dignitaries were active participants. Irvin S. Cobb, who was not in the movie but attended as the master of ceremonies, and Wayne Morris appeared at various civic events prior to the banquet and premiere (an event noted frequently by the visiting Californians in their speeches was that the University of Nebraska football team had just lost to California's Stanford team in the Rose Bowl). There was a public reception, a chamber of commerce dinner, a tea, and a banquet. At the banquet the evening of the premiere, writer Irvin S. Cobb (no relation to John and Clara Cobb), the main speaker, was seated next to Aldrich. From the family table in the guest section, Bob Aldrich, looking up at his mother in her formal dress, amid the glamor of the actors and actresses from Hollywood, couldn't help thinking of her in a more usual role, seeing her "in the kitchen turning pancakes by the dozens." When he told her of this later, Aldrich understood: "They've seen me that way a lot more than the evening clothes way."[13]

The Nebraska reviews of *Cheers for Miss Bishop* came in immediately and the critics were delighted. The most powerful national critic of the time, Louella O. Parsons, called *Cheers* "a great picture—one of the greatest ever made in Hollywood. . . . You see life itself being unfolded for you, with all its drama and its joys and sorrows." Parsons lamented that the picture had not been released in time for Academy Award consideration, "for it would offer definite competition. . . . Yes, I think 'Cheers for Miss Bishop' is as good a picture as 'Goodbye, Mr. Chips,' and in no way is it an imitation, for the stories are entirely different, although they both deal with the devotion of a teacher to a school." An advertisement in *Variety* in early March, quoting directors

David O. Selznick, Walter Wanger, and others, described *Cheers* as a "tender and touching piece of Americana" and called it "MARVELOUS."[14]

Aldrich went to New York for the movie's opening there at Radio City Music Hall in early March. The reviews again were good, one reviewer calling Martha Scott "Tops as Female 'Chips,'" and writing that in both movies there is "the same warm feeling for humanity, the same sympathy for the principal, the same compassionate understanding of what teaching means." About the advertising, Aldrich wrote in amazement to daughter Mary: "Well, I never thought I'd live to see my name in the *subway* at all the underground waiting stations but there it was yesterday even if *smallest* under Scott's and Gargan's big printed names."[15] Aldrich described to Marie Clements how it was to see *Cheers* in the New York setting:

> It did these old eyes good to drive up to the Music Hall and see the place roped off in front, a [police officer] in charge and the rotunda and lobby packed and a string half way down the side street. It holds 6000 people and we couldn't see (from the loge where we sat) a vacant seat. Of course it was Sat. night and that accounts for part of the huge attendance as it's almost impossible to fight your way in to shows on that night. We paid $1.65 each for our seats (reserved) and I suppose I could have had passes if I had made myself known to the manager but preferred this way so I could mingle with the crowd and hear the comments. On all sides we heard good things, 'She's marvelous in it.' 'She should come in for an Acadamy award.' 'Yes, I liked it as well as Mr. Chips.' 'That's the best picture I ever saw.' . . . all good excepting one smart gal in earrings down to her shoulders who was saying: 'She was an old maid and they gave a banquet for her . . . so what?'
>
> The best of all [is that] the picture has been held over a second week. Now that may not seem anything but because the MUSIC HALL is so huge they very seldom hold

a picture, the two before it stayed only a week and one was a Margaret Sullavan picture. VARIETY said [*Miss Bishop*] grossed $75,000 the first week.[16]

Aldrich wrote also to Grace Bailey, telling her, too, about enjoying her anonymous eavesdropping on the audience's after-the-show discussions. The talk, she said, was "frank and uninhibited"; most comments "were all that anyone connected with the picture could wish." Of the time when the "smart gal in earrings" expressed her indifference to the movie, Aldrich, delighted, wrote that she then "knew the joys of obscurity."[17]

Cheers for Miss Bishop was successful throughout the country, and in 1942 was selected as one of the ten best pictures to show American life to oversea countries.[18] Today, with cable television and round-the-clock programming, it is still possible to see *Cheers for Miss Bishop*. Like the Aldrich books, it endures.

During the difficult days of Clara's last illness, Aldrich tried to do some writing, making notes and outlines on the sequel to *Song of Years*. Williams realized she was under stress, but he tempered his understanding with practicality, urging her in a December letter to have the new book completed for fall 1941 publication. In the same letter, he wrote that he had just finished reading her "To the Authors of Tomorrow" in the *Writers' Markets and Methods* and was keeping it to show to young writers because "it is practical advice which is rare for beginning writers . . . a real service for the people I know you want to help."[19]

Williams was not the only publisher trying to acquire more Aldrich work. Erd Brandt stopped in Lincoln in January to meet with her and discuss future story possibilities, as would Williams later that year. But Aldrich did not feel a compelling interest in her work and could not stick with the writing. She was, she admitted, "just tired out from everything."[20] She was also reluctant to get too deeply into new work because there was word that the Hollywood agent was close to another sale, in which case Aldrich would soon go to California. Anyway, March was approaching, and Aldrich generally tried to visit her two sons in the

East that month. When Hollywood hopes for the sale were again deflated, Aldrich went to New York (for the opening of *Cheers*, mentioned above) staying first at the Grosvenor, then, when the man who shared the apartment with Jim was drafted, moving to stay with Jim. On days when Chuck was in town, the three went to plays and movies, including a second viewing of *Cheers for Miss Bishop*.

As always, Aldrich extended her Eastern trip to take in Washington DC and Boston. In Boston, the president of Wellesley College, Mildred McAfee, gave a luncheon for her, which she enjoyed; an even greater pleasure was holding in her hands letters that Robert Browning wrote to Elizabeth at the Barrett house on Wimpole Street and holding, too, an unpublished manuscript of Charlotte Bronte's. A lecturer for the Federated Women's Clubs had film footage made of Aldrich at the Sleepy Hollow Cemetery, walking around the gravesites of Emerson, Louisa May Alcott, and Hawthorne; while Aldrich tried, she admitted that "You can't look soulful at Emerson's grave with a movie camera turned on you." She went also "to Plymouth to see the Rock and to see the John Alden and Priscilla home, as well as to the church yard where Hester Prynne is buried." The cemetery was closed, but, Bess reported, a woman told her that "if I would climb on a pew and look slantwise through the opened window, I could see the grave along by the side of the church. When I climbed down I [said] it was certainly the irony of fate that with all the good and virtuous wives and mothers out in the graveyard, I should be hanging by my heels to see the grave of the one scarlet one. Such is fame." Aldrich exulted in these glimpses of the past, writing that "Oh, I just was drowned in atmosphere of those old places."[21]

By late April, Aldrich, back in Elmwood, was again working off and on at the novel. Williams was resigning himself to putting out a book of her Christmas short stories rather than a new novel. However, Aldrich wrote that she did not like the group of Christmas short stories that had not yet appeared in book format and did not want to go ahead with that project. Williams suggested that in that case they go back to their original plan and issue her short story, *The Drum Goes Dead,* as a small book to appear before Christmas. They would then plan on the novel for the following year (1942). Aldrich could not give wholehearted approval even to *Drum,* but Williams was adamant about its publication, telling her that "my opinion of THE DRUM GOES DEAD is, seemingly, much higher than yours. . . . I am very much pleased to know that we are to have [it] this fall."[22]

Still the new novel would not seem to move. In August she responded to a letter from Erd Brandt, telling him that she was unable to write historical fiction because of the war and concerns for her own and others' sons. Brandt was out of town, but the associate editor who responded noted that currently it is "difficult to attain a sense of proportion in the face of cataclysmic events." He added that "people, [now] more than ever, will turn for relaxation and at least temporary inner peace, to read of the past—even the recent past." Aldrich, in a response to pressure from Williams, said she could not believe that people wanted to read about war, which would be a part of her new work. Williams replied that a new printing of *Lantern* as well as of *Miss Bishop* had been ordered the previous week, and "I do believe you will find in that fact the answer to your wondering whether or not today's public wishes relief from war news, fiction about the war."[23] In both books, young men go off to battle. During this period, Aldrich found articles easier to write than stories of any length, and when A. S. Burak of the *Writer* asked for an article, she quickly completed "The Story Germ," which he published three months later.[24]

That summer (1941), Aldrich received two diaries from Lillie M. Houghton, of Marshalltown, Iowa, that had been written by Miss Houghton's aunt and uncle, Sarah Elizabeth Canfield and Second Lieutenant Andrew Nahum Canfield. Miss Houghton suggested that Aldrich might find material for a novel in the diaries. Sarah's diary covers a little over a year, 30 April 1866 to 9 June 1867, and tells of her trip up the Missouri to join her husband in Dakota Territory. Sarah did not write every day, but she was particularly conscientious that every entry include weather information. The time span for Andrew's diary is January through November 1868. The entries are an almost daily log of his work as a second lieutenant in the post–Civil War regular army, providing brief descriptions of the duties and activities in the forts on the Upper Missouri and the happenings on the trip back down the river at year's end.[25]

While Aldrich found the diaries interesting, she wrote to Brandt in September that she did not really see a novel in them, at least not enough to start working immediately. She offered to send them to him for possible publication with the idea that she would step out of the picture and let the *Post* deal with the diaries' owner. Brandt told her they would be glad to read the material; occasionally, he said, they would "find something in these off the trail manuscripts that we are very glad to get." The conclusion of his letter was acerbic: "I am beginning to believe that, like many other authors, you find it much harder to end a writing vacation than to start one."[26] This comment had not been anticipated, and Aldrich was stung, feeling she was working hard on the *Song* sequel. Nonetheless, she sent the diaries to New York. After a reading, Brandt returned them as not being anything they could work into the pages of the *Post*.

In the meantime, *Lantern* continued to gather new readers. In November, Appleton allowed publication of a less expensive version, but limited the number to 100,000 copies. Williams cheered, "Just think of an edition *limited* to 100,000 copies! That shows what a novel you wrote." Later that month, he wrote that Hollywood agent McCormick had made a tentative arrangement for using *Lantern* in a radio program and that, if she agreed and it went through, she would receive $7,500. She wired, "Approve radio deal, no tampering with story except necessary rearrangement," to prevent the addition of sequences not in the original story. A week later the agent reported that the story had been turned down "because they wanted something more sexy." Another broadcasting company rejected *Lantern* for the same reason.[27]

Aldrich began to reconsider the diaries. On 14 October she wrote to George Landy, of McCormick's in Hollywood, giving him a story outline, and querying if it sounded interesting as movie material. He was "extremely interested." She wrote also to Brandt, and after some correspondence he suggested this would make a two-part *Post* serial. Williams agreed to Appelton publishing it after serialization. Williams also told her on 3 November that *The Drum Goes Dead*, which had been released on 31 October, was already into its second printing. By 1 December it had gone into a fourth printing and further printings were expected before Christmas.[28]

The movie, *Cheers for Miss Bishop*, continued to do well. In the early 1940s, while books could quickly reach small-town markets, the small-town movie theaters did not get first-run movies until many months after their premieres. Thus not until early December, almost a year after the Nebraska opening, did *Cheers* reach Brainerd, Minnesota, which was the home of Aldrich's much older cousin, Louise Barrett, who had been working on her master's degree at Iowa State Normal School while Aldrich was an undergraduate. Plans were made for the three-day run in Brainerd to have a momentous opening. The local weekly newspaper, describing the forthcoming event, said Miss Barrett, "who frankly admits that she is thrilled no end by the prospect of seeing a picture inspired by her life and written by her cousin, Mrs. Aldrich," was to be guest of honor. The report continued: "One of the highlights of the picture is a testimonial dinner. . . . This identical scene was actually enacted in Brainerd on Friday, June 3, 1932, with a banquet at the old Whittier school where Miss Barrett's 52 years of service as a teacher were marked with appropriate ceremonies. . . . There was singing, speech making, and presentations of material tributes to Miss Barrett. Miss Barrett was made very, very happy."[29] This was the scene that appeared in the earlier 1926 short story, "The Woman Who Was Forgotten," as well as the subsequent movie of that name. The Brainerd premiere was cancelled, however: Pearl Harbor was attacked 7 December 1941, the day before *Cheers* was to open. Aldrich, in Lincoln that day to visit with Mary, Milton, and the children, was in a car with them when they heard the news: the United States was at war.

Aldrich now abandoned working on the sequel to *Song,* deciding that it was "for next time," and began in earnest with the diaries to make them into a novel that would provide escape for her readers from contemporary pressures. Aldrich felt the theme of the 1866 story "fits in better with the present times, as it is the story of a young woman who went up the Missouri River in 1867, right after the Civil War, to marry an army man." She used both diaries in writing what became the novel, *The Lieutenant's Lady.* The diary facts became vehicles to carry human emotions. With her passion for authenticity, Aldrich studied all of the informa- tion available about the early-day fortifications on the Missouri River, material from the Montana and Nebraska historical so- cieties, the *Kurtz Journal,* and the translation of a part of the diary of General Phillippe de Trobriand, who was at Fort Berthold in September 1867. That she was successful in keeping close to the facts is clear from a letter she received after the book was pub- lished from a woman reader who, as a child, had been taken to those forts and remembered the general. She remembered also the east window—"out of which I used to peer"—that Aldrich described in the general's house, overlooking the river.[30]

The work provided Aldrich with focus on something other than the war. She had known two conflicts already in her lifetime, the Spanish-American War in which Cap had served, and World War I to which neighbors' sons had gone, and some not returned. Now, with all other mothers, she worried about the men of her family going to war. For a while it seemed that none of the Aldrich sons would go. Chuck, an aircraft-design engineer, was in secret defense work; Jim, called in April, was rejected because of high blood pressure; and Bob was not expected to be eligible, for his vision could be corrected only with very thick glasses. Bob did go into service later, but was not sent overseas. Milton, Mary's hus- band, as the father of two children, was exempt.[31]

By June 1942, Aldrich had completed the manuscript for

the new book. She sent it first to the *Saturday Evening Post,* but Brandt felt it was too long for the two-part serial he wanted, so she sent it on to Appleton for publication. For this latest book, Aldrich wrote a dedication, which was unusual, and which was possibly to those who served their country in all wars and to their wives who stood physically or emotionally beside them. The only other book she had dedicated (to Cap) was *The Rim of the Prairie.* However, in July Aldrich cancelled the dedication, despite Williams telling her the people at Appleton had liked it, and both he and they requested that she let it stand. She did not, and it was lost. Jim again was the dust-jacket artist. The back of the dust jacket carried "A Message to the reader from Bess Streeter Aldrich," urging the public to buy war stamps and bonds. In a corner appeared the Treasury Department's minuteman logo, used in World War II promotions of stamp and bond sales. Aldrich received a letter from the Treasury Department telling her "how delighted we were to get the splendid statement on War Bonds and Stamps which you wrote for the back jacket of your forthcoming book." Appleton scheduled publication of *The Lieutenant's Lady* for 25 September. Before the release date, Aldrich autographed and sent a copy to Lillie Houghton, who responded with thanks, adding, "How proud my aunt would have been could she have known that their diaries would be a help to you in writing this story."[32]

Aldrich begins *The Lieutenant's Lady* by noting that years ago a young woman kept a diary, and "this story is a fictionized version of that diary" (1). The book goes on to tell of Linnie Colsworth, a young New York woman, who, in 1867, makes an extended visit to her Uncle Henry Colsworth's family in the thirteen-year-old town of Omaha, Nebraska. The narrator portrays the growing town and many of its inhabitants and social activities through the actions of the Colsworths. Linnie's cousin, Cynthia, is an attractive but shallow woman of about the same age as Linnie. At a party given in her honor, Linnie meets Lieutenant Norman Stafford, also of New York, who becomes engaged to Cynthia and who then leaves almost immediately for Fort Leavenworth. A few months later he is transferred up the Missouri River to Fort Randall, to help keep the river open to navigation. He wants Cynthia to meet him there, where the couple will be married; however, he is ordered further upriver to Fort Berthold, in Dakota Territory, and Cynthia cannot join him until the following spring. By spring, cousin Cynthia decides instead to marry another young man, saying she has not had a letter from Stafford for several months and that if he cared about her he would have managed some communication. She has, however, received his Christmas gift of riverboat transportation to Fort Berthold. The new fiancé is George Hemming, a clerk in a local Omaha store, in whom Cynthia's father (Linnie's Uncle Henry), lawyer and expert in backroom deals, has taken an interest because he knows that George can be manipulated (and that Stafford cannot). Cynthia and Hemming elope, with unacknowledged aid from Uncle Henry. Cynthia asks Linnie to write to Stafford with news of the marriage.

Before returning to New York, Linnie is to travel to Sioux City to visit a friend from the Eastern school they both attended. She finds she cannot write the letter to Lieutenant Stafford, and, thinking the news would be less harsh given in person than coming in a letter, toys with the idea of remaining on the boat and going up to Ft. Berthold. Not until they have reached Sioux City does Linnie decide to go on upriver. She later acknowledges that, had she understood the length or the difficulties of the trip, she would not have made that decision.

After the long and occasionally dangerous trip, the boat docks at Fort Berthold, and Stafford rushes aboard expecting to find Cynthia, but is instead greeted by Linnie. Stafford is outraged that she has forced herself into his life so foolishly. He tells her there are no women at the fort, there is no extra room in which she might live until the first downriver boat comes, and there is no possibility of her remaining on the boat and continuing upstream until it can turn around and return. Linnie is trapped by the moral conventions of the times. Stafford angrily tells her that he will marry her, however, which will protect her from scandal, and, important to Stafford, he will save face; he does not want his fellow officers and men to know he has been jilted. Stafford reminds Linnie that when she returns later to civilization, she can get a divorce through one of her attorney uncles. He assures her the marriage will be in name only. They leave the boat and return to the post, where the commander performs the brief wedding ceremony.

Stafford is courteous and thoughtful of Linnie and finds time each day to take her to see the sights or activities around the fort. He later requests that she not take the first boat down the river, for, as with the wedding, he knows he will be a laughingstock should his bride desert him so quickly. She agrees. Before the second boat arrives, Stafford is ordered upriver to Camp Cooke. Fort Berthold is to be abandoned, and Linnie cannot remain. The boat that comes to take them further north and west carries other officers and wives, so Linnie no longer will be the only woman at the post. They go up into Montana Territory, past the juncture of the Yellowstone and the Missouri, and finally up to Camp Cooke. Now there is no way to leave until next year.

Summer becomes fall, then winter, and shared dangers and proximity work on the couple. As they watch the northern lights one evening, Stafford and Linnie both realize that she will not leave and that theirs will become a real marriage. The bitter cold and snow of winter give way, and spring arrives. During this second summer, Norman is sent on a three-month mission in command of a company. While he is gone, Camp Cooke comes under a nearly overwhelming Indian attack, and the decision is made that, in the event that the fort cannot be held and capture is imminent, Linnie and the other wives will be put to death by the officers (this is recorded in the diary). The fort, however, is secured.

In October, when the last of the steamboats has gone downriver, Stafford receives orders that he is to leave Camp Cooke with seven men, go to old Fort Buford and pick up fifty more men, and proceed south to Sioux City and Omaha. He will be gone all winter. Linnie, who had not liked being alone through the summer, uncertain of his fate or even her own in that hostile country, angrily rejects the idea of staying seven more months at Cooke without him. Travel will be by flatboat, which Stafford insists she could not stand. In a fury, she tells him that she will go and then wants never to see army quarters, an Indian, a fort, an officer, a buffalo hide, a rat, or Stafford himself ever again.

She goes. He is grimly polite on the trip, occasionally asking if she is all right. At first, while travel is comfortable and temperatures are moderate, it is easy for her to respond. Later, even though the winter becomes vicious, her cramped position in the boat painful, and the hours and days unending and almost unendurable, she refuses to acknowledge her discomfort, managing always to respond, "I can stand it" (245). This journey of incredible cold and hardship leads her to understand that simple survival brings forth in her the same stolid, stoic qualilties she had seen but not understood in Indian women.

In late November, Linnie, Stafford, and the troops arrive in Omaha. The couple visit briefly with Uncle Henry, Aunt Louise, and Cynthia, who has been recently widowed and whom Linnie believes Stafford may now decide to marry after their divorce. Linnie, however, despite her earlier angry words, does not want a divorce, for she had wanted to marry Norman from their first meeting. Stafford realizes that Cynthia cannot compare with the woman whom he married at Fort Berthold and asks Linnie if she can stand another army move. She responds, "I can stand it . . . I can always stand it" (274). The storyteller returns the reader to the present, musing that it is now seventy-five years since that diary was written. And in a closing note: "They say that on the day of her death . . . old Mrs. Stafford roused suddenly," believing she heard bugles sounding. " . . . And maybe they were. Maybe they were the echoes of bugles from a hundred bleak American camps and outposts and frontier forts—from San Juan Hill and Belleau Wood and the Island of Luzon" (275). Aldrich is paying tribute to her country's fighting men in a book that also acknowledged the courage of American women.

Word of the critics' acceptance arrived quickly. Williams

sent an advance copy of the *New York Times*'s favorable review, which called the book "a novel of wholly fresh and convincing quality." On 27 October, Williams noted that the work had moved still further up the *Herald Tribune* list of best-sellers, and that it was selling well.[33] Many described it as "timely." The *El Paso Times* specifically recognised that the book was "praise to the valor of army wives through generations of army history." The *Atlanta Constitution* wrote that "this novel of romance and high adventure is Miss [*sic*] Aldrich at her best, equal to 'Miss Bishop' in clear characterization, superior, perhaps to 'Lantern in Her Hand' in its human interest." Another review called the novel a strange but true history "of an army wife on the American frontier" with a "wholly fresh and convincing quality," adding that "Mrs. Aldrich, who is a good story-teller herself, has had the discretion to leave this material substantially unaltered." The *Knoxville Journal* described *The Lieutenant's Lady* as a "fascinating story that has in it much philosophy. The author has taken an old fashioned diary and by the alchemy of her imagination has transformed it." The *Syracuse Post Standard* in New York contributed that "you always can depend upon a first-class story from the pen of Bess Streeter Aldrich. This one is no exception." George Grimes, of the *Omaha World-Herald,* disagreed with that assessment. Grimes wrote, "One never feels that . . . [the reader] penetrates through the stiff formality that, in the earlier day, masked the kinds of stuff our forebears were made of."[34] Aldrich, however, had been careful to retain the Victorian formalism of her source, the woman diarist who was a product of her times, a point that some reviewers mentioned.

The Lieutenant's Lady helped sales of other Aldrich books, sending *Spring Came On Forever* into another printing and causing Williams to write to Aldrich that "this bears out the fact that new books appearing by you stimulate interest in previous publications."[35]

Scarcely had *The Lieutenant's Lady* reached best-seller status when Williams asked Aldrich to return to the sequel of *Song of*

Years. He wanted her to have a new book out in 1943. He suggested that she go ahead with the Iowa novel because such a work would provide "a message and a meaning that will constitute a real contribution to building up and strengthening morale by showing today's people . . . the lives of their forebears." Other editors, too, were writing her. A. C. McClurg & Company, in Chicago, requested a Christmas article for their *Christmas Book News,* and Aldrich provided " 'Christmas Magic' [which] possesses some of the intangible beauty of the Christmas spirit, as well as the ingenuity of a generation that didn't let gas-rationing or the lack of mechanical toys dim the pleasure of Christmas.' " McClurg was delighted with the article. That same year Aldrich filled the *Chicago Tribune*'s request for a Christmas article, and she had also agreed to do some book reviewing for the *Tribune.* The executive editor of Fawcett Publications, one of the largest of the multimagazine publishers, often requested stories. Aldrich told him that the war had created a block, and she could not write. He replied that he knew how she felt: "I remember when I called on Sir James M. Barrie several years after the finish of the first war and tried to induce him to do an article for me for *Cosmopolitan.* He told me that the war had done something to him and he just couldn't get his mind back to writing."[36]

In April 1943, Aldrich wrote Williams that she was "off fiction," a comment he rejected. "This is no time to be off fiction," he told her. "Your audience needs a good full-length novel by you and I urge you to start writing it now. . . . What has become of your plan for the novel about the characters in Song of Years? Do, please, get to work on it." In August, Williams, hoping to spark interest in a new work, suggested she create a story of a woman whose husband was in the Spanish American War, whose sons were in World War I, and whose grandsons are in World War II. Aldrich, polite as always, replied that it was an interesting theme but that she was still considering the sequel to *Song.* Williams urged her to begin at once so that they might have the book for publication the following year. On 21 December Williams wrote her that he was resigning as of 31 December but gave no further information or reason. A few years later, as an editor for Bobbs-Merrill, he solicited a nonfiction book from her, which he felt would not conflict with her loyalty to Appleton.[37]

Aldrich was no longer worrying so much about money. The sale of *Miss Bishop* to be made into a film had gone far to alleviate her major concerns; further, she had made some good investments over the years. Financially, she no longer had to write. Revenues continued to come in from book sales and from magazine sales in England. In August 1944, Aldrich sold to *Think Magazine* the story of Zimri Streeter's trek to Georgia to pick up the Iowa soldiers' ballots. While she sold it under the title of "There Was No V-Mail in '64," they published it as "The Soldier Vote in '64." *Scholastic Magazine,* published by Jacques Chambrun (as was *Think*), purchased the piece for reprint in their November issue.

During the war, Aldrich wrote bond-sale material for the Treasury and the War Department. The director of the Press and Radio Division of the War Savings Staff, in a letter of appreciation, told her they were offering her material "for syndication to newspapers through one of the national wire services. We feel that you have made a very real contribution toward helping the country's war effort and want you to know how much we appreciate your help."[38]

Aldrich was on the verge of a major change in her personal life. As she looked back through her daily journal and counted the days spent in Elmwood and those spent elsewhere, she realized she was gone more often than she was home. Many of the days away had been spent with daughter Mary and her family in Lincoln, and she felt the time had come to leave her home and her town. In the spring of 1945, she succumbed to Mary's and Milton's urging that she buy the lot in Lincoln next door to them. The war was winding down. On the August day it ended in the Pacific, Aldrich—still in Elmwood—walked downstairs to listen to the 8 A.M. news and learned that, although it was not yet official,

Japan had surrendered. In her journal, she wrote simply, "*The War Is Over!* Thank God." Later that day she and most of Elmwood met at the community building for thanksgiving and a band concert.[39]

The following April, Aldrich received a letter from a Hungarian woman, Maria Ruzitska, who wrote that "I have translated a lot of American books, for instance, your *A Lantern in Her Hand, A White Bird Flying, Song of Years*, etc., and so it is through me that your works moved the minds and hearts of thousands of Hungarian readers. This gives me the courage to implore you, Madam." She told Aldrich of trying to support and care for her blind mother, of living in an apartment in which the only coverings on the windows to keep out the cold were oiled paper. Aldrich began immediately preparing a large box, but the length of time between Aldrich's receiving the letter and Ruzitska's receiving it was such that Ruzitska thought the letter lost. She wrote again: "Believe me it is not easy to write a letter like that for somebody who never asked anything and used to be proud . . . we are now beggars . . . the seige of Budapest ruined everything. My journalist's salary as collaborator [contributor?] of the best and most popular Hungarian weekly, doesn't reach for buying four pounds of cabbages or a dozen of eggs in a month." She asked if Aldrich could send "not money . . . only a small parcel of a few ounces of tea, or coffee, or candy or margerine, of condensed milk, of drugs, of soup, anything. . . . You who know the human heart so well, please try to understand me and if that unhappy letter reaches you, be so kind and send a word, a telegram, and it would give strength and hope again." The package and a letter from Aldrich both arrived very soon after she mailed this second letter. Ruzitska expressed her deep appreciation and added, "You said if I have any sense of humour left I may feel like laughing at some of the things you have put in. I don't see how one could live without a sense of humour nowadays. But I rather felt like crying at the things you filled the littlest cracks and crevices with."[40]

In June 1946, Aldrich received another letter carrying

with it reference to the war—but from a very different source. This one came from Fleet Admiral Chester W. Nimitz. He said his letter was long overdue, for

> it should have been written to you several years ago during the war or perhaps even before we entered the war when I first read your splendid books on the settlement of Nebraska. . . .
>
> I wish to acknowledge to you the great pleasure that I and the members of my private family had in reading your books before the war, and how much I and the members of my official family in the Pacific enjoyed rereading them during the war. They were truly inspirational and you may be sure that we were helped over many a rough spot and through tough going by the knowledge that we had in our forces men—and women too—who possessed those qualities which you so well described in your writing.

Nimitz autographed and enclosed with his letter a "photograph of the Japanese surrender scene on the USS MISSOURI in Tokyo Bay on 2 September 1945."[41]

In July 1946, Aldrich gave up her Elmwood home. She had spent much time sorting which things she would take to Lincoln, which to give away or sell, work she found "emotionally distressing." Writing to Grace Bailey in May 1945, Aldrich had confessed that "I never thought I'd leave this comfortable old home, and I wouldn't now if there were a single [family member] left here. I realize now more than ever that no one is *ever* coming home again unless it is for a few days' visit. I had visions of always living here and keeping the old home to which they could return when they wanted to, but those times get farther and farther apart"[42] In the fall of 1945, Aldrich had sold "The Elms" to Guy and Marie Clements, her friends and neighbors across the road. Guy was now president of the American Exchange Bank (the bank with which Cap and Bess had been associated). Marie was Bess's very good friend; and the Aldrich children had grown up with the Clements children. The close ties eased Aldrich's sale and move. When moving day finally arrived, 15 July 1946, Aldrich noted in her journal: "Van came today. Goodbye, old home. Chapter closed. [Later] At Mary's now.—All so good to me."[43]

Work on the new house could not begin immediately because wartime building restrictions were in place until December, and it was not until the following January that she received permission to begin construction. She had had plans drawn for a Williamsburg style house and was ready to proceed; on 11 April 1947 workers began digging the foundation. However, the nation was still turning from a wartime to a peacetime economy and labor force, and house-building was slow. Not until 8 August 1948 did Aldrich sleep in her new home. She had spent more than two years living with Mary, Milton, and the children, a period they individually described as wonderful. Aldrich wrote a friend that "nothing but the Pyramids ever took so long to build as my new home. Also I suppose I hold the world's record for the oldest woman ever to build a new house, but my forebears all lived to be 86, 90, 94—and ages like that, so it must unconsciously have given me the courage to tackle the project, being only in my sweet sixties yet."[44]

For the next few years, Aldrich wrote something on the order of one short story a year: in September 1947, she sold "Journey into Christmas" to the *Christian Herald;* in 1948, "Star Across the Tracks," which she had originally titled "Mr. Kurtz and Christmas," went to the *Saturday Evening Post;* in 1949, "The Case of Emmaline Smith" was changed to "The Heirs" when purchased by *Collier's;* and in 1950, "The Great Wide World of Men" was published in the *Woman's Home Companion.* Also during 1950, A. S. Burak asked for another article, and she wrote "Working Backwards" for the *Writer.* In 1953, Aldrich sent the *Christian Herald* "The Outsider"; while they paid somewhat less than other major magazines for stories, she was working with them as a reviewer for their Family Bookshelf, and compensation for that was "on a basis equivalent to the New York TIMES book reviews."

During these years, many of her stories were being broadcast on the radio, but she continued to be denied the prize she so wanted: another movie. The pain of this was apparent in a letter to Bess Furman early in 1949. Aldrich wrote she had received word from *Publishers Weekly* that "*A Lantern in Her Hand* was in the final poll of the ten books for foreigners to read in order to understand the U.S. . . . [But] the other nine [have] all been filmed . . . so why haven't they bought mine?"[45]

In the meantime, the book of Christmas stories came yet again under consideration. In 1948, it was decided that Appleton would publish the book the following year, so that the new "Star Across the Tracks" could be included. Jim had been working on sketches and would again be the artist. This time, however, Aldrich required that the contracts be drawn so that he would share in the royalties rather than receive an outright fee, and Appleton complied. In April 1949, an Appleton representative visited Lincoln, and the final shape of the book was discussed. *Journey into Christmas* was released 11 November 1949, and during the next two months Aldrich autographed books in local stores, signing four hundred books in one Omaha bookshop. *Journey* was selected as the December choice for Family Bookshelf—a choice on which reviewer Aldrich was not allowed to vote. As with all the Aldrich books, it sold well, going into three printings before Christmas. Theodore M. Purdy, the Appleton editor who replaced Williams, wrote that the printing and sale of nearly thirty thousand "I know . . . is nothing compared to your novel sales, but considering the fact that it is short stories, and material which has for the most part already appeared, it is nothing less than astonishing." The critics were favorable in their comments. A Nebraska reviewer, aware of Aldrich's decreasing output of new work, concluded his discussion on this latest book with "If *Journey into Christmas* is Mrs. Aldrich's literary farewell (and I hope it is not) she could not have done better than gather these stories into a single volume. They are grand."[46]

The following year (1950), the People's Book Club made arrangements with Appleton-Century-Crofts to publish an Aldrich omnibus as both a dividend for members and a premium for new subscribers; Appleton would be able to sell the omnibus under their own imprint. The collection included the novels *A Lantern in Her Hand* and *A White Bird Flying* and the short stories "The Day of Retaliation," "How Far Is It to Hollywood?" "Juno's Swans," "Will the Romance Be the Same?" and "Welcome Home, Hal!" In May, the book, entitled *The Bess Streeter Aldrich Reader*, came out to good reviews. The *Philadelphia Inquirer* wrote that "from everyone familiar with Mrs. Aldrich's magnificent saga of the American way of life, this *Reader* will receive a real welcome. For those who have never stood in the shining glow of Abbie Deal's warmth and humanness, this book will be a rare treat."[47] Another reviewer said that "taken with her *Journey into Christmas* . . . and containing some of her very best short stories, this volume gives you . . . work that probably will survive for many years to come. . . . You are in for a treat when you return to them."[48] It was her fourteenth book.

It was also her last book. Since the 1942 publication of *The Lieutenant's Lady*, Aldrich had written no new long fiction. There were probably four main reasons for this. First, the war had made fiction-writing seem to her inappropriate in the midst of international anguish. She could not believe that in a world of such horrors people would want to read novels. Because she could not believe that others wanted them, she could not bring herself to write them.

Second, Aldrich was intensely determined to be accurate. When she wrote a book, her personal demands required that even small details be correct, and this took a heavy toll in time and in physical and mental concentration. She became so deeply involved with the characters and facts that she was near exhaustion when a work was completed. A neighbor said Aldrich "was like someone wrung her out of strength when she finished a book." Son Charles noted that "she said many times that, once she started a project, it completely absorbed her night and day. It was extremely difficult to face the task of starting something new."[49]

Third, Aldrich moved from Elmwood to Lincoln. From

the time she sold "The Elms" in the fall of 1945 until she moved to Lincoln in 1946 she was busy sorting and packing. She did not get into her new Lincoln home until August 1948, and did not have her files out of storage until sometime later. By then, she had not written a novel for six years, was sixty-seven years old, and was taking pleasure in the closeness of her Lincoln family, which allowed frequent daily trips back and forth between the two homes. She also had a busy social life, centering around the activities of the Lotus Club, P.E.O., Altrusa, and Quill.

And fourth, she was financially secure. Aldrich no longer felt the need for the intensity of her earlier years' work.

In 1952, Aldrich went to her doctor for a physical, suspecting she had a malignancy. She was correct, and on 19 June 1952, she had a colostomy. The prognosis was excellent, but in late May 1954, Aldrich developed severe headaches and neckaches, and examination indicated that the cancer had returned. She remained at home for two weeks before returning to the hospital. One evening, shortly before Aldrich lapsed into her final coma, she told Mary: "I have written my books. I have raised my family. However this turns out will be all right."[50] Bess Streeter Aldrich died 3 August 1954, at the age of seventy-three. She is buried in the Elmwood, Nebraska, cemetery beside her husband, Charles.

Notes

Introduction

1. J. Berg Esenwein to BSA, 27 June 1918, box 8, mss. & notes, NSHS.

2. BSA, untitled ms. for talk (probably). Page 3 begins, "A few things time has taught me." Box 10, NSHS.

3. BSA, speech notes, p. 15, misc. mss. & notes, box 10, NSHS.

4. BSA, *Journey into Christmas* (New York: Appleton-Century-Crofts, 1949).

1. The Early Days

1. *Journal-Star,* Lincoln. BSA, *A Lantern in Her Hand,* (New York: D. Appleton), 176.

2. BSA, "How I Mixed Stories with Do-nuts," *American Magazine* 91 (February 1921): 32–33.

3. In 1640, Steven Streeter married Ursala Adams, daughter of (John) Henry Adams and Edith Squires Adams. *Henry Adams of Somersetshire, England and Braintree, Massachusetts,* compiled by J. Gordon Bartlett for Edward Dean Adams (New York: privately printed, 1927, pp. 72, 78).

4. BSA, "The Story Behind *A Lantern in Her Hand,*" *Christian Herald,* March 1952, reprinted in *Nebraska History* 56 (summer 1975): 239.

5. BSA, "I Remember," *Journey into Christmas and Other Stories* (New York: Appleton-Century-Crofts, 1949), 237.

6. BSA, draft of "I Remember" (draft hereafter DIR), 7–10, box 8, NSHS).

7. The election was held on 8 November 1864 and Lincoln was declared the winner on 10 November 1864. The Iowa votes were announced in

the weekly *Iowa State Registry* on 7 December 1864. Men from various areas were appointed commissioners by Governor Kirkwood to go to the regiments recruited from their districts and return the ballots in compliance with state law. Zimri Streeter arrived at Richmond as it fell, and trains were no longer running north at that time. Sherman's army did not reach the sea until 21 December 1864. The material was used by BSA in *Journey into Christmas and Other Stories* (New York: Appleton-Century-Crofts, 1949), 240–41.

8. BSA, "The Story Behind *A Lantern in Her Hand*," *Christian Herald*, March 1952, reprinted in *Nebraska History* 56 (summer 1975): 239.

9. BSA, "Midwestern Writers," *Prairie Schooner* 1 (1927): 80–81.

10. BSA, *McCall's Magazine*, 54 (November 1962): 2:11. Draft for unnamed article for Waterloo IA *Daily Courier*, n.d., p. 1, NSHS.

11. BSA, *The Rim of the Prairie* (New York: D. Appleton, 1925), 53.

12. BSA to James Hearst, 30 April 1927, UNIA.

13. MAB, telephone interview with author, 17 July 1990. Mrs. Beechner stated she believed her mother read her stories to her inseparable childhood friend, Grace Simpson [Bailey].

14. BSA, *Mother Mason* (New York: D. Appleton, 1924), 11, 89, ff. Also in *The Cutters* (New York: D. Appleton, 1926).

15. BSA, *Christian Herald* 54, no. 6 (May 1931).

16. BSA, to "Miss Sheffler," 15 February 1937, CFHS.

17. BSA, early draft of high-school reminiscences, n.d., BB.

18. BSA, "Josephine Encounters a Siren," *American Magazine* 94 (December 1922): 50–52.

19. BSA files, UNIA; *The Normal Eyte*, 25 November 1899, 256.

20. BSA files, UNIA.

21. MAB, interview with author, 17 June 1988.

2. The Captain, the Wedding, and Elmwood

1. MAB, telephone interview with author, 6 September 1988.

2. BSA, early draft of article beginning "and I left for Salt Lake City" and apparently never completed. BB.

3. RSA, interview with author, 28 May 1988. BSA outline notes in BB, no page, no date. Vopal Youngberg confirmed the name of the Salt Lake City School. BSA, *A White Bird Flying* (New York: D. Appleton, 1931), 220.

4. Registrar's books card, 13 June 1906, UNIA. Also BSA, "Pie," *Country Gentlemen,* June 1930.

5. BSA Journal, 13 August 1945. BB.

6. BSA, "Madonna of the Purple Dots," *National Home Journal,* no page, no date (hereinafter n.p., n.d.) but 1907. Anna C. White, letter to Aldrich dated 21 September 1907, NSHS.

7. *Cedar Falls Daily Record,* "Marriage of Miss Streeter," Cedar Falls IA, 25 September 1907, 3, col. 5, CFHS.

8. Mary Anderson Streeter, *Mother's Thoughts by the Way,* various poems or comments about or by two sons, Robert and James Streeter, BB. Aldrich's sister, Annie Lauri Streeter Woods, was a poet laureate of Iowa.

9. BSA, speech ms. "Acquaintance with the Wright family," speeches file, box 9, NSHS.

10. Lynelle Greer, *Lincoln Star,* 6 December 1925, n.p. Also, BSA, "Why I Live in a Small Town," *Ladies' Home Journal* 50 (June 1933): 21.

11. BSA, "Why I Live in a Small Town," *Ladies' Home Journal* 50 (June 1933): 21.

12. BSA, "Why I Live in a Small Town," *Ladies' Home Journal* 50 (June 1933): 21.

13. Margaret Dean Stevens, pseudonym for BSA, "The Little House Next Door," *Ladies' Home Journal* 28 (July 1911): 14.

14. Franklin B. Wiley to BSA, 13 March 1911, bus. corres., box 4, NSHS. "Nebraska Author Tells of Her Work," n.p., n.d. item 20, NSHS.

15. BSA, "How I Mixed Stories with Do-Nuts," 33ff; "Nebraska Author Tells of Her Work," n.p., n.d. item 20, NSHS.

16. BSA, ledger book in which she posted all of her prizes and sales throughout her life. All following amounts with dates are from this source; dates differ from publication dates, BB. Annie Russel Marble, "A Daughter of the Pioneers, Bess Streeter Aldrich and Her Books" (New York: D. Appleton, n.d.), 6.

17. *Omaha World Herald,* to BSA, 20 March 1914, "Yellow Page Contest," no further identification, 20 March 1914, "Question no. 3," n.p., 28 March 1914, box 4, NSHS.

18. Doris Greene Lamb, information in "E[lmwood] W[omen's] C[lub] 1923–24" booklet and interview with author 21 April 1988. Janet Sorenson, Elmwood Library Board chair, made minutes of Women's Club available to the author, 9 October 1990.

19. Donna Greene Rueter, letter to the author 8 September 1988 and interview with the author 28 May 1988.

20. BSA, "Advice to the Writers of the Future," *Story World* (April 1924), 9, NSHS. Myra G. Reed, *McCall's*, to BSA, 13 December 1917, box 3, NSHS. Editor, *People's Magazine*, to BSA, 4 January 1918, box 3, NSHS.

21. Margaret Dean Stevens, pseudonymn for BSA, "Mother O' Earth," *The Delineator* 39 (July 1916): 11–12. Margaret Dean Stevens, pseudonymn for BSA, "The Cat Is on the Mat," *Delineator* 39 (October 1916): 18–19. BSA, "Wedding Bells Ring Merrily," *Elmwood Leader-Echo,* 27 June 1917. Marie Clements files from Robert Clements.

22. J. Berg Esenwein to BSA, 7 April 1917, box 8, NSHS. BSA and J. Berg Esenwein correspondence, series 6, manuscripts & notes, box 3, advanced short-story correspondence course letters 1917–21, NSHS.

23. John M. Siddall, editor of *American Magazine,* to BSA, 22 January 1920, box 4, bus. corres., NSHS.

24. Siddall to BSA, 17 May 1918. Austin E. McNeill to Siddall, 10 February 1919, box 10, NSHS. Siddall to BSA, 25 February 1919, box 4, bus. corres., NSHS.

25. Siddall to BSA, 20 June 1919, box 4, bus. corres. file, NSHS.

26. RSA, personal interview with author 28 May 1988, and MAB telephone interview with the author, 6 September 1988. BSA to GSB: Cap "was proud of my work," 24 June 1925, JB archives. BSA, "How I Mixed Stories with Do-nuts," 32–33.

27. Siddall to BSA, 8 October 1919. Siddall to BSA, 16 October 1919. BSA and *Ladies' Home Journal,* box 3, bus. corres file, NSHS. "The Editor" (that is the signature; no name is given), to BSA, 2 December 1916, NSHS. Her note on this letter said she "sold it to *McCall's*"; in fact, however, it was sold to the *Ladies' Home Journal.*

28. Bessie Beatty, ed., *McCall's,* to BSA, 14 December 1918; Mary B. Charlton, managing ed., *People's Home Journal,* to BSA, 25 August 1919; Siddall to BSA, 23 January 1920, box 4, bus. corres., NSHS.

3. The Early 1920s: First Big Sales

1. Siddall to BSA, 22 January 1920, box 4, bus. corres., NSHS. Siddall to BSA, 22 January 1920, box 4, NSHS.

2. MAB telephone interview with author, 6 September 1988. BSA, letter to a Mr. Chapman, 23 November 1932, Iowa University Collection, Iowa City IA.

3. A. P. Watt & Son to BSA, 10 December 1920, box 4, NSHS. BSA to "Al-

pha Girls," reprinted in the "College Eye," n.d., newspaper of the University of Northern Iowa, 1921, 2, UNIA.

4. BSA, "How I Mixed Stories with Do-nuts," *American Magazine* 91 (February 1921): 32ff.

5. Lynnelle Greer, *Lincoln Star,* 2 December 1925.

6. Mary P. Ryan, *Womanhood in America from Colonial Times to the Present,* 3d ed. (New York: Franklin Watts, 1983), 222.

7. *American Magazine* 91 (February 1921): 120–23.

8. Siddall to BSA, 19 November 1919, box 4, NSHS.

9. Margaret E. Thompson Sheldon, *Lincoln Kiwanis Club Distinguished Service Presentation* booklet, 13 December 1949, box 14, file misc. printed matter, NSHS. Mrs. Austin Burt, "What New Book Would You Name as One of the Best? Women of City Explain Their Selections," n.p.,n.d., item 20, NSHS. BSA, "Mother Mason Gives Some Good Advice," *American Magazine* 89 (May 1920): 48–51.

10. BSA to GSB, 22 December 1921, BB and JB files.

11. BSA to GSB, 22 December 1921, BB and JB files.

12. H. V. Davis to BSA, 2 September 1919, box 4, bus. corres files, NSHS. Palmer Photoplay Corp. telegrams to BSA, 14 September 1922 and 8 January 1923, NSHS.

13. BSA to Elizabeth Dickinson, 30 August 1944, box 3, bus. corres., NSHS.

4. The Rim of the Prairie

1. *Lincoln Journal-Star,* "Reception Is Held for Mrs. Aldrich," 3 December 1925, NSHS. Gertrude Kinscella, typed interview with BSA, probably 1936 (the year Bob was a junior in high school). Box 10, NSHS.

2. BSA, "Teachers Grad Declares Lurid Stories Passing," *College Eye* 5, series 1, vol. 1, 18 June 1926, UNIA.

3. BSA, "The Pioneer in Fiction," script for talk on radio station KFAB, Lincoln NE, 1925, 2, box 10, NSHS.

4. BSA, "Teachers Grad Declares," *College Eye,* 18 June 1926, series 1, vol. 1, UNIA. G. K., "The Other Side of Main Street," *Post,* Chicago, n.p., n.d., item 19, NSHH. Decatur IL clipping titled simply "Review" by BSA, n.d. or source given. "*The Rim of the Prairie,*" *Banner,* Nashville TN, n.p., n.d., item 19, NSHS. *Banner,* Greenville TX, March 1926, n.p., item 19, NSHS.

5. BSA, "Long Distance Call from Jim," *American Magazine* 88 (August

1919), 48. BSA, "Marcia Mason's Lucky Star," *American Magazine* 89 (March 1920), 22. BSA, "He Whom a Dream Hath Possest," *American Magazine* 103 (June 1927), 48.

6. BSA, "Teachers Grad Declares," *College Eye,* 18 June 1926, series 1, vol. 1, 5, UNIA.

7. BSA, "Reception Is Held for Mrs. Aldrich," *State Journal,* evening, 4 December 1925, Lincoln NE.

8. RSA, interview with author, 28 May 1988. Robert Aldrich commented that, while his mother said her characters were created from characteristics of various but not particular individuals, there was a great deal of his father in her portraits of bankers. MAB confirmed this, 9 February 1989. Rev. W. Seth Longacre, friend of C. S. Aldrich and former pastor, in *Elmwood Leader-Echo,* 5 May 1925, n.p., n.d., BB. Mary Linhardt telephone interview with author, 7 March 1994.

9. RSA, interview with author, 28 May 1988.

10. MAB, telephone interview with author, 9 February 1989. Clara undoubtedly enjoyed this vignette. Others in Elmwood also mentioned the Cobb's mode of motoring.

11. Vopal Youngberg collection, BSA letter to GSB. New Hartford IA.

12. Margaret Dean Stevens (pseudonymn until 1918 for BSA), "Grandpa Statler," *Harper's Weekly* 60, 26 June 1915, 606.

13. BSA, draft of "The Story Behind *A Lantern in Her Hand,*" prepared for *McClintock's.* The article later appeared in *McClintock's* (October 1929), 6–7. A similar article was published in the *Christian Herald* (March 1952).

5. "There Is Nothing to Do but Go On"

1. *Elmwood Leader-Echo,* 8 May 1925, n.p., BB.

2. *Elmwood Leader-Echo,* 8 May 1925, n.p., BB.

3. BSA to her friend Della Green, May 1925. Copy of letter provided by Green's daughter, Donna Green Reuter, of Elmwood NE, to author.

4. BSA to GSB, 24 June 1925, from JB files. Also BSA to Miss Ewing of the Quill Society, Lincoln, 20 May 1925, Quill files, NSHS.

5. BSA to Della Green, May 1925.

6. BSA to GSB, 24 June 1925, JB files.

7. BSA, ledger containing sales of stories by month, year, and sum, and all income from book royalties, foreign rights sales, and reprints.

8. BSA, day journals, BB.

9. MAB, interview with author, 7 November 1988.

10. RSA, personal interview, Elmwood NE, 28 May 1988. Also comments of P.E.O. members, Lincoln NE, 19 April 1988. Many of those interviewed, both here and in Elmwood, commented that, being younger, they would never have thought of calling her by any name other than Mrs. Aldrich. Many commented on her absolute and unfailing courtesy, which they never considered breaching.

11. BSA, talk to Lincoln Manufacturers, 1 December 1925, 3, box 10, NSHS. The response is not included in her NSHS materials.

12. Aldrich is quoted in the *College Eye,* from a talk at Iowa State Normal School, Cedar Falls IA series 1, vol. 1, 18 June 1926, 5, UNI. She told the students many writers have "almost hopelessly misrepresented [the small town]." Aldrich accused them of suggesting that only three types of people dwell in rural areas and small towns: "the first class 'people are crude'; the second 'intelligent ones who are glad to get away' and the third class, 'are people lumped' . . . 'into a class of half-wits.' " BSA, "Meadows Entertains a Celebrity."

13. *Omaha World-Herald,* reprint of article, "The Charm in Novels," *Kansas City Star,* 18 August [1922?], NSHS.

14. Unnamed newspaper, probably from Lincoln NE, 4 December 1925.

15. MAB, interview with author, 10 October 1990. CSA, letter to author, 21 November 1988. BSA, "Why I Live in a Small Town," *Ladies' Home Journal* 50 (June 1933): 21.

16. RSA, interview with author, 28 May 1988.

17. Lynnelle Greer, "Bess Streeter Aldrich First Glimpsed Nebraska in a Dust Storm, But She Remained to Defend 'Main Street,' " interview in *Lincoln Sunday Star,* 6 December 1925, part 5, p.41.

18. Lillian Lambert, "Bess Streeter Aldrich," *Midland Schools,* Des Moines IA, 42, 8 April 1928, 301, quotes the *Literary Review,* n.p., n.d. The *Star,* n.p., n.d. *New York Evening Post,* n.p., n.d. *New York Times,* 30 January 1925, item 20. Scrapbook, NSHS.

19. BSA to Victor P. Hass, 16 November 1949, *Chicago Sun-Tribune,* "Mrs. Aldrich Star Writer of Yule Tales," 4 December 1949, part 6, p.4. BSA to Victor P. Hass, 16 November 1949. Materials provided by Victor P. Hass to author, 18 March 1987.

20. Vopal Youngberg, New Hartford IA.

21. RSA, interview with author, 28 May 1988.

22. MAB and RSA interviews with author, 9 February 1989 (MAB) and 28 May 1988 (RSA). BSA to GSB, 12 October 1932, JB files. BSA to a Mrs. Brentano, 22 August 1950, NSHS.

23. BSA, "Nebraska History in Nebraska Novels," *Omaha World-Herald*, Sunday Magazine section, 24 October 1929, 11.

6. A Lantern in Her Hand

1. BSA, draft of "Can the Midwest Give Thanks?" n.d., 4, BB.

2. BSA, "The Story Behind *A Lantern In Her Hand*," *McClintock's Magazine* (October 1929). BSA, "The Pioneer in Fiction," script of talk on radio station KFAB, Lincoln NE, n.d., 1925, 2, box 10, NSHS. BSA, "Bess Streeter Aldrich," *Wilson Bulletin* 1929, 608.

3. BSA, "The Pioneer in Fiction," draft of talk given on radio station KFAB, n.d., 1925, 3, box 10, NSHS.

4. "In the same year. . . . 1860s and 1870s." Points made by BSA in draft of a talk, n.d. Also draft prepared for *McClintock's Magazine*, where the final version appeared October 1929. The material is similar to "The Story Behind *A Lantern in Her Hand*," *Christian Herald* (March 1952). All in NSHS. BSA, note card apparently for a speech, n.p., n.d., box 14, NSHS. BSA, draft, "Nebraska History in Nebraska Novels," 9, box 9, NSHS.

5. BSA, draft, "The Story Behind *A Lantern in Her Hand*," for *McClintock's Magazine* (October 1929), 8, NSHS.

6. BSA, draft, "The Story Behind *A Lantern in Her Hand*," for *McClintock's Magazine*, 8, NSHS.

7. BSA, draft, "The Story Behind *A Lantern in Her Hand*," for *McClintock's Magazine*, 8, NSHS.

8. Sandra L. Myres, *Westering Women and the Frontier Experience, 1890–1915* (Albuquerque: Univ. of New Mexico Press, 1982), 8. Myres describes such characterizations as common in nineteenth-century accounts. Myres, page 10, quotes David M. Potter, "American Women and the American Character" in *American History and the Social Sciences*, Edward N. Saveth, ed. (Glenco IL: Free Press of Glenco, 1964), 431–32.

9. BSA, draft, "The Story Behind *A Lantern in Her Hand*," for *McClintock's Magazine*, 6, NSHS.

10. BSA, draft, "The Story Behind *A Lantern in Her Hand*," for *McClintock's Magazine*, 8, NSHS. BSA, "The Story Behind *A Lantern in Her Hand*," *Christian Herald* (March 1952), 2, typed copy in NSHS.

11. BSA, draft of paper, probably for *Christian Herald* or *McClintock's*

Magazine. It is substantially longer than the *McClintock's* article, hence probably was written for the *Herald.* NSHS.

12. See note 11.

13. See note 11; p. 9.

14. BSA, note dated 1 November 1926 in archives, NSHS. MAB stated that, as far as she knew, her mother did not read *Daily Food* on a regular basis. Telephone interview with author 11 April 1989. I am indebted to Charlene Fletcher for deciphering Aldrich's handwriting here and in other places.

15. BSA, draft of "Nebraska History in Nebraska Novels," 11, n.d., box 9, NSHS.

16. MAB and Milton Beechner, interviews with author and telephone confirmation, 11 April 1989.

17. On an envelope marked "Edward P. Sharp Insurance Agency," BSA has noted the information as "Used." Contents include information about Native Americans, the Mormon child with the sore foot, and the boiling down of watermelons for syrup, last folder, box 15, NSHS.

18. *New York City Times,* 20 January 1929, clippings scrapbook, item 20, n.p., NSHS. *Star Telegram,* Fort Worth TX, 8 February 1931, item 20, n.p., NSHS. Hugh Fullerton, "Hugh Fullerton Says." The names of the forty newspapers in the syndication are not given—15 July 1929, item 20, n.p., NSHS. Earl A. Aldrich, "Hokum?: *A Lantern in Her Hand,*" *Saturday Review of Literature,* 17 November 1928, item 20, n.p., NSHS. St. Louis *Times,* 13 October 1928, n.p.

19. Rutger Bleeker Jewett interview in *Tucson Daily Citizen,* n.p., n.d., NSHS. Appleton Book Chat, 15 December 1928, item 20, NSHS. BSA to Bess Furman, 1 January 1929. Library of Congress Bess Furman Papers.

20. *Bookman,* June 1930, and Melbourne, Australia, newspapers, 16 August 1930 and 17 January 1931, item 20, NSHS. Alice G. Harvey, "Nebraska Writers 11, Bess Streeter Aldrich," *Nebraska's Own Magazine* (April 1931): 208, box 15, NSHS. Newspaper clipping from unspecified paper, probably *Lincoln Journal,* Sunday edition, 19 May 1930, item 20, NSHS. *Bookman,* June 1930, and Melbourne, Australia, newspapers, 16 August 1930 and 17 January 1931, item 20, NSHS. *Publishers Weekly,* "In the Bookmarket" (12 April 1930): 201, item 20, NSHS.

21. Harry Carr, *Los Angeles Times,* 1932, n.p., n.d., box 9, NSHS. *Publishers Weekly,* (March 1932): 12, item 20, NSHS. BSA to Herma Naomi Clark, 24 March 1930, Chicago Historical Archives. "Weekly News of Books, A Check List of Old Favorites for New Readers," no. 7, 10, n.p.,

n.d., publisher not traced, item 20, NSHS. Bessie Row, field editor, *Farmer's Wife Magazine*, n.p., n.d., item 20, NSHS. "Prairie Pioneers Had Their Fun, Bess Streeter Aldrich Insists" [*New York Herald Tribune*?], 9 March 1939, box 15, NSHS. Also "The KDKA Bookworm" radio station KDKA, Pittsburgh PA, 1939(?); to which BSA added the words "Book Review of *Song of Years*," box 14, NSHS.

22. JLBW to BSA, 30 June 1942. BSA's response to him granting approval 6 July 1942. Appleton-Century manuscripts department, Lilly Library, Indiana University, Bloomington IN. BSA handwritten notation in scrapbook, item 18, NSHS.

23. Alma E. Henderson, *The American Author*, 14, quote from the *Boston Transcript*, n.p., n.d., box 14, NSHS. BSA to Mrs. Lowell Brentano, 22 August 1959, in Lowell Brentano Papers, the Library, Eugene OR. BSA, speech to P.E.O., Lincoln NE, n.d. box 9, speeches file, NSHS.

24. BSA, note cards for talks, n.p., n.d., box 10, NSHS.

25. BSA, note cards for talks, n.p., n.d., box 10, NSHS. Mothers' Club, Elmwood NE, discussion with author, 14 April 1988.

26. BSA to a Miss Dickinson, 10 August 1944, 2, box 3, letters sent 1941, file, NSHS. Mary Pickford, letter to BSA, 10 February 1935, box 6, bus. corres. file 1935, NSHS.

27. *Town and Country Life*, London, 35, n.d., NSHS. *Dundee Courier*, 35, n.d., NSHS.

28. The identity of the Japanese girl is not known. She wrote Miss Alice Gwinn, of Doshisha, Kyoto, Japan, n.p., n.d., box 15, NSHS. Roger C. Johnson, "China Turns Curious," unspecified Los Angeles newspaper, n.p., n.d., box 15, NSHS. Perhaps from a Lincoln newspaper, 8 November 1936, box 15, NSHS. Bess M. Wilson, "Housework No Bar to Art, Says Bess Streeter Aldrich," *Minneapolis Journal*, 28 August 1934, box 15, NSHS.

29. Mari Sandoz to BSA, 15 January 1954, box 1, letters, 1949–56, NSHS.

30. Probably the *Lincoln Journal-Star*, Lincoln NE, 16 April 1950, n.p., NSHS; "'The Pioneer Woman Statue' . . . was suggested by Bess Streeter Aldrich's *A Lantern in Her Hand* and honors the early comers to this region." Probably *Lincoln Journal-Star*, n.p., n.d., item 18, NSHS. This was a joint effort of the Lincoln Women's Club and the Lincoln Park Department. The statue, six feet tall and on a three-foot base, was created by Ellis Burman, Lincoln sculptor. It is to be found in the Memory Garden at 33rd and Sheridan.

31. BSA to Herma Naomi Clark, 24 March 1930, Chicago Historical So-

ciety Archives, manuscript dept. BSA, draft of "Nebraska History in Nebraska Novels," 11, n.d., box 9, NSHS.

7. A White Bird Flying

1. Ralph H. Graves to BSA, 3 January 1929, box 5, NSHS.

2. Harold Matson and M. V. Dempsey, the McClure Syndicate, letter and contract to BSA, 7 January 1929, box 5, NSHS. The information about the Northwestern Speech College from BSA financial ledger, 26, BB.

3. RBJ to BSA, 25 January 1929, box 5, NSHS.

4. Rejections of "Pie" letters to BSA: *Ladies Home Journal* (3 January 1929), *Saturday Evening Post* (7 February 1929), *Red Book* (7 May 1929), *Smart Set* (18 May 1929), box 5, NSHS. H. C. Paxton, *Country Gentlemen*, letter to BSA, 3 July 1929, box 5, NSHS.

5. H. C. Paxton, *Country Gentlemen*, to BSA, 3 July 1929 and 18 March 1930, box 5, NSHS. CSA telephone conversation with author, 18 June 1989. CSA speculates that Aldrich did not follow this suggestion because she neither knew "sheik" types nor saw them as residents of Elmwood.

6. CSA and RSA, telephone conversations with author, 20 August 1994.

7. Dwight Clements, telephone conversation with author, 7 July 1994. CSA, telephone conversations with author, 3 July 1994 and 20 August 1994. The plane was indeed a Piper Coupe, not a Piper Cub, which was a different plane.

8. MAB, conversation with author, 27 September 1994. CSA, telephone conversation with author, 20 August 1994. RSA, letter to author, 19 August 1994.

9. CSA, telephone conversation with author, 20 August 1994. RSA, letter to author, 19 August 1994.

10. RSA, letter to author, 19 August 1994.

11. Aldrich's son James died 12 March 1972 in New York. CSA, telephone conversation with author, 20 August 1994. RSA, letter to author, 19 August 1994.

12. Dwight Clements, telephone conversation with author, 5 October 1994. RSA, letter to author, 19 August 1994.

13. F. M. Clouter to BSA, 24 June 1929, box 5, NSHS.

14. O. B. McClintock to BSA, 12 June 1929, box 5, NSHS.

15. CSA, telephone conversation with author, 3 July 1994.

16. O. B. McClintock to BSA, 2 July 1929. Also C. D. O'Kieffe to BSA, 20

September 1929, box 5, NSHS. *McClintock's Magazine* omitted the last three lines because they would have otherwise needed to start a new column, making her signature look "very awkward." The omitted lines were "But if you are prairie born . . . or have learned to love the prairie folks in later years . . . you have perhaps paused to remember some of the sacrifice and hard labor that were the portions of *other* Abbie Deals." Box 10, NSHS.

17. Mary Derieux of the *American Magazine* to BSA, 17 June 1929; Ruth D. Champenois of *McCall's*, letter to BSA, 17 June 1929; editor of the *Saturday Evening Post*, letter to BSA, 17 September 1929; Katharine A. Matlock of *Ladies' Home Journal*, letter to BSA, 27 September 1929; James N. Young of *Collier's*, letter to BSA, 14 October 1929; W. F. Bigelow of *Good Housekeeping*, letter to BSA, 30 November 1929, box 5, NSHS.

18. RBJ to BSA, 18 January 1929 and 25 January 1929, box 5, NSHS.

19. JLBW to BSA, 6 February 1929, box 5, NSHS.

20. JLBW to BSA, 26 April 1929. RBJ to BSA, 3 September 1929. RBJ to BSA, 26 June 1929. RBJ to BSA, 10 December 1929. Box 5, NSHS.

21. H. Adelbert White to BSA, 23 November 1929. BSA to a Miss Knobel, 20 January 1930. Box 5, NSHS. Letterhead of the Society of Midland Authors to a Mr. Chapman, 31 January 1933, Iowa University Archives.

22. Katharine A. Matlack of *Ladies' Home Journal* to BSA, 23 April 1930. Bern J. Hawley of *Cosmopolitan* to BSA, 29 May 1930. Sumner Blossom of the *American Magazine* to BSA, 20 June 1930. Stanley High of the *Christian Herald* to BSA, 19 August 1930. F. W. Beckman of the *Farmer's Wife* to BSA, 4 October 1930. *Physical Culture* purchase and price noted in BSA financial ledger, BB.

23. The *Delineator* purchase and price noted in BSA financial ledger, BB.

24. Nina Lewton, an editor with MGM Pictures, to BSA, 6 August 1930. Verne Porter, an editor with Universal Pictures, to BSA, 16 August 1930. Box 5 NSHS.

25. RBJ, letter to BSA, 6 February 1929, box 5, NSHS. BSA, "The Nicest House in Town," *American Magazine* (February 1923): 41.

26. RBJ to BSA, 8 January 1930. RBJ to BSA, 11 February 1930. RBJ to BSA, 17 February 1930 and 3 March 1930. RBJ to BSA, 14 July 1930. Box 5, NSHS.

27. BSA. "Wild Critics I Have Known," *Bookman* (November 1930): 265.

28. RBJ to BSA, 22 July 1932, box 5, NSHS. His words apparently quote Aldrich's, for he replies "No, I don't wonder that you have not been able to dig in, close the mouth of the cave and concentrate upon the novel.

Your letter suggests the activities of a three-ring circus. I congratulate you nevertheless upon getting the chariots safely around the circle."

29. RBJ to BSA, 22 July 1930, box 5, NSHS.

30. RBJ to BSA, 3 December 1930, box 5, NSHS.

31. RBJ to BSA, 17 June 1931, box 5, NSHS.

32. RBJ to BSA, 25 June 1931, box 5, NSHS.

33. D. Appleton release, n.d., box 14, NSHS.

8. Miss Bishop *and the Early 1930s*

1. BSA financial records, BB. RBJ to BSA, 20 August 1931, box 5, bus. corres. file 1931, NSHS.

2. BSA to GSB, 2 January 1932. Original letter in possession of JB, Cedar Falls IA.

3. BSA to GSB, 26 April 1932, BB.

4. BSA to GSB, 26 April 1932, BB.

5. Ivan Kahn to BSA, 18 May 1933, 20 May 1933, box 5, letters received 1933. BSA to Charles Aldrich, 30 March 1932, box 2, letters sent. Mary Pickford to BSA, 10 February 1935, box 5. NSHS.

6. RBJ to BSA, 18 March 1932, letters received 1932. RBJ to BSA, 3 May 1932, box 5, letters received 1932. RBJ to BSA, 26 December 1931, box 5, letters received 1931. NSHS. BSA, "The Runaway Judge," *Ladies' Home Journal* 49 (July 1932). BSA, "The Silent Stars Go By," *Cosmopolitan* (January 1933).

7. RBJ to BSA, 28 October 1932, box 5, bus. corres. RBJ to BSA, 19 February 1935, box 6, bus. corres. 1935. RBJ to BSA, 25 February 1933, in which he refers to her letter of 22 February 1933, box 5, bus. corres. 1933. NSHS. BSA "Why I Live in a Small Town," *Ladies' Home Journal* 50 (June 1933): 21. Helen Geneva Masters, "Bess Streeter Aldrich," *Nebraska Education Journal*, February, n.d., 60, BB.

8. RBJ to BSA, 23 March 1933, 2 April 1933, and 24 May 1933. Box 5, letters received 1933 file, NSHS.

9. Landale note placed in BSA file, *Omaha World-Herald*, 8 December 1950, DCHS. Also "Posthumous Tribute to Bess Streeter Aldrich by George W. Woods, state banking department 1929 to 1934," n.d., BB. The "tin box" description furnished by MAB in various interviews with author.

10. D. Appleton became D. Appleton-Century in 1933. RBJ to BSA, 29 November 1933, box 5, letters received 1933 file, NSHS.

11. "Former Student Is Author of Movie," *College Eye,* 8 September 1931, UNIA, Also BSA draft of article that begins "The idea in a story and the characters are inextricably welded together," 5, box 10, NSHS.

12. BSA, marked "COPY" (of letter), no addressee, 27 March 1936, box 2, NSHS.

13. Miss Bishop may have been a combination of all of these educators. *The Alumnus,* the Univ. of Northern Iowa yearbook (February 1947), says: "Sarah Findlay Rice is believed to have been the model for the main character, Miss Bishop, who was portrayed as a dedicated teacher." Roger Leavitt, a Cedar Falls historian, also accepted Sarah Rice as the model and suggested that the late president of UNI "closely resembles" Midwestern College's new president, *College Eye,* 24 January 1941, n.p., UNIA. Grace Norton, mentioned specifically by Aldrich as one of the "outstanding teachers of those years in the nineties," was one who would regret seeing the old school building destroyed. Louise P. Barrett is noted as Miss Bishop in letter form—Byron G. (Barney) Allen to William V. Anthony of UNI, 26 October 1972, UNIA. "Miss Barrett—'Miss Bishop,'" article published in the *Dispatch,* Brainerd MN, 4 December 1941, UNIA. "Fifty Years" (*Alumnus* of Iowa State Teachers College), vol. 16, no. 4, October 1932, box 10, NSHS: "'This younger generation is not the problem that many think it to be.' She [the retired Miss Barrett] feels that boys and girls of fifty years ago are little different than those of today."

14. JLBW to BSA, 31 July 1933, box 5, letters received 1933, NSHS. BSA, draft of letter to a Mr. Blair, for either the Cedar Falls newspaper or the Paramount Theater in Cedar Falls. No further ID, page 1, n.d., CFHS.

15. Fred Ballard to BSA, 5 December 1932, box 5, letters received, NSHS.

16. Willa Cather, William Faulkner, and Mari Sandoz were among other authors of the time in whose novels could be found traces of earlier short stories. Bess Streeter Aldrich, "The Weakling," *American Magazine* (February 1925).

17. Newspaper clipping from P.E.O. scrapbook, dated only May 1926, n.p., probably *Lincoln Journal-Star.* BSA, "Letter to Alpha" in *College Eye,* n.d. (probably 1921), 3, UNIA.

18. RBJ to BSA, 17 October 1933, box 5, letters received, NSHS. "Spinster," *Time,* n.p. (4 September 1932). "Miss Bishop," *Post,* Houston, n.p., 5 November 1933. *Post Dispatch,* n.p., 24 September 1933. *Christian Science Monitor,* Boston, n.p., 7 October 1933. *Daily Star,* Montreal, n.p., n.d. All from item 24, NSHS.

19. RBJ to BSA, 3 February 1934. RBJ to BSA, 19 February 1934, box 6, NSHS.

20. Edward L. Smith to BSA, 21 September 1933, box 5, NSHS. *Omaha Bee-News*, Louella Parson's column, 14 October 1933, item 28, NSHS. RBJ to BSA, 20 November 1933, box 5, letters received, NSHS. Edward L. Smith to BSA, 26 January 1934, box 6, letters received, NSHS.

9. The Mid-1930s and Spring Came On Forever

1. Manley H. Jones, Houghton Mifflin, to BSA, 1 July 1936 re visit by Manley H. Jones, box 6. BSA, letter to James Hearst, 24 January 1927, Hearst collection, UNIA. James Putnam, Macmillan, to BSA, 25 August 1936. Burton G. Hoffman, Knight Publications, to BSA, 31 August 1936, box 6, bus. corres. file, NSHS. Chesla G. Sherlock to BSA, 26 March 1934, box 6, bus. corres. 1934, NSHS.

2. Letters to BSA: Frank Hanighen, 20 October 1932, 5 January 1934, 2 April 1934, and 26 May 1934; F. M. Holly, 28 January 1933; Paul R. Reynolds 9 and 23 March, 15 May, 17 June, and 15 December 1933; Jean Wick, 29 January 1932; box 5, bus. corres. 1932 and 1933, NSHS. Frank C. Hanighen to BSA, 5 January 1934, box 6, 1934 bus. corres. BSA, draft of "The Soap Kettle," box 9, NSHS. Also RBJ to BSA, 4 April 1934, box 6, bus. corres. file 1934, NSHS.

3. Frank C. Hanighen, letter to BSA, 2 April 1934, box 6, bus. corres., 1934, NSHS.

4. BSA to James Hearst, 24 January 1927, UNIA. RBJ to BSA, 21 November 1932, box 5, bus. corres. 1932, NSHS.

5. Paul R. Reynolds, *The Middle Man: Adventures of a Literary Agent* (New York: Morrow, 1971), 83–84.

6. BSA to GSB, n.d., but December 1934, JB material.

7. BSA, acceptance speech to Kiwanis Club, 13 December 1929, box 9A, speeches file, NSHS. Quoted from Lincoln Kiwanis Club presentation award booklet, BB.

8. JLBW to BSA, 27 June 1934, box 6, bus. corres. 1934, NSHS. BSA to GSB, December 1934, JB materials; also author's telephone conversation with MAB, 27 September 1989. Aldrich had also gone to the World's Fair in 1933; it ran 170 days in 1933 after its 27 May opening, closed for the winter, and reopened in May 1934, running for another 163 days. JLBW to BSA indicates she and Bob were in Minnesota in August, 6 August 1934, box 6, bus. corres. 1934, NSHS.

9. RBJ to BSA, 19 February 1934, box 6, bus. corres. 1934, NSHS.

10. BSA, "Low Lies His Bed," *Cosmopolitan*. Aldrich sold this story on 11 November 1933; *Miss Bishop* was published 25 August 1933. Aldrich financial ledger, BB.

11. BSA, financial ledger, BB.

12. Letters to BSA, box 3, 1934, NSHS.

13. JLBW to BSA, 20 September 1934, box 6, bus. corres. 1934, NSHS.

14. *P.E.O. Record,* November 1934, BB. E. M., *Omaha World-Herald,* "Aldrich's Publisher Said It with Orchids," 15 November 1934, DCHS. JLBW to BSA, 7 November 1934, box 6, bus. corres. file 1934, NSHS.

15. Jack Thall to BSA, 11 October 1934, box 6, bus. corres., NSHS. JLBW to BSA, 30 October 1934, box 6, bus. corres. file, 1934, NSHS.

16. Merritt Hulburd to BSA, 9 November 1934, box 6, bus. corres. 1934, NSHS.

17. Merritt Hulburd to BSA, 16 November 1934, box 6, bus. corres. 1934, NSHS.

18. BSA to GSB, December 1934, JB materials. "Bess Streeter Aldrich Is Going to Hollywood," *Omaha World-Herald,* 2 January 1935, n.p., DCHS. *The World: 1934 Almanac and Book of Facts* (New York: *World Telegram,* 1934), 359 (the statistics are for 1932).

19. BSA, letter to "Dear Children," 26 January 1935, letters sent file, 1935, box 2, NSHS.

20. BSA to Dear Children, 5 February 1935, letters sent 1935, box 2, NSHS. BSA to Dear Children, 26 January 1935, letters sent 1935, box 2, NSHS. BSA to family, 14 April 1935, box 2, letters sent, NSHS.

21. JLBW, letter to BSA; Jewett died 25 January 1935. RBJ letter to BSA, 4 April 1934, box 6, bus. corres. file 1934, NSHS.

22. JLBW to BSA, 25 January 1935, box 6, bus. corres. file 1935. JLBW to BSA, 7 February 1935, box 6, bus. corres. file 1935. BSA to family, 18 February 1935, box 2, letters sent, NSHS.

23. BSA to family, 19 February 1935, box 2, letters sent, NSHS. BSA to Dear Children, 19 February 1935, box 2, letters sent, 1935, NSHS.

24. Margaret Wallace, "Four Generations of Life in Nebraska," *New York Times,* 27 October 1935, item 15, NSHS.

25. JLBW to BSA, 7 March 1935 and 22 March 1935—the latter letter acknowledged permission received, box 6, bus. corres. 1935. JLBW to BSA, 3 April 1935, 11 April 1935, box 6, bus. corres. 1935. NSHS.

26. BSA to Children and Tallie, 15 April 1935, box 2, letters sent. BSA to MAB, 22 April 1935, box 2, letters sent, NSHS.

27. JLBW to BSA, 9 July 1935, box 6, bus. corres. 1935, NSHS.

28. JLBW to BSA, 9 September 1935, box 6, bus. corres. file 1935, NSHS.

29. JLBW to BSA, 9 October 1935, 18 October 1935, 1 November 1935, 8 November 1935, box 6, bus. corres. 1935, NSHS. *Spring Came On Forever* scrapbook, item 25, 1935–36, NSHS.

30. Highland Park IL, *News,* 7 November 1935. *Cleveland Plain Dealer,* 17 November 1935. *St. Louis Globe Democrat,* 16 November 1935. *New York Times* Book Review by Margaret Wallace, 27 October 1935. *Mercury-Herald,* San Jose CA, 10 November 1935. Tom Shaw, Greensboro NC, *Record,* n.p., n.d., item 25, NSHS.

31. BSA, draft of letter to Peggy Haskell Benjamin, 26 November 1935, box 2, letters sent. BSA, letter to George E. Grimes, 26 November 1935, box 2, letters sent. NSHS.

32. BSA to C. Gibson Scheaffer, 23 November 1935, as noted in Scheaffer's letter to BSA, 25 November 1935, box 6, bus. corres. 1935. BSA, letter to George E. Grimes, 26 November 1935, box 2, letters sent. NSHS.

33. BSA to Grimes, 26 November 1935. BSA to Benjamin, 26 November 1935, box 2, letters sent, 1935, NSHS.

34. BSA to Grimes, 26 November 1935, box 2, letters sent, NSHS.

35. BSA, draft of letter to Benjamin, 26 November 1935, box 2, letters sent, 1935.

36. Scheaffer to BSA, 6 December 1935, box 6, bus. corres. 1935.

37. Mari Sandoz to BSA, 18 December 1935, Sandoz archives, University of Nebraska–Lincoln.

10. The Late 1930s and More Best-sellers

1. JLBW to BSA, 31 January 1936, box 6, bus. corres. 1936, NSHS.

2. JLBW to BSA, 17 and 28 March 1936, box 6, bus. corres. file 1936, NSHS.

3. JLBW to BSA, 26 March 1936 with copy of letter from Howard E. Reinheimer, counselor at law, copy of contract to Edward L. Smith of D. Appleton-Century, 24 March 1936, box 6, bus. corres. file 1936. MAB telephone conversation with the author, 28 November 1989. Edward L. Smith to BSA, 6 April 1936, box 6, bus. corres. file 1936, NSHS.

4. JLBW to BSA, 10 April 1936, bus. corres. file, box 6, 1936.

5. JLBW to BSA, 10 April, 15 April, and 24 April 1936, box 6, bus. corres. file 1936, NSHS.

6. BSA to "Dear Mary, Chuck, Jim and Cobbs," 25 February 1935, box 2, letters sent 1935. JLBW to BSA, 10 December 1936, box 6, bus. corres. file 1936, NSHS.

7. JLBW to BSA, 5 August 1936, box 6, bus. corres. file 1936, BSA, letter to "Dear Folks," 3 August 1936, regarding letter from *Reader's Digest,* 29 July 1936, box 2, letters sent 1936. C. Gibson Scheaffer, letter to BSA, 1 May 1936, box 6, bus. corres. file 1936. NSHS.

8. JLBW to BSA, 18 June 1936, box 6, bus. corres. file 1936.

9. BSA to "Dear Folks," 8 July 1936, box 2, letters sent 1936, NSHS.

10. BSA to director of pensions, Veterans Administration, Washington DC, 6 June 1933, box 2, letters sent 1933. BSA, letter to John Cobb, 2 March 1932, box 2, letters sent 1932. NSHS.

11. JLBW to BSA, 21 July 1936, box 6, bus. corres. 1936. BSA response in box 2, letters sent 1936. NHSH.

12. BSA to "Dear Folks," 26 August 1936, box 2, letters sent 1936, NSHS.

13. BSA to Roger Leavitt, 29 January 1937, CFHS. JLBW to BSA, 10 December 1936, box 6, bus. corres. 1936, NSHS.

14. Roger Leavitt to BSA, 14 November 1930, CFHS. BSA to Leavitt, "History from Letters," 8, n.d., CFHS.

15. BSA to Leavitt, 29 January 1937, "History from Letters," 8, CFHS.

16. BSA to Leavitt, 29 January 1937, "History from Letters," 8, CFHS.

17. BSA to Leavitt, 4 February 1937, "History from Letters," 9, CFHS.

18. BSA to Leavitt, 10 February 1937, "History from Letters," 10, CFHS.

19. BSA, draft of article sent to "local newspapers during Centennial year," n.d., box 9A, speeches folder, NSHS.

20. BSA to Leavitt, 31 March 1937, "History from Letters," 12, CFHS. BSA to Florence Dewey Novak, 14 October 1949, CFHS.

21. BSA to Leavitt, 11 May 1937, "History from Letters," 13, CFHS. JLBW to BSA, 27 April 1937, box 6, bus. corres. BSA told Williams she had decided on *Song of Years* as title in a letter, 28 July 1937, box 6, bus. corres. 1937, NSHS. BSA to Leavitt, "History from Letters," 25 October 1937, 14, 15, CFHS.

22. BSA to Leavitt, 21 March 1938, "History from Letters," 15, CFHS and from C. Gibson Scheaffer to BSA, 22 March 1938, box 6, bus. corres. file 1938, NSHS. JLBW to BSA, 26 May 1938, box 6, bus. corres. file 1938, NSHS. C. Gibson Scheaffer to BSA, 22 March 1938, box 6, bus. corres. file 1938, NSHS.

23. Erd Brandt to JLBW, carbon copy to BSA, 19 July 1938. Original letter was written 18 April 1938, bus. corres. file 1938. BSA response re rewrite was telegram of 23 April 1938, as noted in carbon copy of Brandt's letter, box 3. NSHS.

24. *Post* telegram to BSA, 22 April 1938, box 3. Erd Brandt to JLBW, copy to BSA, 19 July 1938, bus. corres. file 1938. BSA response was telegram of 23 April 1938, as noted on carbon copy of Brandt's letter. Box 3, NSHS.

25. Brandt to JLBW, copy to BSA, 19 July 1938, bus. corres. file 1938. BSA response was telegram of 23 April 1938. Brandt to JLBW, copy to BSA, 19 July 1938. Original letter was written by BSA to Brandt, 2 May 1938. Bus. corres. file 1938, NSHS.

26. Brandt to JLBW, copy to BSA, 19 July 1938. Date of original letter not given; nor is date of BSA telegraphed response. Bus. corres. file 1938, NSHS.

27. BSA to GSB, 23 May 1938, JB Files. John McCormick, 9 May 1938, box 6, bus. corres. file 1938, NSHS.

28. Brandt to BSA, 6 June 1938, box 3, telegrams, NSHS. JLBW to BSA, 29 June 1938, box 6, bus. corres. file 1938, NSHS. JLBW to BSA, 6 July 1938, box 6, bus. corres. file 1938, NSHS. BSA did go to California in July. She wrote from the Hollywood-Knickerbocker Hotel to Marie Clements, 28 July 1938; Marie Clements files provided by Robert Clements.

29. Brandt to JLBW, 19 July 1938. Carbon copy of letter by Brandt to BSA, box 6, bus. corres. file 1938, NSHS.

30. BSA to Marie Clements, 28 July 1938. BSA to Leavitt, 7 February 1939, Vopal Youngberg files.

31. JLBW to BSA, 26 July 1938. Brandt to BSA, 24 October 1938, bus. corres. file 1938, NSHS.

32. Raymond Cossett to all studios, 16 November 1938. Brandt to BSA, 12 December 1939, box 6, bus. corres. file 1939, NSHS.

33. "Famed Novelist Gives Intimate Picture of County History," *Waterloo Courier,* sec. 5, p. 6, 20 June 1954, Vopal Youngberg files. BSA to Leavitt, 16 January 1939, CFHS. "Appleton-Century Book Chat," 21 January 1939, John McCormick to movie directors, box 14, n.d. 1939, NSHS.

34. Adelaide W. Neall to BSA, 8 February 1939, bus. corres. file 1939, NSHS; BSA to Leavitt, 7 February 1939, Vopal Youngberg files; Chesla C. Sherlock, "The Place to Begin Is Where You Are," *Opportunity* 29 (August 1938), NSHS.

35. Roger Leavitt, "Local References Used in *Song of Years,*" 9, n.d., CFHS.

36. Wallace Stegner, "American Dream," *Saturday Review of Literature,* n.p., 28 January 1939. "Novel Pulses with Vitalty," *Oakland Tribune* Oakland CA, 12 February 1939. Margaret Wallace, review in the *New*

York Times, 22 January 1939. The *News,* Miami FL, n.p., 19 February 1939, item 26, NSHS.

37. *St. Louis Globe Democrat,* n.p., 28 January 1939. *Pittsburgh Press,* 29 January 1939. *Journal,* Dayton OH, n.p., 5 February 1939. *Post,* Houston TX, n.p., 12 February 1939. Item 26, NSHS.

38. BSA to a Mrs. Pynchon, 27 October 1938, University of Illinois at Chicago Library. Dodd to BSA, 20 February 1939. JLBW to BSA, 17 September 1939. Dodd to BSA, 9 September 1940, box 6, bus. corres. file 1940, NSHS.

39. BSA to Roger Leavitt, 7 February 1939, Vopal Youngberg files.

40. BSA to Marie Clements, 9 March 1939, provided by Robert Clements. JLBW to BSA, 11 February and 3 March 1939, box 6, bus. corres. file 1939, NSHS. BSA to Marie Clements, 9 March 1939. BSA to Bess Furman Armstrong, 5 June 1939, Library of Congress.

41. BSA to Bess Furman Armstrong, 5 June 1939.

42. JLBW to BSA, 7, 14, and 17 July 1939, box 6, bus. corres. file 1939, NSHS.

43. George Landy to E. L. Smith of Appleton-Century, copy to BSA, 23 September 1939, box 6, bus. corres. file 1939. Brandt to BSA, 8 July 1940, box 6, bus. corres. file 1940, NSHS.

44. Mignon Eberhart to BSA, n.d. (probably summer of 1940). Eberhart wrote she had been listening to the Republican convention. Box 3, fan letters, NSHS. Lynn Riggs, *Green Grow the Lilacs* (New York: Samuel French, 1931).

11. The 1940s, A Movie at Last, The Lieutenant's Lady, and the 1950s

1. BSA to GSB, 1 May 1940, JB files, Cedar Falls IA.

2. JLBW to BSA, 8 January 1940, box 6, bus. corres. file 1940, NSHS.

3. BSA to GSB, 21 June 1940, JB files.

4. George Landy to BSA, 2 May 1940, box 6, bus. corres. 1940. Erd Brandt to BSA, 8 July 1940, box 6, bus. corres. 1940. NSHS.

5. BSA, sketch of trip taken in 1939 or 1940, BB.

6. Theodore Roosevelt to BSA, 11 April 1940, BB.

7. Marie Clements files from Robert Clements.

8. BSA to Marie Clements, 26 September 1940, Marie Clements files. BSA to Mrs. Pynchon, of the Society of Midland Authors, about the ribbon,

14 February 1941, University of Chicago Library. BSA to a Mr. Blair, n.d., CFHS. Also Richard Rowland to BSA, 13 November 1940, bus. corres. file 1940. Box 6, NSHS.

9. BSA to Marie Clements, 30 September 1940. BSA to Marie Clements, 8 October 1940. BSA to GSB, 25 January 1941, JB files, Cedar Falls IA.

10. BSA to GSB, 30 October 1942, JB files, Cedar Falls IA.

11. BSA to GSB, 25 January 1941, JB files, Cedar Falls IA.

12. BSA to GSB, 1 May 1940, JB files, Cedar Falls IA; Keith Wilson, "'Bishop' Film Gives Lincoln Hollywood Premiere Thrill," *Omaha World-Herald,* 14 January 1941, n.p., Marie Clements files.

13. Keith Wilson, "'Bishop' Film Gives Lincoln Hollywood Premiere Thrill," *Omaha World-Herald,* 14 January 1941, Marie Clements files. BSA to GSB, 25 January 1941, JB files, Cedar Falls IA.

14. Louella O. Parsons, "'Cheers for Miss Bishop' Great Picture," n.p., n.d., item 24, NSHS. Fred Ballard, Peterborough NH, sent the *Variety* ad, dated 12 March 1941, to BSA, item 28, NSHS.

15. Leo Mishkin, "Screen Presents Martha Scott Tops as Female 'Chips' in Superb 'Cheers for Miss Bishop,'" *New York Telegraph,* 14 March 1941, item 28, NSHS. BSA to MAB, 13 March 1941, box 3, NSHS.

16. BSA to Marie Clements, 21 March 1941, Marie Clements files.

17. BSA to GSB, 20 June 1941, JB files, Cedar Falls IA.

18. BSA to Roger Leavitt, 3 September 1942, Vopal Youngberg files.

19. JLBW to BSA, 13 December 1940, box 6, bus. corres. file 1940, NSHS.

20. BSA to GSB, 25 January 1941, JB files.

21. BSA to GSB, 20 June 1941, JB files. In *The Scarlet Letter,* by Nathanial Hawthorne, Hester Prynne bore a child out of wedlock and was sentenced to wear a scarlet *A* for adulteress for the rest of her life.

22. JLBW to BSA, 11 June 1941, box 7, bus. corres. file 1941.

23. Stuart Roge for Erd Brandt of *Saturday Evening Post* to BSA, 27 August 1941, box 7, bus. corres. file 1941, NSHS. JLBW to BSA, 18 September 1941, box 7, bus. corres. file 1941, NSHS.

24. A. S. Burack to BSA, 21 August and 13 September 1941, box 7, bus. corres. file 1941, NSHS.

25. Box 8, "Lt's Lady File," NSHS.

26. BSA to Mrs. Hamilton Fish Webster, 1 February 1943, misc. file, box 8. Brandt to BSA, 23 September 1941, box 7, bus. corres. file 1941. NSHS.

27. JLBW to BSA, 7 November 1941. JLBW to BSA, 27 November 1941.

George Landy to BSA, 3 December 1941. Box 7, bus. corres. file 1941, NSHS.

28. George Landy to BSA, 14 October 1941. JLBW to BSA, 3 November 1941 and 1 December 1941. Box 7, bus. corres. file 1941, NSHS.

29. "Miss Barrett—Miss Bishop," *Brainerd Dispatch,* Brainerd MN, 4 December 1941, n.p., UNIA.

30. BSA to GSB, 11 June 1942, JB files. BSA to Mrs. Hamilton Fish Webster, 1 February 1943, misc. file, box 8, NSHS.

31. BSA to GSB, 11 June 1942, JB files.

32. JLBW to BSA, 27 July 1942, box 7, bus. corres. file 1942. Julian Street Jr., Treasury Department, Washington DC to BSA, 14 September 1942, box 1, letters received, NSHS. Although he indicated the book was *Lantern,* the *Lieutenant's Lady* jacket has the war-bond message. Lillian Houghton to BSA, 24 September 1942, letters received, box 1, NSHS.

33. JLBW, letters to BSA, 2 and 27 October 1942, box 7, bus. corres. file 1942. Also *Nebraska Writer's Guild,* October 1942, 4, box 13, NSHS.

34. M.H.B. review of *Lieutenant's Lady* in *El Paso Times,* 1 November 1942. *Atlanta Constitution,* 15 November 1942. "A Frontier Romance," 4 October 1942. *Knoxville Journal,* 1 November 1942. *Syracuse Post Standard,* "Another Absorbing Pioneer Story by Mrs. Aldrich," 11 October 1942, box 15, NSHS. George Grimes, *Omaha World-Herald,* 27 September 1942, 20-C, Douglas County Historical Society.

35. JLBW to BSA, 9 September 1942, box 7, bus. corres. file 1942, NSHS.

36. JLBW to BSA, 7 December 1942, box 7, bus corres. file 1942, NSHS. BSA to Alice Hudelson of A. C. McClurg, for "Christmas Book News," 4 November 1942, and letter to BSA from Hudelson, 7 December 1942, box 7, bus corres. file 1942, NSHS. BSA, "Bess Streeter Aldrich Hopes for Gay Reunion Next Year," *Chicago Tribune Sunday Book Section,* 6 December 1942, and letter from JLBW to BSA re book reviews, 27 October 1942, NSHS. William C. Lengel, Fawcett Publications, to BSA, 21 October 1943, box 7, bus. corres. file 1943, NSHS.

37. JLBW to BSA, 16 April, 13 August, and 13 September 1943, box 7, bus. corres. file 1943. JLBW to BSA, 6 March 1946, box 7, bus. corres. file 1946, NSHS.

38. Keith Royer, "Home Plans Take Time of Bess Aldrich," *Lincoln Sunday Journal and Star,* 25 August 1946, Marie Clements files. Vincent Callahan, War Savings Staff, to BSA, 10 October 1944, box 1, letters received, NSHS.

39. BSA, day journal, 14 and 15 August 1945, BB.

40. Ruzitska to bsa, 11 April and 11 October 1946, box 1, nshs.

41. Nimitz to bsa, 1 June 1946, box 1, folder 1945–46, nshs.

42. bsa to gsb, 1 May 1945, jb files.

43. bsa, day journal, 16 March and 15–18 July 1946, bb.

44. Individual interviews with family members by the author. bsa to Bess Furman, 18 February 1949, Library of Congress.

45. Daniel A. Polling to bsa, 4 December 1947, box 7, bus. corres. file 1947, nshs. bsa, letter to Bess Furman, 22 February 1949, Library of Congress.

46. Theodore M. Purdy, Appleton-Century-Crofts, to bsa, 29 November 1948, box 7, bus. corres. file 1948. bsa, day journal, 21 April 1949. bsa day journal, seven entries in November and on 3 December "signed 400 autographs at Matthews Books Store," bb. Patricia Schartle, Appleton-Century-Crofts, to bsa, 3 November 1949. Purdy to bsa, 21 November 1949, box 7, bus. corres. file 1949. Victor P. Hass, "Mrs. Aldrich Gathers Her Beautiful Christmas Stories," *Omaha World-Herald,* 13 November 1949, 24-c, dchs.

47. Appleton-Century had by now become Appleton-Century-Crofts. *Philadelphia Inquirer,* 28 May 1950, box 15, nshs.

48. *Philadelphia Inquirer,* 28 May 1950, box 15, nshs. Victor P. Hass, *Omaha World-Herald,* 11 June 1950, box 15, nshs.

49. John Lee quotes Mrs. Ralph Greene in "Bess Streeter Aldrich 'Cleaned Her Shoes Like Everyone Else,'" *Omaha World-Herald,* n.p., n.d., from Mary Linhardt files. csa to author, 19 February 1990.

50. mab to gsb, 29 August 1954, jb files.

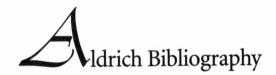

Aldrich Bibliography

Page references in text to Aldrich's works are to the editions given in this bibliography.

Short Stories

In addition to the short stories listed here, Aldrich's shorter works included book reviews for the *Christian Herald*, for which Aldrich was book review editor, and Sunday miscellaneous writings.

1898   "A Late Love," *Baltimore News*

1899   "Xantippe"

1903   "The Highland Shepherd's Chief Mourner," *Young Citizen*, February

       "Discovering America," *Young Citizen*, October

1904   "Abraham Lincoln's Boyhood," *Young Citizen*, February

       "One May Night," *Young Citizen*, May

1907   "The Madonna of the Purple Dots," *National Home Journal of St. Louis*

1911   "The Little House Next Door," *Ladies' Home Journal* (under Margaret Dean Stevens pseudonymn) 28, July

1912   "My Life Test," *Ladies' Home Journal* (published without byline), n.d.

       "How I Knew When the Right Man Came Along," *Ladies' Home Journal* (published without byline), n.d.

1913   "The Heart o' the Giver," *Modern Priscilla*, n.d.

       "Why I am Ashamed of My Wife," *Ladies World* (published without byline), n.d.

"Armour Recipe," *Armour Cook Book,* n.d.

"Picture Game," *Omaha World-Herald,* n.d.

"Criticisms," *Delineator,* n.d.

"Feminist Experience," *Delineator,* n.d.

1914   "Molly Porter," *Harper's Weekly* 59, 19 December

"Christmas Breakfast," *Delineator,* n.d.

1915   "Concerning the Best Man," *Modern Pricilla,* n.d.

"The Old Crowd," *Ladies World,* June

"Grandpa Statler," *Harper's Weekly* 60, 26 June

1916   "Mother o'Earth," *Delineator* 39, July; one of two BSAS selected for mention in *Best Short Stories of 1916,* Edward J. O'Brien, ed.

"The Cat Is on the Mat," *Delineator* 89, October; the other of the two BSAS mentioned for *Best Short Stories of 1916.*

"The Old Monarch," *American Motherhood,* n.d.

"The Patient House," *Designer,* n.d.

"The Light o' Day," *Woman's Home Companion* 43, November

1917   "Crete Plan of Domestic Science," *Housewives League,* n.d.

"Miss Livingston's Nephew," *Designer,* n.d.

"The Rosemary of Remembrance," *Black Cat Magazine,* November

"Lions in the Way," *People's Home Journal,* n.d.

1918   "The Box Behind the Door," *McCall's,* May

"Their House of Dreams," *People's Home Journal,* n.d.

"Mother's Dash for Liberty," *American Magazine,* December

1919   "Through the Hawthorne Hedge," *McCall's,* March

"Mother's Excitement over Father's Old Sweetheart," *American Magazine* 88, July

"Long-Distance Call from Jim," *American Magazine* 88, August

"Two Who Were Incompatible," *McCall's,* August

"The Mason Family Now on Exhibition," *American Magazine* 88, November

"The Theatrical Sensation of Springtown," *American Magazine* 88, December

1920   "Ginger Cookies," *Ladies' Home Journal* 37, January

"Across the Smiling Meadow," *Ladies' Home Journal* 37:20+, February

"Marcia Mason's Lucky Star," *American Magazine* 89:22–25, March

"Tillie Cuts Loose," *American Magazine* 89, April

"Mother Mason Gives Some Good Advice," *American Magazine* 89, May

"Last Night, When You Kissed Blanche Thompson," *American Magazine* 90, August

"Father Mason Retires," *American Magazine* 90, October

1921   "How I Mixed Stories with Do-nuts," *American Magazine* 91, February

"A Message to Mrs. American Banker," *McClintock's Magazine*, May

"The Man Who Dreaded to Go Home," *American Magazine* 92, November

1922   "The Woman Nell Cutter Was Afraid Of," *American Magazine* 93, January

"Mother Gets Back on the Job," *American Magazine* 93, February

"Nell Cutter's White Elephants," *American Magazine* 93, April

"Present Generation," *American Magazine* 93, May

"What God Hath Joined," *American Magazine* 94, September

"Nell Cutter Lets Her Family Shift for Itself," *American Magazine* 94, October

"Josephine Encounters a Siren," *American Magazine* 94, December

"The Cashier and Christmas," *McClintock's Magazine*, December

1923   "The Cashier and the Little Old Lady," *McClintock's Magazine*, January-February

"The Nicest House in Town," *American Magazine* 95, February

"Home-Coming," *American Magazine* 96, July

"Meadows Entertains a Celebrity," *American Magazine* 96, August

"The Victory of Connie Lee," *American Magazine* 96, October

"When the Children Grew Up," *American Magazine* 96, December

1924   "A Few Fagots for the Fire," *Today's Housewife,* January

"Advice to Writers," *Story World,* April

1925   "The Weakling," *American Magazine,* February

"Easy Money," *McCall's,* September

1926   "The Woman Who Was Forgotten," *American Magazine* 101, June

"I Remember," *McCall's,* November

1927   "The Woman Who Was Forgotten," reprint, *National Education Association Journal,* 16

"He Whom a Dream Hath Possest," *American Magazine* 103, June

1928   "The Man Who Caught the Weather," *Century Magazine,* July

1929   "Romance in G Minor," *Delineator,* February

"The Cashier and the Business Woman," *McClintock's Magazine,* June

"The Story Behind *A Lantern in Her Hand,*" *McClintock's Magazine,* October

1930   "The Cashier and the Children," *McClintock's Magazine,* March

"The Cashier and the Old Man," *McClintock's Magazine,* April-May

"Pie," *Country Gentleman,* June

"The Faith that Rode with the Covered Wagon," Part 1, *Christian Herald,* August 9

"The Faith that Rode with the Covered Wagon," Part 2, *Christian Herald,* August 16

"Wild Critics I Have Known," *Bookman,* November

1931   "It's Never Too Late to Live," *Delineator,* January

"Youth Is All Up and Coming," *Physical Culture Magazine,* May

"Will the Romance Be the Same?" *Physical Culture Magazine,* September

1932   "The Day of Retaliation," *Ladies' Home Journal* 49, February

"Trust the Irish for That," *Cosmopolitan,* January

"Runaway Judge," *Ladies' Home Journal* 49, July

1933	"The Silent Stars Go By," *Cosmopolitan,* January
	"Why I Live in a Small Town," *Ladies' Home Journal* 50, June
1934	"Low Lies His Bed," *Cosmopolitan,* January
	"Alma, Meaning to Cherish," *Good Housekeeping* 98, June
	"How Far Is It to Hollywood?" *Cosmopolitan,* July
	"Welcome Home, Hal," *Ladies' Home Journal* 51, September
1935	"Bid the Tapers Twinkle," *Ladies' Home Journal* 52, January
	"Juno's Swans," *Cosmopolitan*
1936	"Another Brought Gifts," *Cosmopolitan,* January
1938	"The Drum Goes Dead," *Cosmopolitan,* January
	"Song of Years," serialized novel, *Saturday Evening Post* 211, 10, 17, 24, 31 December
1939	*"Song of Years,"* serialized novel, *Saturday Evening Post,* 7, 14, 21 January
1941	"Story Germs," *The Writer* 45, December
1942	"Christmas Magic," *Christmas Book News,* December
1944	"Soldier Vote in '64," *Think Magazine,* 25 August 1944
	"Soldier Vote in '64," with biographical note, reprint, *Scholastic* 45, 13 November
1947	"Journey into Christmas," *Christian Herald,* November
1948	"Star Across the Tracks," *Saturday Evening Post* 221, 25 December
1949	"Heirs," *Colliers* 124, 10 September
1950	"Great Wide World of Men," *Woman's Home Companion* 77, May
	"Working Backwards," *The Writer* 63, November
1952	"The Story Behind *A Lantern in Her Hand,*" *Christian Herald,* March
1954	"The Outsider," *Christian Herald,* May

Books

This is a list only of dates of first U.S. publication. All the books have been reprinted, set in braille, and translated into other languages.

1924   *Mother Mason*
        New York: D. Appleton

1925	*The Rim of the Prairie* New York: D. Appleton
1926	*The Cutters* New York: D. Appleton
1928	*A Lantern in Her Hand* New York: D. Appleton
1931	*A White Bird Flying* New York: D. Appleton-Century
1933	*Miss Bishop* New York: D. Appleton-Century
1935	*Spring Came On Forever* New York: D. Appleton-Century
1936	*The Man Who Caught the Weather* New York: D. Appleton-Century
1939	*Song of Years* New York: D. Appleton-Century
1941	*The Drum Goes Dead* New York: D. Appleton-Century
1942	*The Lieutenant's Lady* New York: D. Appleton-Century
1949	*Journey into Christmas* New York: Appleton-Century-Crofts
1950	*The Bess Streeter Aldrich Reader* New York: Appleton-Century-Crofts
1959	*A Bess Streeter Aldrich Treasury* New York: Appleton-Century-Crofts

ndex

"Abraham Lincoln's Boyhood," 16
"Across the Smiling Meadow," 29, 117
Aldrich, Bess Streeter (pseud. Margaret Dean Stevens): awards, 131; *Bess Streeter Aldrich Reader,* 199; in California, 115–16, 118, 138, 155, 170, 172, 177; and Christmas, 21, 114, 116, 132, 136; college degrees of, 16, 21; and Fate, 45, 50–51, 52, 53; and literary agents, 128–29; as member of organizations, 72, 100, 200; and pseudonym, 25, 26, 27; and rejections, 34–35, 45, 73, 102–3, 105; and teaching, 16, 21, 33; on writing, 33, 90, 182, 199
Aldrich, Charles, 26, 97–98, 114, 116, 131, 132, 155, 174, 179, 183, 187, 199
Aldrich, Charles S. (Cap), 1, 17, 18, 31, 55, 61–62, 85, 101; as attorney, 19, 22, 32; as banker, 22, 24; education of, 18; as member of organizations, 62; and Spanish-American War, 19, 187; as U.S. Commissioner in Alaska, 19, 20
Aldrich, James, 25, 97, 114, 132,
167, 168, 171, 174, 179, 183, 187, 188, 198
Aldrich, Mary B. Whitson, 18, 23
Aldrich, Mary Eleanor, 23, 24, 97, 98, 114, 125, 174, 179, 181, 194, 197, 200
Aldrich, Robert, 37, 43, 98, 100, 115, 127, 132, 139, 155, 172, 174, 179, 180, 187
Aldrich, William W., 18
"Alma, Meaning to Cherish," 133, 154
America, 111
American Exchange Bank of Elmwood NE, 22, 28, 55, 119, 196
American Library Association, 146
American Magazine, 29, 30, 31, 34, 36, 41, 43, 44–45, 47, 49, 50, 55, 66, 70, 71, 102, 105, 121–22
American News: Don Gordon, 146
Anderson, Basil, 6, 7
Anderson, James, 7
Anderson, Margaret Stevens Wilson, 5–7, 85
Anderson, Mary Wilson, 6, 7, 8, 84, 85. *See also* Streeter, Mary Wilson Anderson
"Another Brought Gifts," 154

Appleton, D. (also, D. Appleton-Century and Appleton-Century-Crofts), 35, 60, 66, 70, 88, 95, 115, 120, 128, 145, 147, 152, 153, 160, 168, 175, 188, 198
Armour Cook Book, 26
Armstrong, Bess Furman, 171. *See also* Furman, Bess
Atlanta Constitution, 192
Atlantic Monthly: Dr. S. M. Crothers, 68

Bailey, Charley, 148
Bailey, Grace Simpson, 43, 74, 115, 138, 165, 179, 182, 196. *See also* Simpson, Grace
Baker and Taylor lists, 126, 146, 169
Baltimore News, 15
Barrett, Louise P., 123, 160, 186
Barrie, James M., 10, 139, 193
Beechner, David Aldrich, 153
Beechner, Milton, 114, 187, 194, 197
Benjamin, Peggy Haskell, 147–50, 156
Best Short Stories of 1916, 49
"Bid the Tapers Twinkle," 133, 135–36, 154
Black Cat Magazine, 30
Black Hawk County, 159
"Bob and Mabel Meet Tragedy," 42
Bookman, 88, 107
Boston Transcript, 48, 111
Bowker, 88
"The Box Behind the Door," 27, 32
Braille Type, 74, 89
Brandt, Erd, 165, 166, 167–68, 172, 175, 182, 184, 185, 186, 188
Buck, Pearl S., 171
Burnett, E. A., 131

Canfield, Sarah Elizabeth, and Second Lieutenant Andrew Nahum Canfield, 184

"The Cashier and the Business Woman," 101
"The Cashier and the Children," 104
"The Cashier and the Old Man," 104
Cass County NE, 78
Cather, Willa, 69, 75, 112
"The Cat Is on the Mat," 29
Cedar Falls High School, 13–15
Cedar Falls IA, 3, 8, 12, 20, 48, 54, 125, 158
Century Magazine, 73
Charlton, Mary B., 32
Cheers for Miss Bishop, 46, 177, 179, 181–82, 186
Chicago Post, 48
Chicago Record, 15
Chicago Tribune, 146, 193
"The Chinese Nightingale" (Lindsay), 117, 125, 142
Christian Herald, 8, 99, 105, 107, 197
Christian Science Monitor, 126
"Christmas Magic," 193
Cincinnati Post, 111
Clark, Herma Naomi, 88
Clements, Dwight and Marge, 28
Clements, Marie (Lorenz) and Guy, 28, 100, 167, 177, 178, 181, 196
Cleveland Plain Dealer, 146
Cobb, Clara (Tallie) Streeter, 20, 21, 24, 57, 139, 142, 160, 178–79, 182
Cobb, Irvin S., 190
Cobb, John, 20, 21–22, 24, 57, 139, 155, 156, 166
Collier's, 103, 197
Cosmopolitan, 105, 117, 129, 132, 133, 134–35, 155
Costain, Thomas B., 129
Country Gentleman: H. C. Paxton, 96–97, 103, 105, 125
"Crete Plan of Domestic Science," 27
"The Critic," 107

The Cutters, 12, 27, 70–71, 76, 137, 155

Daily Food, 82–83
Darners, 100
Davenport, Marcia, 171
Davis, H. V., 44
"The Day of Retaliation," 154, 199
Delineator, 26, 30, 49, 70, 105
depression (1930s), 75, 78, 105, 109, 110, 113, 117, 118, 126, 129, 133, 142, 144
de Trobriand, General Phillippe, 187
Dickens, Charles, 56, 137
"Discovering America," 16
Dodd, Edward H., Jr. (Dodd Mead Publishing), 170
Doubleday, 130, 176
Douglas, Lloyd, 137, 139, 170
Doyle, Arthur Conan, 36
The Drum Goes Dead, 184, 186
Dundee Courier, 91

"Easy Money," 46, 71
Eberhart, Mignon, 172
Eisley, Loren, 69
Elmwood Leader-Echo, 28, 61, 175
Elmwood NE, 22, 23, 24, 26, 77, 99, 118, 119, 195, 196, 199, 200
El Paso Times, 192
Esenwein, Dr. J. Berg, 28, 29, 30, 41

"The Faith that Rode with the Covered Wagon," 107
Farmer's Wife Magazine, 105; Bessie Rowe, 88–89
"Father Mason Retires," 32
"A Few Fagots for the Fire," 125
Fisher, Dorothy Canfield, 139
Fitch, Ruth, 142
Fosler, Laurence, 124
"Freedom from Her Mountain Height," 29, 30. *See also* "Mother's Dash for Liberty"

Furman, Bess, 88, 140. *See also* Armstrong, Bess Furman

Gargan, William, 177, 181
Garland, Hamlin, 78, 170
Giants in the Earth (Rölvaag), 79
"Ginger Cookies," 31, 44, 153
Goldwyn, Sam, 155
Goodbye, Mr. Chips, 180, 181
The Good Earth (Buck), 88, 91, 112. *See also* Buck, Pearl S.
Good Housekeeping, 103, 105, 111, 133
"Grandpa Statler," 27
"The Greatest Experience of My Life and How I Met It," 26
"The Great Wide World of Men," 197
Greene, Della, 63
Greene (Rueter), Donna, 27
Greene, Inez, 100
Green Grow the Lilacs (Riggs), 173
Grimes, George E., 147–49, 192
Gunther, John, 171

Hammerstein, Oscar, 91, 152, 156, 172–73
Hannighen, Frank G., 129–30
Harding, Ann, 116
Harper's Weekly, 27, 59
Harridan, Frank and Lola, 17, 22
Hayes, Helen, 116
"The Heirs," 197
"He Whom a Dream Hath Possest," 53, 66, 68, 153
"The Highland Shepherd's Chief Mourner," 16
Highland Park News, 146
"The Holy Night," 16
"The Home-Coming," 70
Hoover, Herbert, 107, 118
Houghton, Lillie M., 184, 188
Housewives League, 27
Houston Post, 126
"How Far Is It to Hollywood?," 133, 154, 199

"How I Knew When the Right Man Came Along," 26
"How I Mixed Stories with Donuts," 2, 3, 15, 25, 33, 36, 37, 41, 73
Hulburd, Merritt, 137, 138

Iowa State Historical Society, 175
Iowa State Normal School, 15, 95, 123
Iowa State Teachers College, 15, 21, 48, 123
"I Remember," 9, 46, 155; draft, 7, 12
Irish Christian Advocate, 92
"It's Never Too Late to Live," 105, 154

Jewett, Rutger Bleeker, 88, 95, 103–4, 106, 107, 109, 113–14, 116–17, 120, 127, 130, 131, 140
"Josephine Encounters a Siren," 14
"Journey into Christmas," 197
Journey into Christmas, 5, 6, 7, 9, 12, 198
"Juno's Swans," 133, 135, 154, 199

Kahane, B. B., 116
Kahn, Ivan, 116, 155
Keller, Ernest Gray, 151
Kensington, 26–27, 100
Kern, Jerome, 152
Kipling, Rudyard, 36, 57
Knoxville Journal, 192
Kurtz Journal, 187

Ladies' Home Journal, 24, 25, 26, 29, 31, 32, 44, 95, 103, 105, 118, 133, 135
Landale, Ted, 119
Landy, George, 155, 172, 175, 185
Lansbury, Angela, 117
A Lantern in Her Hand, 3, 5, 7–8, 12, 50, 59, 74, 104, 105, 107–8, 109, 111, 116, 137, 138, 146,

147, 148, 151, 154, 155, 157, 184, 185, 199
"Last Night When You Kissed Blanche Thompson," 31, 44
"Late Love," 15
Leavitt, Roger, 157, 158, 159, 161, 168, 169, 171, 175
The Lieutenant's Lady, 187, 188, 199
Lincoln NE, 92, 180, 199
Lindsay, Vachel, 117, 125; Mrs. Vachel Lindsay, 142
Literary Review, 72
"Little House Next Door," 24, 30, 33
Lloyd, Frank, 91, 116
"A Long Distance Call from Jim," 29, 53, 153
Los Angeles Times: Harry Carr review, 88
"Low Lies His Bed," 132, 154
Luther, Martin: and the Lutheran Church, 152

"The Madonna of the Purple Dots," 21
Main Street (Lewis), 68
"The Man Who Caught the Weather," 73, 95, 153, 154
The Man Who Caught the Weather, 153–54, 164
"Marcia Mason's Lucky Star," 53
Marshalltown IA, 17, 19, 20
McAfee, Mildred, 183
McCall's, 9, 27–28, 29, 30, 32, 70, 71, 103, 105
McClintock's Magazine, 38, 74, 101, 104
McCormick, John, 155, 165, 172, 185
McCullough, Colonel, 81
McNeill, Private, 30
"Meadows Entertains a Celebrity," 71
Menken, H. L., 170
Metro-Goldwyn-Mayer, 127
Miss Bishop, 46, 118, 120, 132,

142, 148, 153, 154, 155, 172, 184, 194. See also *Cheers for Miss Bishop*
Modern Literature Series, 89
Montreal Daily Star, 127
Morris, Wright, 69
"Mother Gets Back on the Job," 176
"Mother Mason," 29, 30–32, 34, 44
Mother Mason, 12, 42–43, 47, 65, 68, 70, 116, 132, 155
"Mother Mason Gives Some Good Advice," 42
"Mother o' Earth," 49, 52
"Mother Renews Her Youth," 125
"Mother's Dash for Liberty," 30, 35, 37–40. *See also* "Freedom from Her Mountain Height"
"Mother's Excitement Over Father's Old Sweetheart," 31
"The Mountain Looks on Marathon," 117, 154
"My Life Test," 49

National Education Association Journal, 45, 122
National Federation of Women's Clubs, 26. *See also* Women's Club
National Historic Register, 28
National Home Journal, 21
"Nebraska History in Nebraska Novels," 75
Nebraska State Historical Society, 69
Nebraska State Journal, 77
Nebraska Writers Guild, 73
Neihardt, John, 69, 75
New York Evening Post, 72
New York Times, 72, 87, 90, 111, 146, 169, 192
"The Nicest House in Town," 106
Nimitz, Fleet Admiral Chester W., 196
North, Sterling, 137
Norton, Grace, 14

O. Henry Memorial Award, 73, 94, 154
Oklahoma!, 173
Omaha World-Herald, 26, 73, 75, 119, 147, 192
"One May Night," 16
Our Town (Wilder), 45
"The Outsider," 197

Paramount Pictures, 137–39, 141
Parsons, Louella A., 127, 180
People's Book Club, 198
People's Home Journal, 30, 32
P.E.O. Record, 137
Philadelphia Inquirer, 199
Philadelphia Public Ledger, 111
Physical Culture Magazine, 105
Pickford, Mary, 91, 116
"Pie," 21, 94, 125
"The Pioneer in Fiction," 77
Pittsburgh Press, 170
Pocket Books series, 89
Polund, Arthur, 137
Publishers' Weekly, 88
Purdy, Theodore M., 198

Quick, Herbert, 79

Radio City Music Hall, 181
Reader's Digest, 54
Remick, Lee, 117
Reynolds, Paul R., 130, 131
The Rim of the Prairie, 3, 12, 13, 17, 27, 45, 47, 52, 69, 70, 76, 77, 116, 120, 123, 137, 155, 156, 172, 188
"The Ring of the Piper's Tune," 46
Robson, May, 116
Rockwell, Norman, 31
Rogers, Richard, 173
"A Romance in G Minor," 70, 153
Roosevelt, Eleanor, 140, 171
Roosevelt, Franklin D., 89, 119
Roosevelt, Theodore, Jr., 176
"Rose Leaves in a Jar," 105
"The Rosemary of Remembrance," 30

Rosenkoetter, Gussie, 43, 100
Rowland, Richard, 172
"The Runaway Judge," 117, 154
Ruzitska, Maria, 195

Sandoz, Mari, 69, 92, 150
Saturday Evening Post, 95, 96, 103, 105, 129, 145, 164–65, 166–68, 188, 197
Saturday Review of Literature: Earl A. Aldrich, 87; Dr. Henry S. Canby, 137; Wallace Stegner, 169
Schmidt, Harold von, 168
Scholastic Magazine, 194
Scott, Martha, 177, 181
Shakespeare, William, 14, 56, 80
Sheaffer, C. Gordon, 147
Sheldon, A. E., 69
Sheldon, Lloyd, 138
Sherlock, Chesla G., 129, 168
Siddall, John M., 29, 30–31, 32, 34, 35, 41, 47, 131
"The Silent Stars Go By," 117, 154
Simpson, Grace, 14. *See also* Bailey, Grace Simpson
Sinclair, Upton, 139
Smith, Edward L., 127, 155
"Soap Kettle," 129, 140, 142
Society of Midland Authors, 104, 150
"The Soldier Vote of '64," 194
"The Song of a Thousand Years" (Work), 160
Song of Years, 2, 3, 5, 15, 59, 161, 164, 167, 172, 175, 182
Spring Came On Forever, 49, 117–18, 132, 141–49, 151, 152, 156, 172, 192
Stanwyck, Barbara, 177
Star (Washington DC), 72
"Star Across the Tracks," 197, 198
Steinbeck, John, 170
Stevens, Margaret Dean. *See* Aldrich, Bess Streeter
St. Louis Globe Democrat, 146, 170
St. Louis Post Dispatch, 126

St. Louis Times, 87
Stone, Irving, 137
"The Story Behind *A Lantern in Her Hand,*" 102
"The Story Germ," 184
Streeter, James, 2, 8, 21
Streeter, Lucinda Dean, 2, 4, 164
Streeter, Mary Wilson Anderson, 8, 23, 24, 25, 76
Streeter, Zimri, 2, 3–4, 27, 59, 194; as model for Jeremiah Martin in *Song of Years,* 5, 164
Sullavan, Margaret, 177
Syracuse Post Standard, 192

Talmadge, Constance, 29
"The Theatrical Sensation of Springtown," 31
"Their House of Dreams," 49
Think Magazine, 194
"Tillie Cuts Loose," 43
Time, 126
Times Library Supplement, 91
"To the Authors of Tomorrow," 182
"The Two Who Were Incompatible," 29
"Traumerei" (Schumann), 22
"Trust the Irish for That," 153
Turnbull, Agnes Sligh, 171

United Artists, 177
Universal Pictures, 105, 137
University of Nebraska, 33, 131, 179
University of Northern Iowa, 15

Van Doren, Carl, 137, 170
Variety, 180–81
"The Victory of Connie Lee," 45, 49, 50, 52, 120

Waterloo IA, 3
Waterloo Daily Courier, 9, 160
Watt, A. P. and Son, 36
"The Weakling," 55, 124
"Weekly News of Books," 88

"Welcome Home, Hal," 133, 135, 154, 199

A White Bird Flying, 20, 49, 101, 106, 109, 112, 113, 117, 126, 154, 179, 199

"The White Elephant Sale," 71

Whiteoaks of Jalna (de la Roche), 101

"Why I Live in a Small Town," 118

Widdemer, Margaret, 171

"Wild Critics I Have Known," 107, 111

Wild Geese (Ostenso), 79

Wiley, Franklin B., 25

Williams, Blanche Colton, 151

Williams, John L. B., 103–4, 106, 131, 132, 136, 140–41, 145, 151, 152, 153, 156, 165, 166, 171, 175, 182, 183, 184–85, 186, 188, 191–94

"Will the Romance Be the Same?," 102, 105, 154, 199

"The Woman Nell Cutter Was Afraid Of," 67, 68

Woman's Home Companion, 197

"The Woman Who Was Forgotten," 45, 118, 121–22, 123, 153, 186

Women's Club, 33, 72, 100; Federated Women's Clubs, 183; of Lincoln NE, 92

Woods, George W., 119–20

Woollcott, Alexander, 137, 171

"Working Backwards," 197

World War I, 37, 38, 187

World War II, 172, 175, 186, 188, 194–96, 199

The Writer: A. S. Burak, 29, 41, 184, 197

Writer's Markets and Methods, 182

"Xanthippi," 16

Young Citizen, 16